The General

**GREAT
WAR
STORIES**

Victory at High Tide
by Robert Debs Heinl,Jr.

The Battle for Guadalcanal
by Samuel B. Griffith

Armageddon:1918
by Cyril Falls

History of the Great War
by John Buchan

The Spider Web
by T. D. Hallam

The Breaking Wave
by Nevil Shute

A Bloody War 1939-1945
by Hal Lawrence

Gallipoli
by Alan Moorehead

C. S. FORESTER

The General

The Nautical & Aviation Publishing
Company of America
ANNAPOLIS, MARYLAND

Library of Congress Catalog Card Number: 82-80140

ISBN: 0933852-27-4

Printed in the United States of America

LIBRARY OF CONGRESS CATALOGING IN PUBLICATION DATA

Forester, C. S. (Cecil Scott), 1899-1966.
   The general.

   Reprint. Originally published: Boston, Little, Brown, 1947.
   1. World War, 1914-1918 — Fiction. I. Title. PR 6011. 056G4
1982   823'.912   82-80140 ISBN 0-933852-27-4   AACR2

Preface

W HEN FORESTER wrote *The General*, there was no short-
age of literary works written in protest and bitterness over the
war. *Good-bye to All That* appeared in 1929. Robert Graves,
the author and former subaltern in the Welch Fusiliers, was so
disgusted that he left England to live abroad. Vera Brittains'
Testament of Youth, a poignant memoir written from the
perspective of a non-combatant who had lost a fiancé and a
brother, was published in 1933. Other works appeared which
underscored the human suffering in prose and poetry. How
could anyone read Wilfred Owen's "Anthem for Doomed
Youth" and not be moved? And there was no short supply of
non-literary reminders of the ordeal; statues commemorating
the fallen appeared in English villages; newspapers carried poignant advertisements in which relatives asked for information
concerning loved ones missing in action.

Although *The General* is a clever and scathing literary
criticism of the way the British fought the war, Forester had
other reasons for writing it. When *The General* was republished
in 1947, C.S. Forester wrote his own foreword. In it, he con-
fessed that his motive in writing this novel was to entertain,
"a self-proclaimed work of fiction." The possibility of influencing the course of history never entered his mind. Or so he
claimed. Yet when *The General* first came out in 1936,

Forester, like so many observers of the European littoral, was convinced that another fateful saga was on the horizon. The "war to end all wars" was only a terrible but oft-repeated occurence punctuating the history of Western civilization. The forces of facism were on the march, and to Forester's dismay, England seemed about to be drawn into another conflict.

The General reflects many of the feelings of Forester's generation. For him and for many others, the world had been turned topsy-turvy in 1914-18 and would never be the same. A generation of Englishmen would spend the rest of their lives trying to forget the noise, lice and mud of the trenches. And Forester was troubled by British indifference to what was happening in Europe. *The General* was meant to remind the British of just what did happen and that it could occur again.

Born in Cairo on 17 August 1899, Forester studied medicine at Guys College, London, but gave up that course when his play, *Payment Deferred* (1924), proved a success. A number of popular works followed. Although best known for his series of novels depicting the fictional saga of an English naval officer of the Napoleonic era, Horatio Hornblower, he wrote other novels as well, including *The Good Shepherd* (1955), and *The African Queen* (1935), the latter which enjoyed a successful Hollywood debut starring Humphrey Bogart and Katherine Hepburn. He also tried his hand at non-fiction with *Napoleon* (1924), *Josephine* (1925), *Louis XIV* (1928), and *Nelson* (1929). Forester's autobiography, *Long Before Forty*, appeared in 1967 just a year after his death.

Forester was a realist. Like all of his fictional works, *The General* is rich with realistic characterizations. Forester's character, Herbert Curzon, has personal and professional traits which are easy to admire. After all, his was the stuff that made the Empire. It is not difficult to imagine Curzon leading a charge of lancers against a group of indolent but rebellious tribesmen in some far-flung corner of the Empire. And he can be counted upon to maintain the highest standards as he does his duty. Curzon was the quintessence of the British Army officer of the nineteenth century: "He was the soul of honour . . . he would give his life for the ideals he stood for, and would be happy if the opportunity presented itself . . . all while the breath was in his body he would not falter in the face of difficulties."

Admirable qualities, yes, but Forester is describing an anachronism. Curzon could have lived nowhere but in England and in no time but his own. He is a fair representative of what Bryon Farwell calls "Kipling's Army". Curzon's world view was shaped by the British regimental system and the social nuances of the officers mess. The socio-intellectual fabric that resulted may seem strange to American audiences. It was a world apart, dictated by the regimental system and a seemingly immature social regimen.

The British regimental system, of which Curzon was a part, was unique. A regiment might consist of only one or two battalions, or an entire arm such as in the case of the artillery. Most had county or regional affiliations. Members, especially the officers, identified strongly with their regiment and not with the British Army as a whole. Even if an officer spent much of his career posted away from regimental duties, he nevertheless wore the uniform of his regiment and observed regimental customs. Rivalry among regiments was keen and the social pecking order was not to be ignored. Family and money were important if a young man aspired to join a fashionable regiment. Forester notes more than once that Curzon's regiment of lancers is definitely not on the highest social scale.

Officers of Curzon's vintage usually entered the Army via the Royal Military College, Sandhurst. Graduates from this institution went into the infantry or cavalry. The former arm was considered the best choice; Winston Churchill scored so low on the entrance examinations for Sandhurst that he was commissioned in a cavalry regiment, an act which earned him a substantial rebuke from his father. Brighter young men might attend a similar course at Woolwich, and then enter the Royal Engineers or Artillery. A cavalry regiment such as Curzon's Twenty-Second Lancers usually consisted of a lieutenant colonel in command, four majors, eight captains, and thirteen to sixteen lieutenants. Promotions were notoriously slow and the system fostered the social institution of the officers mess.

Drawn from the aristocracy or upper middle classes, the British officer of the nineteenth century would find no achievement in living in discomfort while in the field. It was simply expected that one lived as well as circumstances allowed. And the most comfortable way to live was to establish an officers mess, a view that survived long after Curzon's time. An officers mess as a distinct part of a garrison or depot probably originated with the Royal Artillery at Woolwich in 1783. From that time until the exigencies of World War Two obliterated its importance, the officers mess was the cornerstone of the military social institution. Almost all of the officers under age thirty were bachelors, and the mess was their home and the center of their social lives. The marriage allowance was not paid until that age, and in most regiments it took ten-to-fifteen years to make captain in any case. To search elsewhere for entertainment or companionship usually meant that a young officer was exceeding his income. Besides, the comradery in the mess was of the very best, as was the food and drink. Dinners in the mess were usually formal, with guest nights (known in America as "mess nights") held as often as once a week.

It was a world apart, dictated by trivial customs and social taboos. The young officers were ruled over by the senior subaltern, and a rebuke from him was not to be taken lightly. Behavior as a gentleman was essential, of course. As late as the 1930s, it was considered inappropriate for a young officer to carry a parcel while in uniform. Although the chilling cold of an English winter might make the roaring fire in the mess attractive, junior officers did not sit by it unless invited. Every mess had its crusty old major or two, passed over for command and destined for retirement long before their ambitions. For a junior officer to broach a conversation with one of these curmudgeons was anathema. It was life in this strange institution that shaped Curzon's world view and prepared him for his greatest but ill-fated calling.

It is no mere chance that Curzon assumes command of a brigade of cavalry during the opening salvos of the war. Forester uses this scenario to underscore the unwillingness of military leadership to accept the fact that twentieth century technology had made much of the tactics of nineteenth century warfare irrelevant. To the dismay of tradition-minded officers like Curzon, shovels proved to be more valuable than sabres and lances. Armies on both sides burrowed into the ground only to emerge when commanders ordered a series of senseless frontal attacks.

Although this new type of warfare is something that Curzon does not really understand, he gains prominence during the retreat from the Mons and the first battle of Ypres because he understands all too well what the order to hold at all cost means: "there was no limit to his savage energy in the execution of clear-cut task." Other officers might need "stiffening," but not Curzon. His duty is clear, even if his perspective is antiquated and out of touch with reality.

When Curzon assumes command of a division in training, he is frankly puzzled by the new breed of soldier. The men of Kipling's Army were soldiers who had little to fall back on. The sometimes harsh life of the nineteenth century British Army was better than no employment at all. The men who came after 1914 were of a different cloth: motivated not by economics but by a desire to serve their king and country in the Great War. Curzon experiences difficulty with this new breed of soldier. When he attempts to clamp down, they simply go around him.

Certain things are intractable, as Forester notes: "no disciplinary methods on earth could keep British soldiers from wine,
women, and wood."

It is difficult not to attempt to fit the fictional Curzon with
one of several British commanders of the era. In truth, Curzon
is Forester's caricature of the best and worst of them all: hide:
bound, traditional, and utterly devoid of imagination, yet brave
and honorable to a fault. Men of Curzon's ilk did not usually
attend the staff college, and it was important not to appear too
keen. The major battles are easier to apply to historical fact.
Curzon comes to the attention of the high command when his
division holds up its end in the ill-fated offensive at the Somme
in 1916. The attack was preceded by an artillery bombardment
that lasted a week. Yet when the infantry went over the top,
the British lost sixty thousand men the first day and after a
week, they had advanced a half-mile. By that fall, each side had
lost nearly a half-million men and the front lines were fairly
near their original location. Curzon's end as a military commander and near brush with death comes during the German
spring offensive of 1918. The fact that Curzon calls for his
sword as the tide of battle turns for the worst should not be
missed.

Forester's fictional work is not too thinly veiled criticism of
military commanders and civilian leadership that brought about
this calamity. "Men without imagination like Curzon were
necessary to execute a military policy devoid of imagination."
Worse, it appeared in the 1930s as though history was going
to repeat itself.

Merrill L. Bartlett, Lt. Col., USMC
U.S. Naval Academy
Annapolis, Maryland

Foreword

A N OFFICER of the Czech General Staff sat on one side
of the table and I sat on the other, with a map of Bo-
hemia spread between us. He was outlining the defensive
campaign the Czech army hoped to make should Hitler's
demands for the Sudetenland lead to war. Despite the fact
that we were both speaking a language foreign to us the
conversation proceeded with ease and understanding, while
from the outside, periodically, came the roar of aeroplane
engines warming up as the little Czech air force held itself
ready to sacrifice itself in the defence of Prague against the
Luftwaffe.

What had brought that Czech general and me together was
The General. It was one of the few English military books
which had appeared in the Czech language and, having been
studied as a textbook by the Czech army, it saved me much
preliminary trouble in explaining my fears and opinions and
hopes. There had been several other translations, too, in German and Polish and Spanish and Italian, so that a fair proportion of European military opinion had at least been exposed to
the influence of my reading of past events.

During those nightmare months before war began my
German publisher told me with frightened pride that the
book was not only being bought by the masses but was being

carefully studied in the very highest circles. The *Führer* himself had read it and was recommending it to his friends; among the Christmas presents which he gave away in 1938 were several specially bound copies — the publisher could not find out for whom they were destined, but he was sure that it would be great men like Goering and Keitel; he uttered the names with a respectful catch of the breath. He was in continual terror in case I should publish something which had disrespectful remarks about Hitler in it, or that I should utter a protest about the treatment of the Jews, or do something else which would lead to the banning of my books in Germany and at one stroke kill the goose which was laying so many golden eggs for him, and which might even lead to his removal from the perilous but pleasant upper circles of German society to a concentration camp. It was a source of relief to him that chance had led me to embark upon a trilogy of novels dealing with the naval side of the Napoleonic Wars.

Perhaps *The General* may have influenced the history of the world, if Hitler read it with care and yet with that complete lack of sympathetic understanding which was so conspicuous a part of his intellectual make-up. He may have been appreciative of the words and not of the spirit, just as he displayed a complete misunderstanding of the spirit of England both in peace and in war. For all I know, it may have been Hitler who set Lord Haw-Haw to broadcast to England excerpts from *The General* at the same time as the B.B.C. was broadcasting excerpts from *The Ship* — a battle of the books.

Yet when I sat down to write *The General* the possibility of influencing history never entered my mind. Why does a novelist write novels? He may want to exhibit himself, he may want money, but whatever his motive or his end the means he employs is first to catch and then to hold the attention of his readers. All I desired to do was to keep pleasantly occupied for a few hours the minds of the people who would read the book. I was writing a novel, a self-proclaimed work of fiction, and fiction does not mean the truth, and certainly does not mean the whole truth and most certainly does not mean nothing but the truth. I told of one fraction of English society, and I described the development of one trend of English thought, but even if I had told the whole story about these two things — which I did not — I left undescribed an infinity of other aspects of my country and my people. I hope the discerning mind can guess at them.

For although I wrote the book to interest and to entertain, and with never a thought of instruction, there must have been a reason for my choosing this particular theme out of the many which occupied my mind at the time. Something must have impelled me to it and the obvious explanation (and the true one, I believe) is that I was in a state of irritation at the indifference England was displaying towards her future; the groove into which she had settled seemed to be heading towards calamity. Let me repeat that it never occurred to me to try and divert her from that groove; I merely wished to tell a logical and reasoned story, and it was the circumstances in which I found myself which selected for me this particular story.

The American edition of *The General*, which was first published in February 1936, has been out of print since February 1943. I did not mind its being unavailable to readers here during the Second World War but I am glad now that the publishers have decided to reissue it.

C. S. FORESTER

January 1, 1947

The General

Chapter I

NOWADAYS Lieutenant-General Sir Herbert Curzon, K.C.M.G., C.B., D.S.O., is just one of Bournemouth's seven generals, but with the distinction of his record and his social position as a Duke's son-in-law he is really far more eminent than those bare words would imply. He is usually to be seen in his Bath chair, with Lady Emily, tall, rawboned, tweed-skirted, striding behind. He has a large face, which looks as if it had been rough-carved from a block of wood and his white hair and moustache stuck on afterwards, but there is a kindly gleam in his prominent blue eyes when he greets his acquaintances, and he purses up his lips in the queerest old-maidish smile. He clings to the habit of the old fashioned Bath chair largely for the reason that it is easier from a Bath chair to acknowledge one's friends; he has never taught himself to walk with ease with any of the half dozen artificial legs he has acquired since the war, and the stump of his amputated thigh still troubles him occasionally. Besides, now that he is growing old he is a tiny bit nervous in a motor car.

Everybody is glad to have him smile to them on Bournemouth promenade, because his smile is a patent of social eminence in Bournemouth. And he wears his position with dignity, and is generous with his smiles, so that his popularity is great although he plays very bad bridge. He goes his way through the town, a plaid rug over his knees, the steering handle in his gloved hands, and on his approach newcomers are hurriedly informed by residents about his brilliant career and his life of achievement. Nowadays, when the memory of the war is fading, these verbal accounts are growing like folk legends, and public opinion in Bournemouth is inclined to give Sir Herbert Curzon more credit than he has really earned, although perhaps not more than he deserves.

The day on which Curzon first stepped over the threshold of history, the day which was to start him towards the command of a hundred thousand men, towards knighthood — and towards the Bath chair on Bournemouth promenade — found him as a worried subaltern in an early South African battle. The landscape all about him was of a dull reddish brown; even the scanty grass and the scrubby bushes were brown. The arid plain was seamed with a tangle of ravines and gullies, but its monotony was relieved by the elevation in the distance of half a dozen flat-topped rocky hills, each of them like the others, and all of them like nearly every other *kopje* in South Africa.

Curzon was in command of his squadron of the Twenty-Second Lancers, the Duke of Suffolk's Own, an eminence to which he has been raised by the chances of war. Three officers senior to him were sick, left behind at various points on the lines of communication and Captain the Honourable Charles Manningtree-Field, who had been in command when the squadron went into action, was lying dead at Curzon's feet with a Mauser bullet through his head. Curzon was not thinking about Manningtree-Field. His anxiety was such that immediately after the shock of his death, and of the realisation that men really can be killed by bullets his first thought had been that now he could use the Captain's Zeiss binoculars and try and find out what was happening. He stood on the lip of the shallow depression wherein lay Manningtree-Field's body, the two squadron trumpeters, and two or three wounded men, and he stared round him across the featureless landscape.

In a long straggling line to his right and left lay the troopers of the squadron, their forage caps fastened under their chins, firing away industriously at nothing at all, as far as Curzon could see. In a gully to the rear, he knew, were the horses and the horseholders, but beyond that Curzon began to realise that he knew extraordinarily little about the battle which was going on. The squadron was supposed to be out on the right flank of an advancing British firing line, but when they had come galloping up to this position Curzon had not been in command, and he had been so preoccupied with keeping his troop properly closed up that he had not paid sufficient attention to what Manningtree-Field had been doing.

Probably Manningtree-Field had not been too sure himself, because the battle had begun in a muddle amid a cascade of vague orders from the staff, and since then no orders had reached them — and certainly no orders had envisaged their coming under heavy fire at this particular point. As an accompaniment to the sharp rattle of musketry about him Curzon could hear the deeper sound of artillery in the distance, echoing over the plain with a peculiar discordant quality, and against the intense blue of the sky he could see the white puffs of the shrapnel bursts far out to the left, but it was impossible to judge the position of their target at that distance, and there was just enough fold in the flat surface of the plain to conceal from him any sight of troops on the ground.

Meanwhile an invisible enemy was scourging them with a vicious and well-directed fire. The air was full of the sound of rifle bullets spitting and crackling past Curzon's ears as he stood staring through the binoculars. Curzon had an uneasy feeling that they were coming from the flank as well as from

[5]

the front, and in the absence of certain knowledge he was rapidly falling a prey to the fear that the wily Boers were creeping round to encircle him. A fortnight ago a whole squadron of Lancers — not of his regiment, thank God — had been cut off in that way and forced to surrender, with the result that that regiment was now known throughout South Africa as "Kruger's Own." Curzon sweated with fear at the thought of such a fate overtaking him. He would die rather than surrender, but — would his men? He looked anxiously along the straggling skirmishing line.

Troop Sergeant-Major Brown came crawling to him on his hands and knees. Brown was a man of full body, and his face was normally brick red, but this unwonted exertion under a scorching sun coloured his cheeks like a beetroot.

"Ain't no orders come for us, sir?" asked Brown, peering up at him.

"No," said Curzon sharply. "And stand up if you want to speak to me."

Brown stood up reluctantly amid the crackle of the bullets. After twenty years' service, without having had a shot fired at him, and with his pension in sight, it went against his grain to make a target of himself for a lot of farmers whose idea of war was to lay ambushes behind rocks.

"Come down 'ere, sir, please sir," pleaded Brown in a fever of distress. "We don't want to lose *you*, sir, too, sir."

The loss of the only officer the squadron had left would place Sergeant-Major Brown in command, and Brown was not at all desirous of such a responsibility. It was that consideration which caused Curzon to yield to his solicitations, and to step down into the comparative safety of the depression.

"D'you fink we're cut orf, sir?" asked Brown, dropping his voice so as to be unheard by the trumpeters squatting on the rocks at the bottom of the dip.

[6]

"No, of course not," said Curzon. "The infantry will be up in line with us soon."

"Ain't no sign of them, is there, sir?" complained Brown. "Expect the beggars are 'eld up somewhere, or lorst their way, or something."

"Nonsense," said Curzon. All his training, both military and social, had been directed against his showing any loss of composure before his inferiors in rank, even if those inferiors should actually be voicing his own fears. He stepped once more to the side of the hollow and stared out over the rolling plain. There was nothing to be seen except the white shrapnel bursts.

"Our orders was to find their flank," said Brown, fidgeting with his sword hilt. "Looks to me more like as if they've found ours."

"Nonsense," repeated Curzon. But just exactly where the Boer firing line was to be found was more than he could say. Those infernal *kopjes* all looked alike to him. He looked once more along the line of skirmishers crouching among the rocks, and as he looked he saw, here and there, faces turned towards him. That was a bad sign, for men to be looking over their shoulders in the heat of action. The men must be getting anxious. He could hardly blame them, seeing that they had been trained for years to look upon a battle as a series of charges knee to knee and lance in hand against a serried enemy. This lying down to be shot at by hidden enemies a mile off was foreign to their nature. It was his duty to steady them.

"Stay here, Sergeant-Major," he said. "You will take command if I'm hit."

He stepped out from the hollow, his sword at his side, his uniform spick and span, and walked in leisurely fashion along the firing line. He spoke to the men by name, steadily and unemotionally as he reached each in turn. He felt vaguely as he walked that a joke or two, something to raise a laugh, would

[7]

be the most effective method of address, but he never was able to joke, and as it was, his mere presence and unruffled demeanour acted as a tonic on the men. Twice he spoke harshly. Once was when he found Trooper Haynes cowering behind rocks without making any attempt to return the fire, and once was when he found Trooper Macguire drinking from his water bottle. Water out here in the veldt was a most precious possession, to be hoarded like a miser's gold, for when there was no more water there would be no fight left in the men.

He walked down the line to one end; he walked back to the other. Sergeant-Major Brown, peeping out from his hollow, watched his officer's fearless passage, and, with the contrariness of human nature, found himself wishing he was with him. Then, when Curzon was nearly back in safety again, Brown saw him suddenly swing right round. But next instant he was walking steadily down to the hollow, and only when he was out of sight of the men did he sit down sharply.

"Are you hit, sir?" asked Brown, all anxiety.

"Yes. Don't let the men know. I'm still in command."

Brown hastily called the squadron first-aid corporal with his haversack of dressings. They ripped open Curzon's coat and bound up the entrance and exit wounds. The destiny which directs the course of bullets had sent this one clean through the fleshy part of the shoulder without touching bone or artery or nerve.

"I'm all right," said Curzon manfully, getting to his feet and pulling his torn coat about him. The arrival of a crawling trooper interrupted Sergeant-Major Brown's protests.

"Message from Sergeant Hancock, sir," said the trooper. "Ammunition's running short."

"Um," said Curzon thoughtfully, and a pause ensued while he digested the information.

"There ain't fifty rounds left in our troop, sir," supplemented the trooper, with the insistence of his class upon harrowing detail.

"All right," blazed Curzon irritably. "All right. Get back to the line."

" 'Ave to do somethink now, sir," said Sergeant-Major Brown as the trooper crawled away.

"Shut up and be quiet," snapped Curzon.

He was perfectly well aware that he must do something. As long as his men had cartridges to fire they would remain in good heart, but once ammunition failed he might expect any ugly incident to occur. There might be panic, or someone might show a white flag.

"Trumpeter!" called Curzon, and the trumpeter leaped up to attention to receive his orders.

The squadron came trailing back to the gully where the horses were waiting. The wounded were being assisted by their friends, but they were all depressed and ominously quiet. A few were swearing, using words of meaningless filth, under their breath.

"What about the dead, sir?" asked Sergeant Hancock, saluting. "The Captain, sir?"

The regiment was still so unversed in war as to feel anxiety in the heat of action about the disposal of the dead — a reminiscence of the warfare against savage enemies which constituted the British Army's sole recent experience. This new worry on top of all the others nearly broke Curzon down. He was on the point of blazing out with "Blast the dead!" but he managed to check himself. Such a violation of the army's recent etiquette would mean trouble with the men.

"I'll see about that later. Get back into your place," he said. "Prepare to mount!"

The squadron followed him down the ravine, the useless lances cocked up at each man's elbow, amid a squeaking of

leather and a clashing of iron hoofs on the rocks. Curzon's
head was beginning to swim, what with the loss of blood, and
the pain of his wound, and the strain he had undergone, and
the heat of this gully. He had small enough idea of what he
wanted to do — or at least he would not admit to himself that
what he wanted was to make his way back to some area where
the squadron would not be under fire and he might receive
orders. The sense of isolation in the presence of an enemy of
diabolical cunning and strength was overwhelming. He knew
that he must not expose the squadron to fire while in retreat.
The men would begin to quicken their horses' pace in that
event — the walk would become a trot, the trot a gallop, and
his professional reputation would be blasted. The gully they
were in constituted at least a shelter from the deadly hail of
bullets.

The gully changed direction more than once. Soon Curzon
had no idea where he was, nor whither he was going, but he
was too tired and in too much pain to think clearly. The distant gunfire seemed to roll about inside his skull. He drooped
in his saddle and with difficulty straightened himself up. The
fortunate gully continued a long way instead of coming to a
rapid indefinite end as most gullies did in that parched plain,
and the men — and Sergeant-Major Brown — were content to
follow him without question. The sun was by now well down
towards the horizon, and they were in the shade.

It was in fact the sight of the blaze of light which was reflected from the level plain in front which roused Curzon to
the realisation that the gully was about to end beyond the
tangle of rocks just in front. He turned in his saddle and held
up his hand to the column of men behind; they came sleepily
to a halt, the horses cannoning into the hind-quarters of the
horses in front, and then Curzon urged his horse cautiously
forward, his trumpeter close behind.

Peering from the shelter of the rocks Curzon beheld the finest spectacle which could gladden the eyes of a cavalry officer. The gully had led him, all unaware, actually behind the flank of the Boer position. Half a mile in front of him, sited with Boer cunning on the reverse slope of a fold in the ground, was a battery of field guns sunk in shallow pits, the guns' crews clearly visible round them. There were groups of tethered ponies. There was a hint of rifle trenches far in front of the guns, and behind the guns were waggons and mounted staffs. There was all the vulnerable exposed confusion always to be found behind a firing line, and he and his squadron were within easy charging distance of it all, their presence unsuspected.

Curzon fought down the nightmare feeling of unreality which was stealing over him. He filed the squadron out of the gully and brought it up into line before any Boer had noticed them. Then, forgetting to draw his sword, he set his spurs into his horse and rode steadily, three lengths in front of his charging line, straight at the guns. The trumpeters pealed the charge as the pace quickened.

No undisciplined militia force could withstand the shock of an unexpected attack from the flank, however small the force which delivered it. The Boer defence which had all day held up the English attack collapsed like a pricked balloon. The whole space was black with men running for their ponies. Out on the open plain where the sweltering English infantry had barely been maintaining their firing lines the officers sensed what was happening. Some noticed the slackening of the Boer fire. Some saw the Boers rise out of their invisible trenches and run. One officer heard the cavalry trumpets, faint and sweet through the heated air. He yelled to his bugle to sound the charge. The skirmishing line rose up from flank to flank as bugler after bugler took up the call. Curzon had brought them the last necessary impetus for the attack. They poured over the Boer lines to where Curzon, his sword still in its sheath, was sitting dazed upon his horse amid the captured guns.

The battle of Volkslaagte — a very great battle in the eyes of the British public of 1899, wherein nearly five thousand men a side had been engaged — was won, and Curzon was marked for his captaincy and the D.S.O. He was not a man of dreams, but even if he had been, his wildest dreams would not have envisaged the future command of a hundred thousand British soldiers — nor the Bath chair on Bournemouth promenade.

Chapter II

TO CURZON the rest of the South African War was a time of tedium and weariness. His wound kept him in hospital during the Black Week, while England mourned three coincident defeats inflicted by an enemy whom she had begun to regard as already at her mercy. He was only convalescent during Roberts' triumphant advance to Pretoria. He found himself second in command of a detail of recruits and reservists on the long and vulnerable line of communications when the period of great battles had come to an end.

There were months of tedium, of army biscuit and tough beef, of scant water and no tobacco. There were sometimes weeks of desperate marching, when the horses died and the men grumbled and the elusive enemy escaped by some new device from the net which had been drawn round him. There were days of scorching sun and nights of bitter cold. There was water discipline to be enforced so as to prevent the men from drinking from the polluted supplies which crammed the hospitals with cases of enteric fever. There was the continuous nagging difficulty of obtaining fodder so as to keep horses in a condition to satisfy the exacting demands of column commanders. There were six occasions in eighteen months during which Curzon heard once more the sizzle and crack of bullets overhead, but he did not set eyes on an enemy — except prisoners — during that period. Altogether it was a time of inconceivable dreariness and monotony.

But it could not be said that Curzon was actively unhappy. He was not of the type to chafe at monotony. The dreariness of an officers' mess of only two or three members did not react seriously upon him — he was not a man who needed mental diversion. His chill reserve and ingrained frigid good manners kept him out of mess room squabbles when nerves were fraying and tempers were on edge; besides, a good many of the officers who came out towards the end of the war were not gentlemen and were not worth troubling one's mind about. Yet all the same it was pleasant when the war ended at last, and Curzon could say good-bye to the mixed rabble of mounted infantry who had made up the column of which he was second in command.

He rejoined the Twenty-Second Lancers at Cape Town — all the squadrons together again for the first time for two years — and sailed for home. The new King himself reviewed them after their arrival, having granted them time enough to discard their khaki and put on again the glories of blue and gold, *schapska* and plume, lance pennons and embroidered saddle cloths. Then they settled down in their barracks with the fixed determination (as the Colonel expressed it, setting his lips firmly) of "teaching the men to be soldiers again."

The pleasure of that return to England was intense enough, even to a man as self-contained as Curzon. There were green fields to see, and hedgerows, and there was the imminent prospect of hunting. And there were musical comedies to go to, and good food to eat, and pretty women to be seen in every street, and the Leicester Lounge to visit, with a thrill reminiscent of old Sandhurst days. And there was the homage of society to the returned warriors to be received — although that was not quite as fulsome as it might have been, because public enthusiasm had begun to decline slowly since the relief of Mafeking, and there was actually a fair proportion of people who had forgotten the reported details of the battle of Volkslaagte.

There was naturally one man who knew all about it — a portly, kindly gentleman with a keen blue eye and a deep guttural voice who had been known as H.R.H. at the time when the Lancers had been ordered to South Africa but who was now King of England. He said several kindly words to Curzon at the investiture to which Curzon was summoned by the Lord Chamberlain. And Curzon bowed and stammered as he received his D.S.O. — he was not a man made for courts and palaces. In the intimacy of his hotel bedroom he had felt thrilled and pleased with himself in his Lancer full dress, with his plastron and his *schapska,* his gold lace and glittering boots and sword, and he had even found a sneaking pleasure in the stir among the people on the pavement as he walked out to get into the waiting cab, but his knees knocked and his throat dried up in Buckingham Palace.

On the same leave Curzon had in duty bound to go and visit Aunt Kate, who lived in Brixton. The late Mr. Curzon, Captain Herbert Curzon's father, had married a trifle beneath him, and his wife's sister had married a trifle beneath her, and the Mr. Cole whom she had married had not met with much success in life, and after marriage Mr. Curzon had met with much, so that the gap between Curzon and his only surviving relatives — between the Captain in the Duke of Suffolk's Own and the hard-up city clerk with his swarm of shrieking children — was wide and far too deep to plumb. Curzon drove to Brixton in a cab, and the appearance of the cab caused as much excitement in that street as did his full dress uniform in the West End. Aunt Kate opened the door to him — a paint-blistered door at the end of a tiled path three yards long, leading from a gate in the iron railings past a few depressed laurels in the tiny "front garden." Aunt Kate was momentarily disconcerted at the sight of the well-dressed gentleman who had rat-tat-tatted on her door, but she recovered herself.

"Why, it's Bertie," she said. "Come in, dear. Uncle Stanley ought to be home soon. Come in here and sit down. Maud! Dick! Gertie! Here's your cousin Bertie home from South Africa!"

The shabby children came clustering into the shabby parlour; at first they were shy and constrained, and when the constraint wore off they grew riotous, making conversation difficult and hindering Aunt Kate in her efforts to extract from her nephew details of his visit to Buckingham Palace.

"What's it like in there?" she asked. "Is it all gold? I suppose there's cut glass chandeliers?"

Curzon had not the least idea. And —

"Did the King *really* speak to you? What was he wearing?"

"Field Marshal's uniform," said Curzon briefly.

"Of course, you've been presented to him before, when you went into the army," said Aunt Kate, enviously. "That was in the dear Queen's time."

"Yes," said Curzon.

"It must be lovely to know all these people," said Aunt Kate. "Are there any Lords in your regiment now?"

"Yes," said Curzon. "One or two."

It was irritating, because he himself found secret pleasure in serving in the same regiment as lords, and in addressing them without their titles, but the pleasure was all spoilt now at finding that Aunt Kate was of the same mind.

More irritating still was the arrival of Stanley Cole, Aunt Kate's husband, whom Curzon felt he could not possibly address now as "Uncle Stanley," although he had done so as a boy. Mr. Cole was an uncompromising Radical, and no respecter of persons, as he was ready to inform anyone.

"I didn't 'old with your doings in South Africa," he announced, almost before he was seated. "I didn't 'old with them at all, and I said so all along. We didn't ought to 'ave fought with the Boers in the first place. And burning farms, and those concentration camps. Sheer wickedness, that was. You shouldn't have done it, you know, Bertie."

Curzon, with an effort, maintained an appearance of mild good manners, and pointed out that all he had done was to obey orders.

"Orders! Yes! It's all a system. That's what it is."

Mr. Cole seemed to think that in this case the word "system" was deeply condemnatory — to Curzon, of course, the word was, if anything, of the opposite implication. He was roused far enough to suggest to his uncle that if he had undergone the discomforts of two years of guerrilla warfare he might not be so particular as to the methods employed to suppress it.

"I wouldn't have gone," said Mr. Cole. "Not if they had tried to make me. Lord Roberts, now. 'E's trying to introduce conscription. Ought to 'ave more sense. And now there's all this talk about a big navy. Big fiddlestick!"

There was clearly no ground at all which was common to Mr. Cole and his nephew by marriage.

"Look at the rise in the income tax!" said Mr. Cole. "Two shillings in the pound! Peace, retrenchment, and reform. That's what we want. And a sane government, and no protection."

Curzon might have replied that Mr. Cole had nothing to complain about in the matter of income tax, seeing that his income was clearly below the taxable limit, but his good manners would not permit him to say so while he was conscious of his own seven hundred a year from his private means. Instead, he rose to go, apologizing for the briefness of his visit and pleading further urgent matters demanding his attention. He declined the tea which Aunt Kate belatedly remembered to offer him; he said, truthfully enough, that he never had tea, and the children goggled up in surprise at a man who could so lightly decline tea, and Aunt Kate said, "You'll be going to have late dinner, I suppose."

She accompanied him to the door.

"Good-bye, then, Bertie," she said. "It was nice of you to come. We'll be seeing you again soon, I suppose?"

"Yes, of course," said Curzon, and he knew it was a lie as he said it, that he would never be able to bring himself again to penetrate into Brixton. He thought the lie had succeeded, if he thought about it at all, but Aunt Kate dabbed furtively at her eyes before she went back into the parlour to talk over the visitor with her family. She knew perfectly well that she would never see "Lily's boy" again.

Meanwhile Curzon, out in the cabless suburban street, had to make his way on foot to the main road to some means of conveyance to take him back to his hotel. Before he took a cab he was constrained to go into a saloon bar and order himself a large whisky and soda, and while he drank it he had to mop his forehead and run his finger round underneath his collar as recollections of his visit surged up within him. He thanked God fervently that he was an orphan, that he was an only child, and that his father was an only child, and that his mother had had only one sister. He thanked God that his father's speculations in Mincing Lane had been early successful, so that preparatory school and Haileybury and Sandhurst had come naturally to his son.

In a moment of shuddering self-revelation he realised that in other circumstances it might have been just possible that he should have breathed naturally in the air of Brixton. Worse still he felt for a nauseating moment that in that environment he too might have been uncertain with his aitches and spoken about late dinner in a respectful tone of voice. It was bad enough to remember that as a child he had lived in Bayswater — although he could only just remember it, as they had early moved to Lancaster Gate. He had ridden in the Park, then, and his father had already decided that he should go into the Army and if possible into the cavalry among the real swells.

He could remember his father using that very expression, and he could remember his father's innocent pride in him at Sandhurst and when he had received his commission in the Duke of Suffolk's Own. Curzon struggled for a moment — so black was his mood — with the realisation that the Twenty-Second Lancers was not really a crack regiment. He could condescend to infantry men and native Indian army — poor devils — of course, but he knew perfectly well when he came to admit it to himself, as on this black occasion, that the House-holds and Horse Gunners and people like the Second Dragoons could condescend to him in their turn.

His father, of course, could not appreciate these distinctions and could have no realisation that it was impossible for a son of a Mincing Lane merchant to obtain a nomination to one of these exclusive regiments.

Perhaps it was as well that the old man had died when he did, leaving his twenty-year-old son the whole of his fortune — when his partnership had been realised and everything safely invested it brought in seven hundred a year. Seven hundred a year was rather on the small side, regarded as the private means of a cavalry subaltern, but it sufficed, and as during the South African War he had been unable to spend even his pay he was clear of debt for once and could look forward to a good time.

The world was growing rosier again now, with his second

whisky and soda inside him. He was able to light a cigar and plan his evening. By the time his cab had carried him up to town he was able to change into dress clothes without its crossing his mind even once that in other circumstances to change might not have been so much of a matter-of-course.

Chapter III

THERE were twelve years of peace between the two wars. It was those twelve years which saw Herbert Curzon undergo transformation from a young man into a middle-aged, from a subaltern into a senior major of cavalry. A complete record in detail of those twelve years would need twelve years in the telling to do it justice, so as to make it perfectly plain that nothing whatever happened during those twelve years; the professional life of an officer in a regiment of cavalry of the line is likely to be uneventful, and Curzon was of the type which has no other life to record.

They were twelve years of mess and orderly room; twelve years of inspection of horses' feet and of inquiry why Trooper Jones had been for three days absent without leave. Perhaps the clue to Curzon's development during this time is given by his desire to conform to type, and that desire is perhaps rooted too deep for examination. Presumably preparatory school and Haileybury and Sandhurst had something to do with it. Frequently it is assumed that it is inherent in the English character to wish not to appear different from one's fellows, but that is a bold assumption to make regarding a nation which has produced more original personalities than any other in modern times. It is safer to assume that the boldness and insensitiveness which is found sporadically among the English have developed despite all the influences which are brought to bear to nip them in the bud, and are therefore, should they survive to bear fruit, plants of sturdy growth.

Whether or not Herbert Curzon would have displayed originality, even eccentricity, if he had been brought up in another environment — in that of his cousins, Maudie and Gertie and Dick Cole, for instance — it is impossible to say. It sounds inconceivable to those of us who know him now, but it might be so. There can be no doubt whatever, on the other hand, that during the middle period of his life Curzon was distinguished by nothing more than his desire to be undistinguishable. The things which he did, he did because other people had done before him, and if a tactful person had been able to persuade him to defend himself for so doing he could only have said that to him that appeared an entirely adequate reason for doing them.

When as a senior captain in the regiment he quelled with crushing rudeness the self-assertiveness of some newly arrived subaltern in the mess, he did not do so from any feeling of personal animosity towards the wart in question (although the wart could not help feeling that this was the case) but because senior captains have always quelled self-assertive young subalterns.

He was a firm supporter of the rule that professional subjects should not be discussed in the mess. Whether the subject rashly brought up was "The Tactical Employment of Cavalry in the Next War" or the new regulations regarding heel-ropes, Curzon was always on the side of propriety, and saw to it that the discussion was short-lived. It did not matter to him — probably he did not know — that the convention prohibiting the discussion in mess of professional matters and of women dated back to the days of duelling, and that these two subjects about which men are more likely to grow angry had been barred then out of an instinct for self-preservation. It was sufficient to him that the convention was established; it was that fact which justified the convention.

And that his conviction was sincere in this respect was obvious. No one who knew him could possibly doubt that he would far rather receive another wound as bad as the one at Volkslaagte — more, that he would far rather go again through all the mental agony of Volkslaagte — than appear in public wearing a bowler hat and a morning coat. Even if he had thought such a combination beautiful (and he really never stopped to wonder whether anything was beautiful or not) he could not have worn it; indeed, it is difficult to imagine anything which would have induced him to do so. The example of the royal family over a series of years might have contrived it, but even then he would have been filled with misgivings.

The feeling of distaste for everything not done by the majority of those among whom he moved (wherever this feeling originated, in the germ or in the womb or at school or in the army) had its effect too on his professional career. The majority of his fellows did not apply to go through the Staff College; therefore he did not apply. There was only a small proportion of officers who by their ebullient personalities attracted the attention of their seniors; therefore Curzon made no effort to be ebullient in his personality — quite apart from his dislike of attracting attention.

These pushful, forceful persons had a black mark set against them in Curzon's mind for another reason as well, distinct although closely connected. They disturbed the steady even tenor of life which it was right and proper to expect. If routine made life more comfortable and respectable (just as did the prohibition of shop in mess) the man who disturbed that routine was an enemy of society. More than that, no man had any right whatever to upset the arrangements of his seniors.

There was a very painful occasion when Curzon was commanding a squadron and had just arranged a much desired shooting leave — it was during the five years that the regiment was stationed in India. Squires, his senior captain, came to him in high spirits, and announced that the War Office had at last seen fit to sanction his application for the Staff College; Squires would be leaving in a month. Curzon's face fell. A month from now his leave was due; a fortnight from now would arrive the new draft of recruits and remounts — hairy of heel all of them, as years of experience of recruits and remounts had taught him to expect. He had counted on Squires to get them into shape; Squires could be relied upon to keep the squadron up to the mark (as Curzon frankly admitted to himself) better than any of the remaining officers. Curzon had no hesitation when it came to choosing between the squadron and his leave. He must postpone his shooting, and he had been looking forward so much to the thrill and danger of following a gaur through blind cover.

"If the orders come through of course you must go," said Curzon. "But it's devilishly inconsiderate of you, Squires. I'll have to disappoint Marlowe and Colonel Webb."

"Blame the War House, don't blame me," said Squires, lightly, but of course it was Squires whom Curzon really blamed. The situation would never have arisen if he had not made his untimely application. It was years before Curzon could meet without instinctive distrust officers with p.s.c. after their name.

That may have been at the root of Curzon's distrust of theorists about war. It was not often that Curzon could be brought to discuss the theory of war, although he would argue gladly about its practical details, such as the most suitable ration of fodder or the pros and cons of a bit and snaffle. But apart from this distrust of theorists because of their tend-

[24]

ency to be different, there was also the more obvious reason that the majority of theorists were mad as hatters, or even madder. As soon as any man started to talk about the theory of war one could be nearly sure that he would bring forward some idiotic suggestion, to the effect that cavalry had had its day and that dismounted action was all that could be expected of it, or that machine guns and barbed wire had wrought a fundamental change in tactics, or even — wildest lunacy of all — that these rattletrap aeroplanes were going to be of some military value in the next war.

There was even a feather-brained subaltern in Curzon's regiment who voluntarily, in his misguided enthusiasm, quitted the ranks of the Twenty-Second Lancers, the Duke of Suffolk's Own, to serve in the Royal Flying Corps. He actually had the infernal impudence to suggest to the senior major of his regiment, a man with ribbons on his breast, who had seen real fighting, and who had won the battle of Volkslaagte by a cavalry charge, that the time was at hand when aeroplane reconnaissance would usurp the last useful function which could be performed by cavalry. When Major Curzon, simply boiling with fury at this treachery, fell back on the sole argument which occurred to him at the moment, and accused him of assailing the honour of the regiment with all its glorious traditions, he declared lightheartedly that he would far sooner serve in an arm with only a future than in one with only a past, and that he had no intention whatever of saying anything to the discredit of a regiment which was cut to pieces at Waterloo because they did not know when to stop charging, and that Major Curzon's argument was a non sequitur anyway.

With that he took his departure, leaving the Major livid with rage; it was agony to the Major that the young man's confidential report from the regiment had already gone in to the War Office and could not be recalled for alteration (as the young man had been well aware). Curzon could only fume and mutter, complaining to himself that the army was not what it was, that the manners of the new generation were infinitely worse than when he was a young man, and that their ideas were dangerously subversive of everything worth preserving.

This picture of Curzon in the years immediately before the war seems to verge closely on the conventional caricature of the army major, peppery, red-faced, liable under provocation to gobble like a turkey-cock, hidebound in his ideas and conventional in his way of thought, and it is no more exact than any other caricature. It ignores all the good qualities which were present at the same time. He was the soul of honour; he could be guilty of no meannesses, even boggling at those which convention permits. He would give his life for the ideals he stood for, and would be happy if the opportunity presented itself. His patriotism was a real and living force, even if its symbols were childish. His courage was unflinching. The necessity of assuming responsibility troubled him no more than the necessity of breathing. He could administer the regulations of his service with an impartiality and a practised leniency admirably suited to the needs of the class of man for which those regulations were drawn up. He shirked no duty, however tedious or inconvenient; it did not even occur to him to try to do so. He would never allow the instinctive deference which he felt towards great names and old lineage to influence him in the execution of anything he conceived to be his duty. The man with a claim on his friendship could make any demand upon his generosity. And while the breath was in his body he would not falter in the face of difficulties.

So much for an analysis of Curzon's character at the time when he was about to become one of the instruments of destiny. Yet there is something sinister in the coincidence that when Destiny had so much to do she should find tools of such high quality ready to hand. It might have been — though it would be a bold man who would say so — more advantageous for England if the British Army had not been quite so full of men of high rank who were so ready for responsibility, so unflinchingly devoted to their duty, so unmoved in the face of difficulties, of such unfaltering courage.

It might be so. But in recounting the career of Lieutenant-General Sir Herbert Curzon it would be incongruous to dwell on "mays" or "mights." There are more definite matters to record in describing the drama of his rise.

Chapter IV

THE first step came even before the declaration of war, during the tense forty-eight hours which followed mobilisation. Curzon was in the stables supervising the arrival of the remounts which were streaming in when a trooper came running up to him and saluted.

"Colonel's compliments, sir, and would you mind coming and speaking to him for a minute."

Curzon found the Colonel alone — he had passed the adjutant emerging as he entered — and the Colonel was standing erect with an opened letter in his hand. His face was the same colour as the paper he held.

"You're in command of the regiment, Curzon," said the Colonel.

"I — I beg your pardon, sir?" said Curzon.

"You heard what I said," snapped the Colonel, and then recovered himself with an effort and went on with pathetic calm. "These are War Office orders. You are to take command of the regiment with the temporary rank of Lieutenant-Colonel. I suppose it'll be in the *Gazette* to-morrow."

"And what about you, sir?" asked Curzon.

"I? Oh, I'm being given command of a brigade of Yeomanry. Up in the Northern Command somewhere."

"Good God!" said Curzon, genuinely moved.

"Yes, Yeomanry, man," blazed the Colonel. "Yokels on plough horses. It'll take a year to do anything with them at all, and the war'll be over in three months. And *you* are to take the regiment overseas."

"I'm damned sorry, sir," said Curzon, trying his best to soften the blow, "but it's promotion for you, after all."

"Promotion? Who cares a damn about promotion? I wanted to go with the regiment. You'll look after them, won't you, Curzon?"

"Of course I will, sir."

"You'll be in France in a fortnight."

"France, sir?" said Curzon, mildly surprised. The destination of the Expeditionary Force had been an object of some speculation. It might possibly have been Belgium or Schleswig.

"Yes," said the Colonel. "Of course, you don't know about that. It's in the secret mobilisation orders for commanding officers. You had better start reading them now, hadn't you? The British Army comes up on the left of the French. Maubeuge, and thereabouts. Here you are."

That moment when he was given the printed sheets, marked "Most Secret. For Commanding Officers of Cavalry Units Only" was to Curzon the most important and vital of his career. It marked the definite change from a junior officer's position to a senior officer's. It was the opening of the door to real promotion. It made it possible that the end of the war would find him a General. Naturally it was not given to Curzon to foresee that before the war should end he would be in command of more men than Wellington or Marlborough ever commanded in the field. And he never knew to what fortunate combination of circumstances he owed this most fortunate bit of promotion, for the secrets of War Office patronage are impenetrable. Of course, the memory of the battle of Volkslaagte had something to do with it. But presumably someone in the War Office had marked the fact that the Colonel of the Twenty-Second Lancers was verging on the age of retirement and had debated whether it would not be better for the regiment to be commanded by a forceful younger man, and at the same time the question of the Yeomanry brigade command had arisen, so that Curzon's promotion had solved a double difficulty. It maintained a reputable trainer of peace-time cavalry in a situation where his talents could be usefully employed, and it gave a man of proved ability in war a command in which he would find full scope.

If Curzon had had time to think about it at all, and if his self-conscious modesty had permitted it, he would undoubtedly have attributed these motives to the War Office; and as it was, his sub-conscious approval of them sent up his opinion of the Higher Command a good many degrees. Moreover, this approval of his was heightened by the marvellous way in which mobilisation was carried through. Reservists and remounts poured in with perfect smoothness. His indents for equipment were met instantly by the Command headquarters. In six brief days the Twenty-Second Lancers had expanded into a regiment of four full squadrons, complete in men and horses and transport, ammunition and supplies, ready to move on the first word from London — nor was the word long in coming.

Curzon, of course, had worked like a slave. He had interviewed every returning reservist; he had inspected every horse; he had studied his orders until he knew them by heart. Nor was this from personal motives, either. His anxiety about the efficiency of the regiment sprang not at all from the consideration that his professional future depended upon it. The job was there to be done, and done well, and it was his business to do it. Somewhere within his inarticulate depths was the feeling that England's future turned to some small extent upon his efforts, but he could not put that feeling into words even to himself. He could faintly voice his feelings regarding the credit of the Army, and of the Cavalry Arm in particular. He could speak and think freely about the honour of the regiment, because that was a subject people did speak about. But he could not speak of England; not even of the King — in just the same way the inarticulate regiment which followed its inarticulate colonel sang popular ballads instead of hymns to the Motherland.

Someone in London had done his work extraordinarily well. There never had been a mobilisation like this in all British history. In contrast with the methods of the past, which had scraped units together from all parts and flung them pellmell onto the Continental shore, without guns or transport or cavalry like Wellington in Portugal, or to die of disease and privation like the army in the Crimea, the present system had built up a real army ready for anything, and had means and arrangements perfected to put that army ashore lacking absolutely nothing which might contribute to its efficiency and its mobility.

One morning at dawn Curzon's servant called him exceptionally early; that same evening Curzon was on the quay at Le Havre supervising the disembarkation of the horses. That day had for Curzon a sort of dream-like quality; certain details stood out with extraordinary clarity although the general effect was blurred and unreal. All his life Curzon could remember the faces of the officers whom he had ordered to remain with the depot squadron looking on unhappily at the dawn parade, while the band played "God Save the King" and the men cheered themselves hoarse. He remembered the fussy self-importance of Carruthers, the Brigade-Major, who came galloping up to the railway sidings at which the regiment was entraining, to be greeted with cool self-confidence by Valentine, the Adjutant, who had every detail of the business at his fingers' ends. There was the lunch on board the transport, interrupted by the flight overhead of a non-rigid airship which formed part of the escort. And then finally the landing at Le Havre, and the business of getting men and horses into their billets — and someone here had done his work again so efficiently that there was no need for Curzon to recall to himself the cavalry colonel's active service maxim — "Feed the horses before the men, and the men before the officers, and the officers before yourself."

The feeling of unreality persisted during the long train journey which followed. The conveyance of the three thousand horses which belonged to the brigade was a business ineffably tedious. Feeding and watering the horses took up much time, and the men needed to have a sharp eye kept on them, because everyone in France seemed to have entered into a conspiracy to make the men drunk — there was free wine for them wherever they came in contact with civilians, and the young soldiers drank in ignorance of its potency and the old soldiers drank with delighted appreciation.

Curzon could not understand the French which the civilians talked with such disconcerting readiness. He had early formed a theory that French could only be spoken by people with a malformed larynx, and in his few visits to Paris he had always managed very well without knowing French; in fact he had been known to declare that "everyone in France knows English." That this was not the case was speedily shown in frequent contacts with village *maires* and with French railway officers, but Curzon did not allow the fact to distress him. Valentine spoke good French, and so did half a dozen of the other officers. It was sufficient for Curzon to give orders about what was to be said — in fact an inattentive observer of Curzon's impassive countenance would never have guessed at his ignorance of the language.

[32]

Then at last, on a day of sweltering sunshine, the regiment detrained in some gloomy sidings in the heart of a manufacturing and mining district. The brigade formed a column of sections two miles long on a dreary paved road and began to move along it, with halts and delays as orders came in afresh. The officers were bubbling with excitement, looking keenly at their maps and scanning the countryside eagerly to see if it would be suitable for mounted action; and in that they were disappointed. There were slag heaps, and enclosures. There was barbed wire in the hedges, and there were deep, muddy ditches — there could be no hell-for-leather charging, ten squadrons together, on this terrain.

Curzon rode at the head of his regiment. Frequently he turned and looked back along the long column of sections, the khaki-clad men and the winding caterpillar of lance points. Try after self-control as he would, his heart persisted in beating faster. He even noticed a slight trembling of his hands as he held his reins, which was a symptom which roused his contempt and made him spurn himself as being as excitable as a woman. The Brigadier, riding along the column, reined in beside him for a moment and dropped a compliment about the condition of the regiment, but the brief conversation was suddenly interrupted by the roar of artillery close ahead. The General galloped forward to be on hand when orders should arrive, and Curzon was left riding wordlessly with Valentine at his elbow, waiting with all his acquired taciturnity for the moment for action.

Unhappily it was not given to the Twenty-Second Lancers to distinguish themselves at Mons. To this day, when Curzon can be induced to talk about his experiences in the war, he always slurs over the opening period. Other regiments, more fortunate, fought real cavalry actions — but they were divisional cavalry or part of the brigade out on the left, who were lucky in encountering German cavalry of like mind to themselves, without wanton interference by cyclists or infantry. Curzon's brigade stayed in reserve behind the line while the battle of Mons was being fought. Twice during that dreary day, they were moved hither and thither as the fortune of the battle in their front swayed back and forth. They heard the wild roar of the firing; they saw the river of wounded flowing back past them, and they saw the British batteries in action, but that was all. Even the Brigadier knew no more than they, until, towards evening, the wounded told them that Mons had been lost to a converging attack by overwhelming numbers. Night fell with the men in bivouac; the general opinion was that next day would see a great counter attack in which the cavalry would find its opportunity.

Curzon lay down to sleep in the shelter of a hedge; he did not share the opinion of his officers, but neither could he oppose it. That feeling of unreality still held him fast, numbing the action of his mind. It was absurd to feel as he did, as if these things were not really happening, as if nothing would ever happen, and yet he could not shake himself free from the feeling. Then he was wakened with a start in the darkness by someone shaking his shoulder.

"Orders, sir," said Valentine's voice.

He read the scrap of paper by the light of the electric torch which Valentine held. It told him briefly that the brigade was to form on the road preparatory to a fresh march — nothing more.

"Get the regiment ready to move off at once," he said, forcing himself into wakefulness.

There was a rush and bustle in the darkness, the whinnying of horses and the clattering of hoofs as the troopers, stupid with cold and sleep, prepared for the march. There was an interminable delay as the brigade formed up on the road, and dawn was just breaking as the march began. The march went on for eleven mortal days.

Curzon remembered little enough about those eleven days. At first there was a sense of shame and disappointment, for the British Army was in retreat, and the Twenty-Second Lancers were in the lead, while far in the rear the boom and volleying of the guns told how the rearguard was still hotly engaged. But as the retreat went on the artillery fire waned, and exhaustion increased. Every day was one of blazing sun and suffocating dust. Sometimes the marches were prolonged far into the night; sometimes they began long before day was come, so that the men fell asleep in their saddles. The horses fell away in condition until even Curzon's fine black hunter could hardly be forced into a trot by the stab of the sharpened spurs into his thickcoated flanks. The trim khaki uniforms were stained and untidy; beards sprouted on every cheek. Every day saw the number of absentees increase — two or three one day, ten or twelve the next, twenty or thirty the next, as the horses broke down and the regimental bad characters drank themselves into stupor to forget their fatigue. In the rear of the regiment trailed a little band of dismounted men, limping along with blistered feet under the burden of as much of their cavalry equipment as they could carry. Curzon scanned the nightly lists of missing with dumb horror. At the halts he hobbled stiffly among the men, exhorting them to the best of his limited ability to keep moving for the honour of the regiment, but something more than dust dried up his throat, and he was not a good enough actor to conceal entirely the despondency which was overpowering him.

Then there came a blessed day when the orders to continue the retreat were countermanded at the very moment when the brigade was formed up on the road. A moment later the Brigadier himself came up. He could give Curzon no reason for the change, but after half an hour's wait he gave permission for the regiment to fall out. There were pleasant meadows there, marshy presumably in winter, but hardly damp at the moment, by the side of a little stream of black water. They had a whole day of rest in those meadows. They cleaned and polished and shaved. As many as forty stragglers came drifting in during the morning — they had not been permanently lost, but having fallen out for a moment they had got jammed in the column farther to the rear and had never been able to rejoin. Everybody's spirits rose amazingly during those sunny hours. The Quartermaster-General's department achieved its daily miracle and heaped rations upon them, so that the men drank quarts of tea, brewed over bivouac fires, and then slept in heaps all over the meadows.

Curzon was able to find time to sit in his portable bath in a screened corner of the field, and to shave himself carefully and to cut his ragged moustache into its trim Lancer shape again — it was that afternoon that he first noticed grey hairs in it (there had been a few in his temples for some time now) and characteristically it never occurred to him to attribute their presence to the fatigues and anxieties of the last month. One servant brushed his clothes, the other groomed his horse, until by late afternoon Curzon for the first time since he landed in France began to feel his old efficient, clear-thinking self again.

A motor cyclist with a blue and white brassard came tearing along the road and stopped his machine at the entrance to the field. Valentine tore his dispatch from him and came running across the grass to Curzon.

"Are we going to advance, sir?" he asked eagerly, and Curzon nodded as he read the orders.

"Trumpeter!" yelled Valentine, all on fire with excitement.

The whole regiment seemed to have caught the infection, for as soon as the men saw that the column was headed back

[36]

the way they had come they began to cheer, and went on cheering madly for several minutes as they got under way. They went back up the white road, over the little bridge with its R.E. demolition party still waiting, and forward towards where the distant low muttering of the guns was beginning to increase in volume and rise in pitch.

And yet the advance soon became as wearisome as the retreat had been. The regiment marched and marched and marched, at first in the familiar choking white dust, and then, when the weather broke, in a chilly and depressing rain. They saw signs of the fighting they had missed — wrecked lorries in the ditches, occasional abandoned guns, and sometimes dead Englishmen, dead Frenchmen, dead Germans. It seemed as if the Twenty-Second Lancers were doomed to be always too late. They had not lost a man at Mons; the Marne had been fought while they were twenty miles away; they arrived on the Aisne just as the attempt to push back the German line farther still died away.

The Brigadier saw fit to rage in confidence to Curzon about this one evening in Curzon's billet. He bore it as a personal grudge that his brigade should have had no casualties save stragglers during a month's active service. But before midnight that same evening the situation changed. Curzon hurried round to brigade headquarters, his sword at his side, in response to a brief note summoning commanding officers. The Brigadier greeted his three colonels with a smile of welcome.

"There's work for us now, gentlemen," he said eagerly, leading them to the map spread on the table. "There's more marching ahead of us, but — "

He poured out voluble explanations. It appeared that during the retreat the Expeditionary Force's base had been transferred from Havre to St. Nazaire, and now would be changed again to the Channel ports. The German right flank was "in the air" somewhere here, at Armentières. Clearly it would be best if it were the British army which was dispatched to find that flank and turn the German line so as to roll it back on the Rhine and Berlin. The transfer was to begin next day, infantry and artillery by rail, cavalry by road, and he, the Brigadier, had been given a promise that the brigade would be in the advanced guard this time. It would be *here,* said the General, pointing to Ypres, that the attack would be delivered, up *this* road, he went on, pointing to Menin. The Belgian army cavalry school was at Ypres, so that was clear proof that the country roundabout was suitable for mounted action. There were six men bending over that map — the General, three Colonels, the Brigade Major, and some unknown staff officer, and five of them were to find their graves at the point where the General's gnarled finger was stabbing at the map. Yet with Curzon at the moment his only reaction at this, his first hearing of the dread name of Ypres, was that it should be spelt in such an odd fashion and pronounced in a still odder one.

Chapter V

THE weary marches were resumed, mostly in the rain. The brigade toiled along by byroads to the rear of the French line, crossing, often only after long delays, one line of communication after the other. They saw unsoldierly French territorial divisions, French coloured divisions, French ammunition and supply columns. After the second day came the order to hasten their march, with the result that they were on the move now from dawn till dark, hurrying through the rain, while the list of the absent lengthened with each day.

For the flank of the allies was as much "in the air" as was that of the Germans, and Falkenhayn was making a thrust at the weak point just as was Joffre. The units which were gathering about Ypres were being pushed forward hurriedly into action, and every reinforcement which could be scraped together was being called upon to prolong the line. At Hazebrouck the roar of battle round about Armentières was clearly to be heard; it was the sight of British ammunition columns pouring up the road from Poperinghe and the stream of English wounded down it which first told Curzon that this was to be no case of heading an advance upon an unprotected and sensitive German flank.

It had been soon after midnight that fresh orders came to call them out of their muddy bivouac. Dawn found them plodding along the road through the rain. There were motor cars, motor cycle despatch riders, mounted orderlies hastening along the straight tree-lined road. An order came back to Curzon to quicken his pace; before very long Carruthers, the Brigade Major, came back at the gallop to reiterate it. But the horses were very weary. It was only a spiritless trot which could be got out of them as the regiment with jingling of accoutrements and squeaking of leather pounded heavily down the road.

The rain fell pitilessly, numbing the faculties. Suddenly there was a roar like an express train overhead, a shattering explosion, and a column of black smoke at the very edge of the road twenty yards behind Curzon. Somebody yelped with dismay. A horse screamed. Curzon looked back over his shoulder. There was a gap in the long column of dancing lance points.

"Keep them closed up, Browning," he growled to the Major at his side commanding the squadron, and Browning swung his horse out of the column, while Curzon rode on, Valentine at his side, jinglety-bump, jinglety-bump, over the slippery pavé.

More shells followed. Curzon found himself riding round the edge of a gaping hole in the road. There was a horrible litter of fragments of men and horses there, but Curzon found he was able to look at it without sensation; he could even note that none of the dead men had lances, and therefore belonged to the Dragoon regiment at the head of the brigade, of which two squadrons had sabres only. They were in among houses now — several houses had shell holes in walls or roof — and a pale staff officer with his left sleeve missing and a bloodstained bandage round his bare arm suddenly appeared and guided Curzon off by a by-road.

"Halt here, please, sir," he said. "You will receive orders in a minute."

And the regiment stood still in the narrow street, the horses steaming in the rain, while the shells burst round them and Curzon tugged at his moustache. To judge by the noise, there were half a dozen batteries in action close at hand; the regiment was in the heart of a battle greater than Mons. The rain began to fall more heavily still, suddenly, just at the moment when the Brigadier came round the corner with his staff and the pale staff officer. Curzon moved to meet them, to be abruptly greeted.

"What in hell are you doing, Curzon?" blazed the General. "Get your men dismounted and horseholders told off. Quick!"

Generals, of course, had to be allowed their fits of bad temper. It was only natural that a colonel of a cavalry regiment should keep his men ready for mounted action in the absence of express orders to the contrary. Curzon left Valentine to see to the dismounting of the men, while he got off his horse and looked at the map which the Brigade Major held open.

"The brigade is to prolong the line *here,*" said the Brigade Major. "You will come up on the left of the Surreys *here.* The Dragoons will be on your right."

Curzon stared at the map, on which the raindrops fell with a steady pitter-patter. It was a featureless affair, with featureless names like St. Eloi and Kemmel and Messines — he had one like it in his leather map case.

"Major Durrant here will guide you," went on the Brigade Major. "Site your machine guns with a good field of fire and get your line entrenched as quick as you can."

"Very good," said Curzon. It seemed incredible that Carruthers could be talking to a cavalry colonel about machine guns and entrenchments like this — Carruthers, who, that very summer in England, had argued so vehemently in favour of lance versus sabre. The words brought back that nightmare feeling of unreality again, but the General dispelled it a moment afterwards.

"Curzon," he said quietly. "We're the last troops that can arrive, and we're going straight into the line. There's nothing behind us. Nothing at all. If we give way, the war's lost. So there's nothing for you to do except to hold your position to the last man. At all costs, Curzon."

"Yes, sir," said Curzon, and the mist lifted from his brain immediately. That was the kind of order he could understand.

"Right," said the General, and then, to Carruthers, "Let's get along to the Dragoons."

"Bring your regiment this way, sir," said the wounded staff officer, and then, seeing the regimental officers still mounted, he added. "They won't want their horses. You won't want your horse, sir, either."

They marched, already weary with much riding, through the streets. Curzon took notice slightly of a long building which reminded him a little of the Houses of Parliament, and then they were out of the town again in flat green fields rising before them in the faintest of elevations.

"There go the Surreys," said the staff officer, pointing over to their left front. "You come up on their right."

As he said the words, the First Battle of Ypres engulfed the Twenty-Second Lancers. For two days now each successive parcel of British troops as it arrived had just sufficed to patch or extend the wavering front in face of the masses which the Germans were hurrying to the same point. The arrival of the last cavalry brigade enabled the British command to close the last gap with less than a quarter of an hour to spare, for the German attack here was launched just as the Twenty-Second Lancers extended into line. There was no time for Curzon to think about entrenchments or a good field of fire for his machine guns. A sudden hail of bullets and shells fell all

[42]

about the regiment, and then even as cavalry tradition evapo-
rated and primeval instinct asserted itself in a search for cover,
monstrous grey masses came looming through the rain over
the slight crest half a mile in front.

There was no time for orders or scientific fire control. It
was every man's business to seize his rifle and begin firing as
rapidly as he could at the advancing lines. They wavered and
hesitated, came on again, and finally shredded away. Immediately afterwards, fresh masses came pouring over the crest,
gathering up with them the remains of their predecessors.
There were mounted officers in the front, waving swords over
their heads as if this was Malplaquet or Waterloo. Curzon,
standing staring through his glasses, watched them toppling
down one by one as the attack died away. He stared mes-
merised until he suddenly awoke to the realisation that bullets
were crackling all around him. The enemy were lying down
firing until fresh impetus could be gathered to renew the attack.

He looked along the line of his regiment. There was no
trace of order there; half the men had established themselves
in a drainage ditch which miraculously ran roughly in the
desired direction and afforded cover to anyone who could
bring himself to lie down in its thick black mud. That meant
the centre was as solidly established as one could hope to be.
Young Borthwick — Lieutenant the Honourable George Borthwick — was in an angle of a tributary ditch to the front with
his machine gun section, the men digging frantically with anything that came to hand so as to burrow into the bank for
shelter. Borthwick had been given the machine guns not as
the most promising machine gun officer in the regiment (a
distinction the whole mess scorned) but because he had the
most slovenly seat on a horse that had ever disgraced the ranks
of the Twenty-Second Lancers. Curzon realised with a twinge

[43]

of anxiety that the reputation of the regiment suddenly had come to depend to a remarkable extent on how much efficiency young Borthwick had acquired at his job.

He strode over to inspect Borthwick's efforts, Valentine beside him. He leaped the muddy ditch, in which the regiment was crouching, so as not to soil his boots, and stood on the lip of the bank looking down at where Borthwick was sitting in the mud with the lock of a machine gun on his lap.

"Are you all right, Borthwick?" he asked.

"Yes, sir," said Borthwick, sparing him just a glance, and then to his Sergeant. "Is that belt ready?"

Curzon left him to his own devices; this much was certain, that however little Borthwick knew about machine guns it was more than Curzon did. They went back to the ditch.

"Better have a look at the flanks," said Curzon, and took his leisurely way to the right. The men stared at him. In that pelting hail of bullets they felt as if they could not get close enough to the ground, and yet here was the Colonel standing up and walking about as cool as a cucumber. It was not so much that Curzon was unafraid, but that in the heat of action and under the burden of his responsibility he had not stopped to realise that there was any cause for fear.

The right flank was not nearly so satisfactorily posted as the centre. The little groups of men scattered along here were almost without cover. They were cowering close to the ground behind casual inequalities of level — several men were taking cover behind the dead bodies of their comrades — and only the accident that there were three shell craters close together at this point gave any semblance of solidity to the line. Moreover, there was only a pretence of touch maintained with the Dragoons on the right; there was a full hundred yards bare of defenders between the Lancers' right and the beginning of the ditch wherein was established the Dragoons' left.

"Not so good," said Curzon over his shoulder to Valentine and received no reply. He looked round. Ten yards back one of those bullets had killed Valentine, silently, instantly, as Curzon saw when he bent over the dead body.

And as he stooped, he heard all the rifles in the line redouble their fire. Borthwick's two machine guns began to stammer away on his left. The Germans were renewing their advance; once more there were solid masses of grey-clad figures pouring over the fields towards them. But one man with a rifle can stop two hundred advancing in a crowd, — more still if he is helped by machine guns. Curzon saw the columns reel under the fire, and marvelled at their bravery as they strove to struggle on. They bore terrible losses before they fell back again over the crest.

Curzon did not know — and he did not have either time or inclination at the moment to ponder over the enemy's tactics — that the attacking troops at this point were drawn from the six German divisions of volunteers, men without any military training whatever, who were being sent forward in these vicious formations because they simply could not manoeuvre in any other. What he did realise was that as soon as the enemy realised the hopelessness of these attacks, and turned his artillery against the regiment, the latter would be blasted into nothingness in an hour of bombardment unless it could contrive shelter. He walked along the line, with the bullets still crackling round him.

"Get your men digging," he said to Captain Phelps, the first officer he saw.

"Yes, sir," said Phelps. "Er — what are they going to dig with, sir?"

Curzon looked Phelps up and down from his cropped fair hair and pop-eyes to his sword belt and his boots. It was a question which might reasonably have been asked on ma-

[45]

noeuvres. Cavalry had no entrenching tools, and the Twenty-Second Lancers had, from motives of pride, evaded throughout their corporate existence the annual two hours' instruction in field fortification which the regulations prescribed for cavalry. But this was war now. A battle would be lost, England would be endangered, if the men did not entrench. Curzon boiled with contempt for Phelps at that moment. He felt he could even see trembling on Phelps's lips a protest about the chance of the men soiling their uniforms, and he was angered because he suspected that he himself would have been stupid and obstructive if his brain had not been activated by his urgent, imminent responsibility.

"God damn it, man!" he blazed. "Get your men digging, and don't ask damn-fool questions."

The fear of death or dishonour will make even cavalry dig, even without tools; especially when they were urged on by a man like Curzon, and when they were helped by finding themselves in muddy fields whose soil yielded beneath the most primitive make-shift tools. A man could dig in that mud with his bare hands — many men did. The Twenty-Second sank into the earth just as will a mole released upon a lawn. The crudest, shallowest grave and parapet quadrupled a man's chance of life.

The fortunate ditch which constituted the greater part of the regiment's frontage, and the shallow holes dug on the rest of it, linked together subsequently by succeeding garrisons, constituted for months afterwards the front line of the British trench system in the Salient — a haphazard line, its convolutions dictated by pure chance, and in it many men were to lose their lives for the barren honour of retaining that worthless ground, overlooked and searched out by observation from the slight crests above (each of which, from Hill 60 round to Pilckem, was to acquire a name of ill omen) which the cavalry brigade had chanced to be too late by a quarter of an hour to occupy.

For the moment there could be no question of readjustment of the line. Some time in the late afternoon the bombardment began — a rain of shells compared with which anything Curzon had seen in South Africa was as a park lake to the ocean. It seemed impossible for anything to live through it. The bombardment seemed to reduce men to the significance of ants, but, like ants, they sought and found shelter in cracks in the ground; the very pits the shells dug gave them protection, for this bombardment, so colossal to their dazed minds, was not to be compared with the later bombardments of the war when mathematical calculations showed that every patch of ground must be hit by three separate shells.

When it was falling dark the bombardment ceased and the German volunteers came forward in a new attack, climbing over their heaped dead, to leave fresh swathes of corpses only a few yards farther on. It was the lifting of the bombardment and the roar of musketry from the Surreys on the left which the dazed men, huddled in the mud, first noticed, but it was Curzon who repelled that attack. There was no limit to his savage energy in the execution of a clear-cut task. He had no intention in the least of impressing his men with his ability to be everywhere at once, but that was the impression which the weary troopers formed of him. In his anxiety to see that every rifle was in action he hurried about the line rasping out his orders. The wounded and the faint-hearted alike brought their rifles to their shoulders again under the stimulus of his presence. It was this kind of leadership for which all his native talents, all his experience and all his training were best suited. While Curzon was at hand not the most fleeting thought of retreat could cross a man's mind.

The attack withered away, and darkness came, and the pitiless chilling rain continued to fall. Curzon, with every nerve at strain with the responsibility on his shoulders, felt no need for rest. There was much to be done — ammunition to be gathered from the pouches of the dead, patrols to be sent out to the front to guard against a night surprise, wounded to be got out of the way, back to the shell hole where the medical officer crouched trying to save life by the last glimmerings of a dying electric torch. The earth still shook to the guns, the sky was still lighted by the flame of the explosions. Shells were still coming over, and every little while a tremor of alarm ran down the attenuated line and men grabbed their rifles and fired blindly into the darkness while the patrols out in front fell flat on their faces and cursed their own countrymen.

There was an alarm from the rear while Curzon was stumbling along through the dark seeing that the line was evenly occupied. He heard the well remembered voice of the Brigadier saying "Point that rifle the other way, you fool," and he hastened back to where a trooper was sheepishly allowing the General and a dozen looming forms behind him to approach.

"Ah, Curzon," said the General when he heard his voice. "All well here?"

"Yes, sir," said Curzon.

"I've had to bring up the supply column myself," said the General.

A brighter flash then usual lit up the forms of the men in his train; the leader was in R.E. uniform and bent under a load of spades.

"Thank God for those," said Curzon. He would not have believed, three months back, that he would ever have thanked God for a gift of spades, but now he saw no incongruity.

"I thought you'd be glad of 'em," chuckled the General. "I've got you fifty spades. The rest's S.A.A. I suppose you can do with that, too?"

"My God, yes," said Curzon. The supply of small arms ammunition had fallen away to less than a dozen rounds a man. He had not dared to think what would happen when it was finished.

"Take it over, then," said the General. "I've got a lot more for these men to do."

"Can't they stay here, sir?" said Curzon. He longed inexpressibly for a reinforcement of a dozen riflemen.

"No," snapped the General, and then, to the carrying party. "Put that stuff down and get back as quick as you can."

There was a bustle in the darkness as the regiment took charge of the loads. The voice of Lieutenant Borthwick could be heard demanding ammunition for his precious guns. Curzon left Major Browning to supervise the distribution while, obedient to a plucked sleeve, he followed the General away out of earshot of the men.

"I couldn't send you up any food," said the General. "But you're all right until to-morrow for that, with your emergency rations. You'll have two a man, I suppose, counting what you'll get off the dead."

"Pretty nearly, sir," said Curzon.

"You'll be able to hold on, I suppose?" went on the General, his voice dropping still lower. His face was invisible in the darkness.

"Of course, sir," said Curzon.

"Speak the truth — lying's no use."

Curzon ran his mind's eye over the line, visualising the improvements those fifty spades would bring about, the new life the fresh ammunition would bring to Borthwick's guns, the piled dead on the hilltop above, the exhaustion of his troopers.

"Yes, we ought to get through to-morrow all right," he said.

"To-morrow? You'll have to hold on for a fortnight, perhaps. But let's get through to-morrow first. You've got patrols out? You're strengthening your line?"

"Yes, sir."

"I knew I could trust you all right. I couldn't get over here during the day — had to stay with the Surreys. Browne's dead, you know."

"Not really, sir?"

"Yes. And so's Harvey of the Dragoons. You succeed to the brigade if I'm hit."

"Don't say that, sir."

"Of course I must say it. But I've got no orders to give you in case I am. It'll just mean holding on to the last man."

"Yes, sir."

"There's two hundred men in the brigade reserve. Horse holders, R.E.'s. A.S.C. Don't be lavish with 'em, because that's all there are between here and Havre. And don't trust that major who's commanding the Surreys now. You know who I mean — Carver's his name."

"Yes, sir."

"I'm getting a second line dug on the edge of the wood back there. But it won't be any use if they break through. Not enough men to man it. So you've got to hold on. That's all."

"Yes, sir."

"Goodnight, Curzon."

"Goodnight, sir."

The darkness engulfed the General as he plodded back alone across the sodden earth, and Curzon went back into the trench, to goad the men into more furious digging, to see that the sentries were alert. Yet even despite Curzon's activity, despite the guns, and the shells, and the pitiless rain, there were men who slept, half buried in the mire — there never was a time when at least a few British private soldiers in any unit could not contrive an opportunity for sleep.

Chapter VI

PERHAPS it had been a premonition which had caused the Brigadier General to talk so freely to Curzon about what should be done should the latter succeed to his command. It was no later than next morning, when the German bombardment was searching for the shallow seam in the earth wherein crouched the Twenty-Second Lancers, that a mud-daubed runner came crawling up the drainage ditch which had already assumed the function of a communication trench in this section, and gave Curzon a folded scrap of paper. The writing was blurred and shaky, and the signature was indecipherable, but the meaning was clear. The General was dead and Curzon was in command of the brigade. The runner was able to supplement the information — a shell had hit the brigade headquarters and had killed or wounded everyone there and left everything disorganised. It was clearly necessary that Curzon should waste no time in taking over his duties.

He passed the word for Major Browning, and briefly handed over the command of the regiment to him.

"What are the orders, sir?" asked Browning.

A Frenchman would have shrugged his shoulders at that question. Curzon could only eye Browning with a stony expressionless gaze.

"None, except to hold on to the last man," he said, not taking his eyes off Browning's face. Perhaps this was as well, for he saw a flicker of despair in Browning's eyes. "You understand, Browning?"

"Yes, sir," said Browning, but Curzon had already made a mental note that Browning of the Twenty-Second Lancers would need stiffening as much as Carver of the Surreys.

"Those are positive orders, Browning," he said. "There's no chance of their being modified, and you have no discretion."

"Yes, sir," said Browning. Whatever motives had led Browning to join the Twenty-Second Lancers as a pink-faced subaltern twenty years ago he was being condemned for them now to mutilation or death, and Curzon did not feel sorry for him, only irritated. Men who stopped to think about their chances of being killed were a nuisance to their superior officers.

"Right," said Curzon. "I'll come up again and inspect as soon as I can."

He picked his way along the ditch, the runner crawling behind him. But such was his appreciation of the need for haste that Curzon ignored the danger of exposing himself, and walked upright across the fields pitted with shell holes while the runner cursed him to himself. The cottage beside the lane to which the runner guided him had been almost completely demolished by a high explosive shell. As Curzon approached, the first sound to strike his ear was a high pitched, querulous stream of groans and blasphemies. There were some dead bodies and fragments of bodies lying on the edge of the lane, and the red tabs on one obscene fragment showed what had happened to the Brigadier. The groans and blasphemies came from Carruthers, the Brigade Major, or what was left of him. There was an orderly bending over him, as he lay on the grass, but the orderly was despairing of inducing this shrieking thing which had graced so many race meetings ever to be silent. Five or six runners were squatting stoically in the ditch near the cottage; there was an R.E. detachment stumbling through the cabbages in the garden with a reel of telephone wire.

Within the shattered walls, down in the cellar now exposed to the light of day, lay Durrant, the staff officer who yesterday had guided the Twenty-Second into action. His left arm was still bare, but the bandage round it was no longer red but black, and his tunic was torn open at the breast showing white skin. He was putting a field telephone back on its hook as Curzon arrived, and, catching sight of him, he snatched it up again with a hasty —

"Hullo. Hold on. Here he is."

Then he looked up at Curzon and went on:

"We're through to the First Corps, sir. Just re-established communication."

Curzon lowered himself into the cellar and took up the instrument. There was a moment of murmurings and grumblings before the earpiece spoke.

"Commanding the Cavalry Brigade?" it asked.

"Yes. This is Colonel Curzon, Twenty-Second Lancers, just taken over."

"Right. You'll go on reporting to us for the present. We've told your division."

"Very well. Any orders?"

"You are to hold your position at all costs. At — all — costs. Good-bye."

Curzon put down the receiver and stood silent. The pain-extorted ravings of Carruthers, twenty yards away, came pouring down to him, cutting through the roar of the battle, but he heard neither sound. He was tugging at his moustache; his rather full, rather loose lips were set hard and straight. He was adjusting his mind to the business of commanding a brigade; and he was ready for the responsibility in ten seconds, and turned to the wounded staff officer.

[53]

"Any report from the Dragoons?" he demanded.

That was the beginning of eleven days of anxiety and danger and responsibility and desperate hard work. Even if Curzon had the necessary literary ability, he could never write an account of the First Battle of Ypres in which he took so prominent a part, for his later recollections of it could never be sorted out from the tangle into which they lapsed. He could never recover the order in which events occurred. He could never remember which day it was that the commander of the First Corps, beautifully groomed, superbly mounted, came riding up the lane to see for himself what were the chances of the cavalry brigade maintaining its precarious hold upon its seemingly untenable position, nor which day it was that he had spent in the trenches of the Surreys, leading the counter attack which caused the Germans to give back at the moment when there were only a hundred or two exhausted Englishmen to oppose the advance of an army corps.

Curzon's work during these eleven days resembled that of a man trying to keep in repair a dam which is being undermined by an unusual flood. He had to be here, there, and everywhere plastering up weak points — the materials at his disposal being the two hundred men of the brigade reserve whom he had found ready to his hand, and the scrapings of other units, reservists, L. of C. troops, which were sent up to him once or twice from G.H.Q. There was the ammunition supply to be maintained, food to be sent up into the line — for water the troops drank from the stagnant pools in the shell holes — and bombs to be doled out from the niggardly supply which the R.E. detachments in the field were just beginning to make.

He had to watch over his reserves like a miser, for he was pestered every minute with pathetic appeals from his subordinates for aid — and in this conservation of his resources his natural temperament was of use of him, because he found no difficulty in saying "no," however urgently the request was drafted, if his judgment decided against it. He put new heart into the men by the way in which he disregarded danger, for to his natural courage was added the mental preoccupation which gave him no chance to think about personal risks. No soldier in the world could have remained unmoved by the nonchalant fashion in which he was always ready to lead into danger. In every crisis his big arrogant nose and heavy black moustache were to be seen as he came thrusting forward to judge for himself. Over and over again during those eleven days it was his arrival which turned the scale.

He was one of the fortunate ones. In the battle where the old British Army found its grave, where more than two-thirds of the fighting men met with wounds or death, he came through unscathed even though there were bullet holes in his clothes. It was as unlikely that he should survive as that a spun penny should come down heads ten times running, and yet he did; it was only men with that amount of good fortune who could come through long enough to make the tale of their lives worth the telling.

He was fortunate, too, in the chance of war which had put his brigade into line separate from the rest of the cavalry corps. There was no divisional general to reap the credit of the work done by his men, and the Corps Headquarters under whose direction he was placed regarded with approval the officer who carried out his orders with so little protest or complaint or appeal for further assistance, and who was always ready to try and wring another ounce of effort out of his exhausted men.

The old army died so gloriously at Ypres because the battle they had to fight called for those qualities of unflinching courage and dogged self-sacrifice in which they were pre-eminent. They were given the opportunity of dying for their country and they died uncomplaining. It occurred to no one that they had to die in that fashion because the men responsible for their training had never learned any lessons from history, had never realised what resources modern invention had opened to them, with the consequence that men had to do at the cost of their lives the work which could have been done with one-quarter the losses and at one-tenth the risk of defeat if they had been adequately armed and equipped. And of the surviving officers the ones who would be marked out for promotion and high command in the new army to be formed were naturally the ones who had proved themselves in the old fashioned battle—men like Curzon of the Twenty-Second Lancers.

For there could be no doubt at all that the High Command looked with approval on Curzon. When eventually the arrival of new units from distant garrisons and of an army corps from India enabled the exhausted front line troops to be withdrawn, a very great general indeed sent for Curzon at headquarters. The message arrived the very day that Curzon brought the cavalry brigade out of the line. He saw the brigade into billets—not much accommodation was necessary for those few score survivors, filthy, vermin-ridden men who fell asleep every few minutes—and did his best to smarten himself up. Then he got on his horse—it was good to feel a horse again between his knees—and rode slowly over in the dark of the late afternoon.

To Curzon there was something incredibly satisfying in his arrival at that pleasant château. He had seen enough of ruin and desolation, of haggard men in tatters, of death and wounds and misery, during the past weeks. Some of his beliefs and convictions had been almost shaken lately. It was a nightmare world from which he had emerged—a world in which cavalry regiments had clamoured for barbed wire, reels and reels of it, and in which horses had been left ungroomed and neglected so that their holders could be sent into action with rifles and bayonets, and in which he had almost begun to feel doubts as to England's ultimate victory.

It was like emerging from a bad dream to ride in at the gates of the château, to have a guard turn out to him all spick and span, and to have his horse taken in charge by a groom whose uniform did not detract in the least from his general appearance of an old family retainer. There were beautiful horses looking out from loose-boxes; there were half a dozen motor cars polished to a dazzling glitter.

Then inside the house the atmosphere changed a little. Outside, it was like a country house with a military flavour. Inside it was like a court with a dash of monastery. There were the court functionaries moving about here and there, suave, calm, and with an air of unfathomable discretion. There were the established favourites, with a bit of swagger. There were anxious hangers-on, wondering what sort of reception would be accorded them to-day, and the rare visitors of Curzon's type who were not in the court uniform — the red tabs — and who only knew by sight the great ones who went to and fro.

The man who occupied the position corresponding to that of Grand Chamberlain came up to greet Curzon. Anyone better acquainted with courts would have been delighted with the cordiality of his reception, but to Curzon it only appeared as if he were receiving the politeness expected from a gentleman. It was good to drink whisky and soda again — only yesterday he had been drinking army rum out of an enamelled mug — and to exchange a few polite platitudes about the weather with no bearing on the military situation. The nightmare feeling of desperate novelty dropped away from Curzon as he stood and talked. This was life as it should be. His very weariness and the ache in his temples from lack of sleep was no more than he had often felt on his first return to the mess after a night in town. He was inexpressibly glad that he had recovered his kit at his billet and so had been able to change from his muddy tunic with the bullet holes in the skirt. A junior chamberlain came out of a blanket-hung door on the far side of the hall and came up to them with a significant glance at his senior. The time had come for Curzon's admission to the presence.

They went through the blanket-covered door into a long room, with windows extending along the whole of one side giving a fine view over a beautiful park. There were tables covered with papers; clerks at work with typewriters; maps on the wall; more green baize tables; half a dozen red-tabbed officers with telephones before them at work in a very pleasant smell of cigars; and a door at the far end which gave entrance to a smaller room with the same view, the same green baize tables, and a chair which was politely offered to Curzon.

The actual interview was brief enough. Curzon had the impression that he was being sized up, but he felt no resentment at this — after all, less than four months ago he had been a mere major of cavalry, and his recent tenure of the command of a brigade began to assume an unsubstantial form in his mind in the presence of all this solid evidence of the existence of another world. He conducted himself with the modesty of his humble station. Nevertheless, he must have made a personal impression good enough to support that given by his record, for he came out of that room with a promise of his confirmation in a brigade command.

Not of his present brigade — that would be too much to expect, of course. The command of a regular brigade of cavalry was not the sort of appointment likely to be given to a newly promoted brigadier — and the speaker hastened to point out in additional consolation that the brigade would hardly be fit for action again for months after its recent losses even though by the special dispensation of Providence it had lost very few horses. But in England there were new armies being raised. There seemed to be a growing conviction (and here the speaker was elaborately noncommittal) that the war would last long enough for them to be used as new formations and not as drafts. A mere hint to the War Office would ensure Curzon's appointment to a new army brigade. With his regiment out of action as it was at present Curzon might just as well take leave and go to London to see about it.

Curzon hesitated. There was not much attraction for him in the command of four raw battalions of infantry. But he knew the army well enough; a man who declined a proffered promotion was likely to be left on the shelf from that time onwards unless he had powerful friends; and moreover he was only a temporary lieutenant-colonel. For all he knew, he might at any moment have to revert to his substantive rank of major. Better an infantry brigade than that. If good fortune came his way he might have a chance of commanding the brigade in action during the closing campaign of the war next summer. He left off tugging at his moustache and accepted the offer.

"Good!" said his host. "And I think it's time for dinner now."

Chapter VII

OUTWARDLY the London to which Curzon returned was not very different from the London he had always known. The streets were darker and there were more uniforms to be seen, but that was all. After the first paralysing blow of the declaration of war the city had made haste to recover its balance to the cry of "Business as Usual". The theatres were as gay as ever — gayer, if anything; the restaurants more crowded. Most of the people in the streets were so convinced of England's approaching victory in the war that now that the front was stabilised the war had ceased to be a matter of more interest to them than their own personal concerns.

But here and there were oases of interest. The Club, for instance. When Curzon went in there he found the place crowded with men he did not recognise. In addition to many men in the khaki which had scarcely ever been seen in the Club in the old days, all the retired officers who hardly set foot in the Club from year's end to year's end had now crowded up to London to besiege the War Office for employment, and were spending their time of waiting listening, all agog, for rumours. Curzon had not realised the efficiency of the censorship until he found men crowding round him all intent on acquiring first hand information. Birtles started it — Birtles had been a major in the regiment when Curzon was only a subaltern.

" 'Morning, Curzon," said Birtles when they encountered each other on the stairs, and would have passed him by if he had not suddenly remembered that Curzon must have come back from France on leave from the regiment; he halted abruptly. "On leave, eh?"

"Yes," said Curzon.

"What — er — " said Birtles, checking himself in the midst of a question as he suddenly had a spasm of doubt lest Curzon had been "sent home." But he reassured himself quickly on that point, because no man who had been sent home would show his face in the Club — at least, not for years. So he was able to continue. "What's the regiment doing?"

Curzon said what he could about the regiment's achievements.

"Dismounted action, eh?" said Birtles. "That's bad. Very bad. And what about you? Short leave, or something?"

Curzon was in civilian clothes, so that Birtles had nothing to go on. Yet he was obviously painfully anxious to ask questions. His old eyes were watering with anxiety. Curzon said he was home to take up a fresh command.

"Yeomanry or something?"

"No, an infantry brigade," said Curzon.

"A brigade? A brigade!" gasped Birtles, who, naturally, having once known Curzon as a subaltern could not think of him as anything else. "Here, come and have a drink. I mean — have you time for a drink?"

Curzon was in need of a drink after his busy morning. He had called at the War Office and had had a very satisfactory interview, because a note about him from G.H.Q. in France had already arrived; and he had been told that his promotion to the temporary rank of Brigadier-General would appear in the next *Gazette*. Not merely that, either. There would undoubtedly be a brigade for him at the end of his fortnight's leave. More still; besides his inevitable mention in despatches there would be a decoration for him — most likely a commandership of the Most Honourable Order of the Bath. Three eminent soldiers had cross-examined him in turn about the state of affairs in Flanders — there was a general anxiety to try and supplement the information doled out by telegram from G.H.Q. — and he had answered questions as well as he knew how.

And from the War Office he had gone to his military tailor's. They did not seem to remember him at first, which had annoyed him, and they had expressed doubt about their ability, in face of a torrent of orders, to supply his demands in the next week. Their attitude had changed a little when he told them who he was, and still more when he gave his order for a general's uniform with the red tabs and crossed sword and bâton of his rank. There had been more excitement than he had expected in giving that order — Curzon was still conscious of a little thrill when he remembered it, and he really badly needed his drink.

Yet by the time the drink had come to him he had precious little opportunity of drinking it, because Birtles hastened to spread the news that he was entertaining a Brigadier-General home from the Front, and from every corner of the Club men came crowding to hear his news and to ask him questions, or merely to look at the man newly returned from a European war. They were grey-headed old men, most of them, and they eyed him with envy. With anxiety, too; they had been gathering their information from the all-too-meagre communiqués and from the all-too-extensive casualty lists. They feared to know the worst at the same time as they asked, and they raised their voices in quavering questions about this unit and that, and to every question Curzon could only give a painful answer. There was not a unit in the Expeditionary Force which had

[62]

not poured out its best blood at Mons or at Le Cateau or at Ypres.

For a long time Curzon dealt out death and despair among those old men; it was fortunate that he did not feel the awkwardness which a more sensitive man might have felt. After all, casualties were a perfectly natural subject for a military man to discuss. It was need for his lunch which caused him in the end to break off the conversation, and even at lunch he was not free from interruption. Someone came up and spoke to him as he began on his soup — a tall, heavily built bald old man in the uniform of a Captain of a very notable regiment of infantry. He displayed all the embarrassment of an English gentleman addressing a stranger with an unconventional request.

"I beg your pardon for interrupting you," he began. Curzon tried to be polite, although it was a strain when he had hardly begun his lunch.

"The fact is — " went on the Captain " — of course I must apologise for being unconventional — I was wondering if you had made any arrangements for dinner to-night?"

Curzon stared at him. But his arrangements were of the vague sort an officer home on leave without a relation in the world might be expected to have.

"Well — " began Curzon. It was the fact that this stranger belonged to that very crack regiment which caused him to temporise.

"You see," went on the captain hastily. "I was hoping — I know all this sounds most impertinent — I was hoping that I could induce you to dine at my brother's to-night."

He had fumbled out his card case by now, and proffered a card with embarrassed fingers. Curzon read upon it the simple words "Lord George Winter-Willoughby." He only half heard what Lord George, voluble at last, went on to say, while

[63]

he coördinated in his mind what the name meant to him. The Winter-Willoughbys were the Bude family, whose head was the Duke of Bude with a score of other titles, who had held office in the last Conservative government. The courtesy title of Lord implied that the present speaker was a son of a Duke — more, it meant that he was brother of the present Duke — in fact it meant that the invitation now being given was to dine with the Duke of Bude. Confirmation trickled through into Curzon's consciousness from the bits of Lord George's speech which Curzon heard — "Bude House" — "Eight o'clock" — "Quite informal — wartime, you know" — "Telephone" — "The Duke and Duchess will be delighted if you can come."

The self-control which had enabled Curzon for fifteen years to conceal the part which chance had played in the battle of Volkslaagte made it possible for him to accept an invitation to dine at one of the greatest London houses as though he were thoroughly accustomed to such invitations; and Lord George displayed immense relief at not being snubbed, apologised once more for the informality of his behaviour, pleaded the present national crisis as his excuse, and withdrew gracefully.

It was fortunate that Curzon was not a man given to analysis of sociological conditions; if he had been he would certainly have wasted the rest of that day in thinking about how extensive must be the present upheaval if it resulted in hasty invitations to Bude House addressed to men of no family at all — he was fully aware that six months ago there would have been no perceptible difference between such an invitation and a Royal Command. As it was, he merely savoured pleasantly of his success and went out and bought a new set of buttons for his white waistcoat.

In December 1914 "wartime informality" at Bude House implied something quite different from what those words meant

[64]

in, say, Bloomsbury in 1918. There was a footman as well as a butler to open the door to Curzon, but they were both over military age and the footman's livery was inconspicuous. For the first time in his life Curzon described himself as "General Curzon" for the butler to announce him.

"It's very good of you to come, General," said a tall woman with dyed hair, offering her hand as he approached her across the deep carpet of the not-too-large drawing room.

"It's very good of you to ask me," Curzon managed to say. The bulky figure of Lord George showed itself at the Duchess' side, and beside it a bulkier counterpart of itself, as if the law of primogeniture ensured that the holder of the title should be a size larger than the younger son. There were introductions effected. The Duke was as bald as his brother — only a wisp of grey hair remaining round his ears. Lady Constance Winter-Willoughby was apparently Lord George's wife, and was as lovely and as dignified as was to be expected of a daughter of an earldom six generations older than the Dukedom of Bude.

Lady Emily Winter-Willoughby was the Duke's daughter; she was nearly as tall as her father, but she was not conspicuous for beauty of feature or of dress. For a fleeting moment Curzon, as his eyes wandered over her face, was conscious of a likeness between her features and those of Bingo, the best polo pony he ever had, but the thought vanished as quickly as it came when he met her kindly grey eyes. Lady Emily, especially now that she had left thirty behind, had always been a woman who preferred the country to London, and felt more at home with horses and dogs and flowers than with the politicians whom she was likely to encounter at Bude House. A few more years might see her an embittered spinster; but at the moment she only felt slightly the tediousness of this life — just enough to sense the slight awkwardness Curzon was careful not to display. When their eyes met they were both suddenly conscious of a fellow feeling, and they smiled at each other almost as if they were members of some secret society.

It was with an odd reluctance that Curzon left the warm glow of Lady Emily's proximity to meet the other two guests, a Sir Henry Somebody (Curzon did not catch the name) and his wife. They were a sharp-featured pair, both of them. Curzon formed the impression that Sir Henry must be some sort of lawyer, and that his wife had wits just as keen. There was a depressing moment of impersonal conversation with them before dinner was announced.

The advent of the war had accelerated the already noticeable decline from the great days of the Edwardians; dinners were very different now from the huge meals and elaborate service of ten years before; twelve courses had diminished to six; there was some attempt to please by simplicity instead of to impress by elaboration. The dining room was lit by candles so that it was hard to see the painted arched roof; there was not a great deal of silver displayed upon the circular table. But the food was perfection, and the wine marvellous — Bude House had not seen fit to follow the example of Buckingham Palace and eschew all alcoholic liquor for the duration of the war.

As the Vouvray was being served Lady Constance on Curzon's right recounted how, a short time before, at another dinner party, where the hostess had tried to be like Queen Mary and confine her guests to lemonade and barley water, the guests had one and all produced pocket flasks to make up for the absence of liquor. With eight people at a circular table general conversation was easy, and the Duchess on Curzon's left announced incisively that if she had been the hostess in question she would never receive one of those guests again, but she went on to agree that only the dear Queen could expect people to dine without drinking.

[66]

"It's bad enough having to do without German wines," she said. "We had some Hock that the Duke was very proud of, but of course we can't drink it *now,* can we?"

Curzon agreed with her, and not out of deference, either. He was quite as convinced as she was that there was no virtue left in Hock or in Wagner or in Goethe or in Dürer. From the innate badness of German art to the recent deeds of the German government was but a step in the conversation — a step easily taken as at least seven of the eight people present were anxious to take it. Before very long Curzon found himself talking about his recent experiences, and he was listened to with rapt attention. It was generally a question either from Sir Henry (on the other side of the Duchess) or from Sir Henry's wife (on the other side of the Duke) which moved him steadily on from one point to the next — at one moment Curzon noted to himself that Sir Henry simply must be a lawyer of some sort, as he had already surmised, because the tone of his questions had a ring of the law courts about it.

The conversation had a different trend from that at the Club in the morning. There was not so much anxiety displayed as to the fates of regiments and battalions. The party seemed to be far more interested in the general conduct of the war — Sir Henry, in particular, seemed to know a good deal more already about Mons and Le Cateau than Curzon did. Curzon almost began to form the idea that they would have relished criticism of the Higher Command, but he put the notion away before it crystallised. That was inconceivable; moreover, there was no chance of his disparaging his superiors to anyone — to say nothing of the fact that he had only the haziest ideas about the conduct of a great deal of the war. The British Army had been pitted against superior numbers over and over again, and had emerged each time from the ordeal with honour. Of crisis at headquarters he knew no more than any subaltern, and he denied their existence with all his soldier's pride. Besides, no soldier who had served under Kitchener could lightly give away anything approaching a military secret.

If the company, as it appeared reasonable to suppose, had been expecting any juicy bits of scandal, they were doomed to disappointment. In fact, the disappointment on the faces of the Duchess, Lady Constance, and Sir Henry's wife was almost noticeable even to Curzon, who got as far as feeling that his conversation was not as brilliant as it should have been — a feeling which did not surprise him in the least. It only made him take more notice of Lady Emily, who showed no disappointment at all.

When the conversation moved from the general to the particular, Curzon was still rather at sea. All his life he had been a regimental officer; these people were far more familiar with individuals on the General Staff than he was — to him they were only surnames, while at this table they were spoken of as "Bertie" and "Harry" and "Arthur." There was only one moment of tense reality, and that was when young Carruthers was mentioned. For a tiny interval Curzon forgot where he was; he forgot the polished table, and the glittering silver, and the exquisite food within him, and the butler brooding over his shoulder like a benevolent deity. It seemed as if he was back at brigade headquarters again, with the tortured screams of Carruthers sounding in his ears. A flood of memories followed — of Major Browning combating the deadly fear which was shaking him like a leaf, of the four headless troopers lying in a huddled heap in one bay of the trench, of the mud and the stench and the sleeplessness.

It was only for a moment. The extraordinary feeling that these men and women here should be forced somehow to realise that these things were part of the same framework as Arthur's appointment to the Adjutant General's department passed away, killed by its own absurdity, before the others had finished their kind words about Carruthers' fate and had passed on to the discussion of someone still alive. After all, it would be bad taste to force these inevitable details of war upon the notice of these women and civilians as it would be to do the same with the details of digestive processes or any other natural occurrence.

Then the women rose to leave the table and gave Curzon a further opportunity to come back to normal again, as the men closed up round the Duke. The war tended to disappear from the conversation from that moment, while later in the vast drawing room where they rejoined the ladies Lady Constance played the piano very brilliantly indeed so that conversation was not necessary. The music was a little over Curzon's head, but he had a very good dinner inside him and some excellent port, and he was quite content to sit beside Lady Emily and listen vaguely. It was with a shock that he found himself nodding in his chair — it was typical of Curzon not to realise what enormous demands those eleven days of furious action and eleven nights of little sleep at Ypres had made upon his strength.

So that it was with relief that he saw Lord George and Lady Constance rise to take their leave, making it possible for him to go immediately afterwards. And Sir Henry's wife said to him as he said good-bye to her, "Perhaps you'll come and dine with *us* if you can spare another evening of your leave?" so that he felt he had not been quite a failure in society.

Chapter VIII

THE same morning that Curzon's promotion to the temporary rank of Brigadier-General appeared in the press, there arrived the invitation to dinner, which enabled Curzon to confirm his suspicion that Sir Henry was really Sir Henry Cross, the barrister and Conservative Member of Parliament; and the other letter which the waiter brought him was a note from the War Office —

DEAR CURZON,
    Sorry to interrupt your leave, but could you possibly come and see me here in room 231 at your earliest convenience?
                            Yours,
                                G. MACKENZIE, Major-Gen.

Curzon puzzled over this note as he ate his kidneys and bacon solitary in the hotel dining room — his early rising habit persisted even in a West End hotel so that he was bound to be the only one having breakfast at that gloomy hour. It was a surprise to him to be addressed as "Dear Curzon" by General Mackenzie. Mackenzie had been one of the eminent officers who had discussed the war with him two days before, but half an hour's conversation did not seem sufficient reason for the Director-General of Strategical Services to address him without a prefix and to preface with an apology what might just as well have been a simple order. It was possible that now that he was a General himself he was being admitted into the confraternity of Generals who might have their own conventions of behaviour among themselves, but Curzon did not think that very likely.

He smoked a comfortable cigar while he read *The Times* —he could not help reading the announcement of his promotion three times over—and then he walked across St. James's Park and the Horse Guards to the War Office. Relays of commissionaries and Boy Scouts led him through the corridors to Room 231. There was only the briefest of delays before he was brought into the office of the Director General of Tactical Services, and Mackenzie offered him a chair and a cigar and made three remarks about the weather before he began to say what he meant to say.

"I didn't know you were acquainted with the Budes, Curzon?" he began.

"I know them slightly," replied Curzon cautiously. "I dined there a night or two ago."

"Yes, I know that" was the surprising rejoinder. Mackenzie drummed with his fingers, and looked across his desk at Curzon with a hint of embarrassment on his large pink face. His ginger hair was horribly out of harmony with the red tabs on his collar. "That fellow Cross was there, too."

"Yes," said Curzon.

"You've never had anything to do with politicians, Curzon," went on Mackenzie. "You've no idea how gossip spreads."

"I don't gossip, sir," said Curzon indignantly.

"No," said Mackenzie. "Of course not."

He looked meditatively at his finger nails before he spoke again.

"Cross has put down a question to ask in the House to-day —the House of Commons, I mean. It's about Le Cateau."

"That's nothing to do with me," said Curzon, more indignantly still, as the implication became obvious to him.

"That was all I wanted to know," said Mackenzie, simply. His bright eyes, of a pale grey, were scrutinising Curzon very closely, all the same. Mackenzie could not make up his mind as to whether or not this was yet another example of the plain blunt soldier with secret political affiliations.

"We can put the lid on friend Cross all right," he went on. "We can always say that it is opposed to public interest to answer his question, if we want to."

"I suppose so," agreed Curzon.

"But the House of Commons is not a very important place just now, thank God," said Mackenzie. "It isn't there that things happen."

Curzon felt bewildered at that. If Mackenzie was not accusing him of betraying military secrets he could not imagine what he was driving at. He had no conception of the power residing in the casual conversation of about fifty or so luncheon and dinner tables in London. He did not realise that high position in the army — even the post of Director-General of Tactical Services — was, if not exactly at the mercy of, at any rate profoundly influenced by, whispers which might circulate in a particular stratum of society. More especially was this the case when a rigid censorship left public opinion unable to distribute praise or blame except under the influence of gossip or of prejudice. All these circumstances were aggravated by the fact that England had entered upon the war under a government not at all representative of the class accustomed to the dispensing of military patronage; there were already hints and signs that to prolong its existence the government must allow some of the opposition to enter its ranks, and in that case the foolish ones who had staked their careers on its continuance unchanged in power would be called upon to pay forfeit.

Mackenzie felt strongly opposed to explaining all this to Curzon. It might be construed as a confession of weakness. Instead, he harked back to the original subject.

"The Bude House set," he said, " — the women, I mean, not men — want a finger in every pie."

"I didn't know that," said Curzon, perfectly truthfully. Of course, throughout his life, he had heard gossip about petticoat influence. But he had not believed — in fact, he still did not believe — that people played at politics as at a game, in which the amount of patronage dispensed acted as a useful measure of the score, so that to have brought about the appointment of one's own particular nominee to an Undersecretaryship of State was like bringing off a little slam at bridge.

Now that the war had become such a prominent feature in the news, and friends and relations were taking commissions or returning from retirement the value of military appointments as counters in the game was higher than ever before. And at the moment the army was especially entangled in politics, thanks to the Irish business. When certain people returned to power there would be a good many old scores to pay off. There would be distinctions drawn between the men who had declared their unwillingness to obey orders and the men who had not seen fit to make a similar declaration. Besides, in some strange way the fact that there was a war in progress accentuated the intensity of this hidden strife between the Ins and the Outs, and made it more of a cut and thrust business than ever before.

"Well, you know now," said Mackenzie, grimly.

"Yes," said Curzon. He was no fool. He could see that he was in a strong position, even if he could not guess what it was that constituted its strength. "I'm due to dine with Cross next week, too."

"Really?" said Mackenzie, contriving to give no hint of

[73]

meaning at all in his intonation, but drumming with his fingers all the same. He was convinced now that if the man he was talking to was not yet a political soldier, he would be quite soon, and one with very valuable connections. In fact, he did not feel strong enough to nip the development in the bud by commanding Curzon, on pain of losing his promised brigade, to have nothing to do with the Bude House set.

"Cross gives damned good dinners," he said. "I don't know why these lawyer sharks should always be able to get the best chefs. More money, I suppose."

"I suppose so," agreed Curzon, and Mackenzie changed the subject.

"By the way, the Foreign Office has just been through to us on the telephone," he said. "The Belgian Government wants to present decorations to some English officers, and I have to give my opinion about their distribution. Seeing what you did at Ypres it would be appropriate if one came to you, don't you think? I suppose you wouldn't mind?"

"Of course not," said Curzon.

"Right," said Mackenzie, making a note on a memorandum tablet. "I expect it will be the Order of Leopold — a nice watered red ribbon. It'll look well with your C.M.G. and D.S.O."

"Thank you very much," said Curzon.

"Don't thank me," said Mackenzie, with a certain peculiar emphasis in his tone. "It's yourself you have to thank."

Curzon came away from that momentous interview with no very clear idea of what had happened. He was delighted, of course, with the offer of the Belgian decoration. Including his two South African medals he would have five ribbons on his breast now; it would not be long before he could start a second row. Ribbons and promotion were the two signs of success in his profession and now he had both. Success was sweet; he

[74]

swung his walking stick lightheartedly as he strode across the park. He even laughed when a spiteful old lady said to him as he passed, "Why aren't you in the army?"

That Curzon could perceive the humour of a situation and laugh at it was a remarkable state of affairs in itself. As he walked, he debated with himself as to whether or no he should telephone Cissie Barnes and see if he could spend the afternoon with her — Cissie Barnes was a lady with whom he had often spent afternoons and weekends before the war began. If Curzon had been given to self-analysis he might have been seriously alarmed at finding that he was not specially anxious to go and see Cissie.

And then although he was quite sure what he wanted to do he ran through in his mind the other ways open to him of spending the afternoon. He might go round to the Club, and at the Club he might talk or play bridge — the latter, more likely. There would be more than a chance that at the Club he might run across an acquaintance with whom he could share a couple of stalls at a musical comedy or at one of these revues which seemed to have suddenly become fashionable. That might serve very well for the evening. He was not so sure about the afternoon.

There were a few houses at which he might call — he ran over them in his mind and decided against each one in turn. He could go down into Leicestershire so as to hunt next day; presumably Clayton could be relied upon to produce a hireling, and he could stay at the Somerset Arms. The illustrated papers he had read yesterday had informed him that of course hunting was still being carried on in the Shires. He could do that to-morrow, though. This afternoon — he admitted it to himself now, having decided that there was a good reason to put forward against all the other courses — he would call at Bude House. It was growing a little old-fashioned to pay a call two days after dinner, but, damn it, he was content to be old-fashioned. Lady Emily might be there. Once he had formed this decision the hours seemed to drag as he ate his lunch and waited for the earliest possible moment at which he could ring the bell at Bude House.

"Her Grace is not at home, sir," said the butler at the door. By a miracle of elocution he managed to drop just enough of each aitch to prove himself a butler without dropping the rest.

"Is Lady Emily at home?" asked Curzon.

"I will inquire, sir."

Lady Emily was glad to see the General. She gave him her hand and a smile. She offered him tea, which he declined, and a whisky and soda which he accepted.

Lady Emily had been brought up very strictly, in the way a child should during the 'eighties and 'nineties, especially when she had had the impertinence to be a girl instead of the boy who would inherit the title. Men, she had been taught, were the lords of the universe, under God. With regard to the subjection of women an important exception was to be made in the case of her mother — the Duchess undoubtedly occupied a place between men and God. What with her parents' ill-concealed disappointment at the accident of her sex, and the prevailing doctrine of the unimportance of women, and her mother's rapacious personality, and the homeliness of her own looks, there was not much self-assertiveness about Lady Emily. To such a pitch had her conviction of innate sin been raised that she even felt vaguely guilty that Lloyd George's pestilent budgets from 1911 onwards had weighed so heavily upon the ducal income.

It was no wonder she had never married. Of course, there were plenty of men who would have been glad of the opportunity of marrying a Duke's only child, but, being a Duke's only child, it had been easy to make sure that she never met that kind of man, and suitable matches had never been attracted. It might be said that Curzon was the first adventurer she had ever met — Curzon would have been furious if anyone had called him an adventurer, but such he was to pay his respects to Lady Emily when he had no more than seven hundred a year of private means, however ample might be his prospects of professional eminence.

Curzon's motives were hardly susceptible to analysis. There could be no denying that for some very obscure reason he liked Lady Emily very much indeed. When her eyes met his as she drank her tea he felt a warm unusual pleasure inside him — but there is nothing that so defies examination as the mutual attraction of two apparently not very attractive people. He was glad to be near her, in a fashion whose like he could not remember regarding any of his light loves or the wives of brother officers with whom he had exchanged glances.

Women had never paid much attention to Curzon; it was gratifying to find one who did, and especially gratifying (there is no shirking this point) in that she was the daughter of a Duke. Success was a stimulating thing. He had risen in four months from Major to Brigadier General. He had always fully intended to marry at forty, and here he was at forty-one with nothing impossible to him — why should a Duke's daughter be impossible to him? The daring of the thought was part of the attraction; and that business with Mackenzie this morning added to the feeling of daring.

He was so much above himself that he was able to talk more readily than he had ever been able to talk to a woman in his life, and Lady Emily listened and nodded and smiled until they both of them felt very much the better for each other's company. They talked about horses and dogs. Lady Emily had much experience of one kind of sport which Curzon had never sampled — staghunting in Somersetshire, where lay the greater part of the Duke's estates. She actually found herself talking about this with animation, and Curzon, foxhunting man though he was, found himself listening with something more than toleration. They exchanged reminiscences, and Curzon told his two tall foxhunting stories (the regimental mess had grown tired of them away back in 1912) with complete success. They found, of course, that they had friends in common in the Shires, and they were talking about them when the Duchess came in with a fragile old gentleman trailing behind her.

Her Grace was mildly surprised at finding Curzon in her house, and she endeavoured to freeze him by displaying exactly that mildness of surprise which could not be construed as rudeness but which most definitely could not be called overwhelming hospitality. It was all very well to have a successful general to dinner at a time when successful generals were more fashionable than poets or pianists, but that gave him no excuse for presuming on his position — especially when he promised to be of no use at all in her political maneuvres. But before Curzon had time to take note of the drop in temperature and to take his leave Lady Emily had interposed — unconsciously, perhaps.

"Tea, Mr. Anstey?" she asked.

"Thank you, yes," said the frail old gentleman. "I shall be glad of some tea. My work at the Palace is unusually tiring nowadays in consequence of the war."

The Duchess made the introductions.

"General Curzon — Mr. Anstey."

"Curzon?" repeated Mr. Anstey with mild animation. "Brigadier-General Herbert Curzon?"

"Yes," said Curzon.

"Then you are one of the people responsible for my present fatigue."

"I'm sorry to hear you say that, sir," said Curzon.

"Oh, there's no need to be sorry, I assure you. I am only too delighted to have the honour of doing the work I do. It is only to-day that I made out two warrants for you."

"Indeed, sir?" said Curzon vaguely.

"Yes. There is of course no harm in my telling you about them, seeing that they are already in the post and will be delivered to you to-morrow. One of them deals with the Companionship of the Bath and the other with the Belgian Order of Leopold — I must explain that I combine in my humble person an official position both in the department of the Lord Chamberlain and in the registry of the Order of the Bath. You will find you have been commanded to be present at an investiture to be held next week."

"Thank you," said Curzon. He remembered vaguely having heard of the Ansteys as one of the "Court families" who occupied positions at the Palace from one generation to the next.

"The Order of Leopold," went on Mr. Anstey, "is a very distinguished order indeed. It is the Second Class which is being awarded to you, General — the First Class is generally reserved for reigning monarchs and people in corresponding positions. Of course, it is not an order with a very lengthy history — it can hardly be that, can it? — but I think an order presented by a crowned head far more distinguished than any decoration a republic can award. I hope you agree with me, General?"

"Oh yes, of course," said Curzon, perfectly sincerely.

The Duchess merely nodded. The orders her husband wore were such as no mere general could ever hope to attain, and possessed the further recommendation (as has frequently been pointed out) that there was no "damned nonsense about merit" attached to them. The Duke's ribbons and stars were given him, if a reason must be assigned, because his great-great-great-great grandfather had come over in the train of William of

Orange — certainly not because ten years ago he had been chivvied by his wife into accepting minor office under a tottering Conservative government. Her Grace was sublimely confident in her share of the universal opinion that it was far better to receive distinctions for being someone than for doing something.

"You are one of the Derbyshire Curzons, I suppose, General?" said Mr. Anstey.

Curzon was ready for that. He had been an officer in India during Lord Curzon's vice-royalty and had grown accustomed to having a relationship suggested — in the course of years even his unimaginative mind had been able to hammer out a suitable answer.

"Yes, but a long way back," he said. "My branch has been settled in Staffordshire for some time, and I am the only representative now."

Curzon always remembered that his father had a vague notion that *his* father had come to London from the Potteries as a boy; moreover he thought it quite unnecessary to add that these mystic Staffordshire Curzons had progressed from Staffordshire to the Twenty-Second Lancers via Mincing Lane.

"That is extremely interesting," said Mr. Anstey. "Even though the Scarsdale peerage is of comparatively recent creation the Curzons are one of the few English families of undoubtedly Norman descent."

Mr. Anstey checked himself with a jerk. Despite his Court tact, he had allowed himself to mention Norman descent from a follower of William the Conqueror in the presence of a representative of a family of Dutch descent from a follower of William of Orange. To his mind the difference was abysmal and the gaffe he had committed inexcusable. He glanced with apprehension at the Duchess, but he need not have worried. Coronets meant far more to her than did Norman blood.

"How very interesting," said the Duchess, coldly.

"Yes, isn't it?" said Lady Emily eagerly, and attracted every eye by the warmth with which she said it.

The Duchess ran a cold glance over every inch of her thirty-year-old daughter's shrinking form.

"There are a great number of fresh letters arrived," she said "about the Belgian Relief Clothing Association. You will find them in the library, Emily. I think they had better be answered at once."

Curzon saw Lady Emily's face fall a little, and it was that which made him take the plunge. He cut in with what he had to say just as Lady Emily, with the obedience resulting from years of subjection, was rising from her armchair.

"I was wondering, Lady Emily," he said, "if I might have the pleasure of your company at the theatre this evening?"

Lady Emily looked at her mother, as ingrained instinct directed. Mr. Anstey sensed an awkwardness, and hastened to try and smooth it over with his well known tact.

"We all of us need a little relaxation in these strenuous days," he said.

"Thank you, I should very much like to come," said Lady Emily — perhaps she too was infected by the surge of revolt against convention and parental control which the newspapers had noted as the concomitant of wartime. The Duchess could hardly countermand a decision publicly reached by a daughter of full age and more.

"What is the play to which you are proposing so kindly to take my daughter?" she asked, icily, which was all she could do.

"I was going to leave the choice to Lady Emily," said Curzon — a reply, made from sheer ignorance, which left the Duchess with no objection to raise; and this emboldened Curzon still further.

"Shall we dine together first?" he asked.

"That would be very nice," said Lady Emily, her bonnet soaring clean over the windmill in this, her first flourish of emancipation.

"Seven o'clock?" said Curzon. "It's a pity having to dine so early, but it's hard to avoid it. Shall I call for you?"

"Yes," said Lady Emily.

Chapter IX

DAMN it all, Maud," said the Duke of Bude to the Duchess, a week after Curzon had gone to the theatre with Lady Emily. "Anyone would think you didn't want the girl to get married."

That was so true that the Duchess had to deny it.

"I don't want Emily to marry a man of no family at all — a mere adventurer," said she, and the Duke chuckled as he made one of his irritating silly jokes.

"As long as he's got no family it doesn't matter. We won't have to invite his Kensington cousins to the Hall, then. The man assured us only yesterday that he hasn't a relation in the world. And as for being an adventurer — well, a man can't help having adventures in time of war, can he?"

"Tcha," said the Duchess. "You know perfectly well what I mean."

"He's a perfectly presentable man. He's Haileybury, after all — everyone can't be a Wykehamist. Colonel of a good regiment —"

"The Twenty-Second Lancers," sneered the Duchess.

"It might have been black infantry," said the Duke. "He's got a C.B. and a D.S.O., and Borthwick at the Lords was telling me that his boy wrote reams about him from the Front. He's a man with a future."

"But they hardly know each other," said the Duchess.

"Well, they're old enough to be able to make up their minds. Emily's thirty-two, isn't she, or is it thirty-three? And he's turned forty. I think it's very suitable. I can't imagine why you're objecting so much."

That, of course, was a lie. The Duke knew perfectly well why the Duchess was objecting, and in his heart of hearts he objected too. But he could bow gracefully to the inevitable, in a way his stiff-necked wife found more difficult.

"Marrying's in the air these wartime days," went on the Duke. "There'll be no stopping 'em if they set their minds on it. Much better start getting used to the idea now. Besides, we may as well be in the fashion."

"Fashion, indeed!" said the Duchess. Her disregard for fashion was one of the things about her which no one who saw her even once could possibly avoid remarking.

"Besides," said the Duchess, unanswerably, "he's got no money."

"M'yes," said the Duke, undoubtedly shaken. "That's a point I shall have to go into very carefully when the time comes."

The time came no later than the day after to-morrow. The courtship had blossomed with extraordinary rapidity in the hothouse air of wartime London. So high above the windmill had Lady Emily's bonnet soared that she had actually accompanied Curzon to a night club so as to dance. They had shuffled and stumbled through the ultra-modern one-steps and two-steps until the pampered orchestra had at last consented to play a waltz. Curzon certainly could waltz; he had learned the art in the great days of waltzing. And it might have been the extra glass of rather poor champagne which she had drunk at dinner which made Lady Emily's feet so light and her eyes so bright. As the last heart-broken wail of the violins died away and they stopped and looked at each other the thing was as good as settled. No sooner had they sat down than Curzon was able to stumble through a proposal of marriage with less difficulty than he had found in the one-step; and to his delighted surprise he found himself accepted.

Lady Emily's eyes were like stars. They made Curzon's head swim a little. His heart had plunged so madly after his inclinations that never again, not once, did it occur to him that her face was not unlike a horse's. To Curzon Lady Emily's gaunt figure stiffly corseted — almost an old maid's figure — was a miracle of willowy grace, and her capable ugly hands, when he kissed them in the taxicab on the way home, were more beautiful than the white hands of Tristan's Yseult.

The interview with the Duke in the morning was not too terrible. It was a relief to the Duke to discover that the General actually had seven hundred pounds a year — especially as under the stimulus of wartime demands some of the dividends which contributed to make up this sum showed an undoubted tendency to multiply. It might have been a much smaller income and still not have been incompatible with Curzon's position in life. Besides, the General offered, in the most handsome fashion, to settle every penny of his means upon his future wife. No one could make a fairer offer than that, after all. And when one came to total up his general's pay, and his allowances, under the new scale just established, and his forage allowances, and so forth, it did not fall far short of twelve hundred a year, without reckoning on the possibility of promotion or command pay or the less likely sources of income. A general's widow's pension (after all, every contingency must be considered) was only a small amount, of course, but it was as good as any investment in the Funds.

And two thousand a year (for so the Duke, in an expansive moment, generously estimated Curzon's income) really could not be called poverty, not even by a Duke with thirty thousand a year, especially when the Duke belonged to a generation whose young men about town had often contrived to make a passable appearance on eight hundred. The Duke proposed to supplement the newly married couple's income with two thousand a year from his private purse, and they ought to be able to manage very well, especially while the General was on active service.

"I think you've been weak, Gilbert," said the Duchess, later.

"Oh, for goodness' sake, Maud!" said the Duke. "I don't see that at all. We owe our national existence at present to the army. And we can spare the money all right. You know that. It'll only go to George and his boys if Emily doesn't get it. That is, if these blasted death duties leave anything over at all."

"I don't think," said the Duchess, "that there is any need for you to use disgusting language to me even though your daughter is marrying beneath her."

The Duchess grew more reconciled to her daughter's marriage when she came to realise that at least while Curzon was on active service she would still be able to tyrannise over her daughter, and the public interest in the wedding reconciled her still more. The formal announcement was very formal, of course. "A marriage has been arranged and will shortly take place between Lady Emily Gertrude Maud Winter-Willoughby, only daughter of the Duke and Duchess of Bude, and Brigadier-General Herbert Curzon, C.B., D.S.O., Twenty-Second Lancers."

The newspapers built a marvellous edifice upon this bare foundation. "Duke's Daughter to Wed War Hero" they said, "Lightning Wooing." It was not every day of the week, by any manner of means, that a duke's daughter married; and war news, now that the campaign in Flanders had dwindled away into a stalemate in the mud and rain, was not likely to stimulate sales. There was something piquant about the union of a Winter of the bluest blood with a Curzon whose relationship to Lord Curzon of Kedlerton was at best only ill defined. All the same, the press played up nobly. The daily press had a great deal to say about the future bridegroom's military achievements — although the exigencies of the censorship compelled them to say more about Volkslaagte than about Ypres — and the snobbish weekly papers laid stress upon the splendours of Bude Hall in Somersetshire, and the interest the Royal Family was taking in the wedding; there were dozens of photographs taken showing the happy pair walking in the Park or at some party in aid of something. A wartime bride had more popular appeal, undoubtedly, than a wartime widow, or than those other ladies underneath whose photographs the papers could only publish the already hackneyed caption "Takes great interest in war work." (Lady Emily and her mother the Duchess were always represented as the hardest workers in the Belgian Relief Clothing Association, and perhaps they were.) And because a Duke's daughter at the time of her betrothal could not possibly be other than young and beautiful all the press loyally forbore to mention the fact that Emily was thirty-two years old, and no one dreamed of mentioning that her features were large and irregular nor that her clothes always had a look of the second hand about them.

Meanwhile, a Field Marshal and a General and a Major General were in conference at the War Office.

"The man's on the verge of senile decay," said the General. "Over the verge, I should say. He's no more fit to be trusted with a division than to darn the Alhambra chorus's tights."

"Who are his brigadiers?" asked the Field Marshal.

"Watson and Webb," said the Major General, apologetically. "Yes, sir, I know they're no good, but where am I to get three hundred brigadiers from?"

"That's your pigeon," said the Field Marshal.

"I'm sending Curzon down there to-morrow," said the Major General. "The third brigade of the division has never had a general yet. I think he'll stiffen them up all right."

"He'll have his work cut out, from what I've seen of that lot," said the General.

"Curzon?" said the Field Marshal. "That's the Volkslaagte fellow, isn't it?"

"Yes, sir," said the Major General. "You read the letter a fortnight ago which G.H.Q. wrote about him."

"I remember," said the Field Marshal. He raised his big heavy face to the window, and stared out contemplatively with squinting blue eyes, while he called up isolated recollections out of a packed memory. Volkslaagte had been fought before he went to South Africa, but he remembered reading the despatches about it very plainly indeed — it was in this very room in the War Office. There was that race meeting in India, and the mob of horses all coming over the last hurdle together, and a Lancer officer doing a brilliant bit of riding in shouldering off a riderless horse which got in the way and might have caused a nasty accident. That was Curzon. That was not the first time he had been pointed out to him, though. Where was that? Oh yes, at the Aldershot review in the old days before India. That was the chap. A big nosed fellow with the centre squadron.

"How old is he now?" asked the Field Marshal.

"Forty-one, sir," said the Major General.

At forty-one the Field Marshal had been Sirdar of the Egyptian army. He would like to be forty-one again, instead of sixty-five with a game leg — but that was nothing to do with the business under discussion. It was this Curzon fellow he was thinking about. He had never put in any time holding a regimental command, apparently, except for a few weeks in France.

[88]

But that was nothing against him, except that it made it a bit harder to judge him by ordinary standards. The Field Marshal had done no regimental duty in his life, and it hadn't hurt him.

But there was something else he had heard, or read, about Curzon, somewhere, quite recently. He could not remember what it was, and was vaguely puzzled.

"Is there anything against this Curzon fellow?" he asked tentatively. It was a little pathetic to see him labouring under the burden of all the work he had been doing during these months of war.

"No, sir," said the Major General, and because Curzon was obviously allied by now to the Bude House set, and would be a valuable friend in the approaching Government reshuffle, he added, "He's a man of very decided character."

That turned the scale. What the Field Marshal had seen, of course, had been the flaming headlines that very morning announcing Curzon's betrothal. He had put the triviality aside, and yet the memory lingered in his subconscious mind. It was because of that that he had pricked up his ears at the first mention of Curzon's name. Neither the General nor the Major General saw fit to waste the Field Marshal's time by a mention of to-day's newspaper gossip, and the vague memory remained to tease him into action. His mind was not fully made up when he began to speak, but he was positive in his decision by the time the sentence was completed.

"You must unstick Coppinger-Brown," he said. "Shunt him off gracefully, though. There's no need to be too hard on him. He's done good work in his time. And Watson'll have to go, too. He's no good. I never thought he was. Give Webb another chance. He can still turn out all right if he's properly looked after. You'll have to give the division to Curzon, though. He ought to make a good job of it."

"Yes, sir," said the Major General. He was reluctant to continue, because it was not safe to pester his chief with a request for further instructions once a decision had been reached, but in this case the service regulation left him no option. "He's junior to Webb as Brigadier, of course."

"Then you'll have to promote him to Major General. Get the orders out to-day."

A wave of the Field Marshal's massive hand told the General and the Major General that their presence was no longer required, and they left the Field Marshal to plunge once more into the mass of work piled before him — into the business of constructing a modern army out of the few antiquated remains left over after the departure of the Expeditionary Force.

That was how Curzon obtained his appointment to the command of the Ninety-First Division and his promotion to the temporary rank of Major General. There were not wanting unkind people who hinted that he owed his new rank to his prospective father-in-law, but the Duke had not raised a finger in the matter. There had been no scheming or bargaining, not even by the little scheming group which centred round the Duke and Lady Constance. He had been selected out of a hundred possible officers who could have filled the vacancy because, while their capacities were all equally unexplored, an adventitious circumstance had singled him out for particular notice. Without that, the Major General would never have had the opportunity of putting in the single sentence which ultimately turned the scale. And it must be specially noticed that the Major General had not the slightest hint that he might receive favours in return; neither Curzon nor his new relations had been parties to anything underhand of that sort.

Chapter X

CURZON was at Bude House when the butler came in to announce — the tone of his voice indicating that he realised the importance of this official business — that the War Office was asking on the telephone if they could speak to General Curzon. Curzon left his lady's side and went out to the telephone.

"Hullo?" he said.

"Is that General Curzon?" asked a sharp female voice.

"Speaking."

"Hold on a minute, please. General Mackenzie would like to speak to you."

There was a click and a gurgle and then Mackenzie's voice.

"Hullo, Curzon. I thought I'd find you at Bude House when you weren't at your hotel. Hope I'm not disturbing you?"

"Not very much."

"I think you'll find it's worth being disturbed for. You've been given the Ninety-First Division."

"I beg your pardon?"

"You've been given the Ninety-First Division — the one you were going to have a brigade in. And you're promoted to Major General with seniority from to-day."

"That's very good news."

"I said you'd think so, didn't I? When can you take up your command?"

"Whenever you like."

"To-morrow?"

"Yes."

"Very well. Call here in the morning. I want to hear your ideas about a staff. It'll be a pretty makeshift one, anyway, I'm afraid, but that can't be helped."

"I suppose not."

"But there's a good house as headquarters, with stabling just as it should be. Trust old Coppinger-Brown for that. You'll have a use for the house, won't you?"

"Yes, I suppose so."

"That reminds me. I haven't congratulated you on your engagement yet. My very best wishes."

"Thanks very much."

"I was wondering when you were going to offer me thanks. You haven't sounded very grateful up to now."

"Oh, thank you very much."

"That's better. You remember this, Curzon; the closer you and I stay by each other, the better it will be for both of us. That's a word to the wise."

"Er — yes."

"But that can wait a bit. I'll be seeing you to-morrow morning. Nine o'clock?"

"Very well."

"All right, then. Good-bye."

"Good-bye."

Back in Emily's sitting room he told the glad news, his eyes bright with pleasure and excitement, and, because of that, Emily's eyes shone too. Until a week or two ago Emily had hardly known that such things as brigades and divisions existed, and she had been decidedly vague about the difference between them, but already she was beginning to grasp the essentials of this army business. The Duke's valet was sent out hurriedly to buy stars at a military tailor's, and then, with a note to the hotel management admitting him to Curzon's room, he was sent on to sew those stars above the crossed swords and bâtons on the shoulder straps of Curzon's tunics all ready for the morning, while Curzon and Emily carried on a muddled conversation in which army promotion and houses and horses and future domesticity were all intermingled.

But next day had its awkward moments. A War Office motor car took Curzon and his kit down into Hampshire, where the division was scattered in billets or under canvas over a five mile radius, and stopped at the end of the long gravelled drive outside Narling Priory, the headquarters of the Ninety-First Division. A young red-tabbed subaltern led Curzon round the side of the house through French windows into a spacious room wherein stood a group of khaki-clad figures with a tall, thin officer, bent and feeble, the sword of ceremony hanging from his belt, standing in advance of them.

"Good morning," he said, standing very stiff and still.

Curzon nodded.

"General Coppinger-Brown?" he asked in return.

"Yes."

It was then that Curzon realised what an embarrassing business it was to relieve a man of his command, because Coppinger-Brown made no effort to put him at ease, but merely stood and waited.

"I have been sent down by the War Office," began Curzon, hesitantly; he waited for help, received none, and had to continue without it. "I am to take command of the division."

"So I understood from orders I received this morning," said Coppinger-Brown. There was the faintest of accents upon the last two words. Curzon realised that it was dashed hard luck on the old chap to be flung out of his command like this at an hour's notice. He wanted for a moment to say "I'm sorry," but one man could hardly say that to another especially in the presence of inferiors. He could only stand and feel awkward while Coppinger-Brown left him to drink the cup of his embarrassment to the full. By the time Coppinger-Brown relented Curzon was decidedly uncomfortable.

"I must introduce," said Coppinger-Brown at last, "the officers of my staff — of your staff, I mean; I beg your pardon, General."

He waved his hand at the group behind him, and each officer in turn came up to attention as his name was spoken.

"General Webb, commanding the Three Hundredth Brigade. General Webb is the only brigadier in the division at present. I made so bold as to give General Watson immediate leave of absence, as I wished to spare him the humiliation of having to leave under orders."

There was something very acid in Coppinger-Brown's tone as he made this speech, but Curzon did not notice it, as he was too busy sizing up his second in command, a beefy red-faced infantry man, of whom Mackenzie at the War Office that morning had said that he was being given one more chance.

"Colonel Miller, my G.S.O.1. Captain Frobisher, G.S.O.3. Colonel Hill, C.R.A. Colonel Septimus, A.D.M.S. — "

For a space it simply rained initials in a manner which would have left a civilian gasping, but Curzon was more accustomed to hearing these initials used than to the words they stood for. He nodded formally to each in turn, to the officers of the General Staff, to the officer Commanding Royal Artillery, to the Assistant Director of Medical Services, and the Assistant Director of Veterinary Services, and the Deputy Assistant Quartermaster General, and the Assistant Provost

Marshal, and the Officer Commanding Royal Engineers, and the rag tag and bobtail of aides-de-camp.

Mackenzie at the War Office had given him thumbnail character portraits of each of these officers; Curzon himself had no knowledge of most of them, and only a hearsay acquaintance with the rest. Hill the Gunner had won a D.S.O. in the Tirah. Webb had commanded a battalion before Curzon had been given a squadron. Runcorn the Sapper had left the army before the war on account of some scandal about drink and women, which was a very remarkable thing to have occurred to a Sapper, so that Runcorn had better be watched with all the attention a freak merited. Miller of the General Staff had been described by Mackenzie as "a bloke with twice the brains of you and me put together," and had left it to Curzon to form his own opinion after this somewhat ominous beginning.

"What's been the matter down there," Mackenzie had said, "as far as I can make out from what Somerset says — he's just been inspecting them — is just sheer dam' laziness on someone's part or other. They've had their troubles, of course. We've let 'em down badly from here once or twice, but you couldn't have run the old army, let alone a new one ten times the size, on the staff I've got left to me here. But old Coppinger-Brown's the real cause of the trouble. He's too old. You can't expect an old boy of seventy-two with bronchial tubes or something to go out in all weathers in the sort of winters we're having and go charging about on a horse keeping an eye on twelve raw battalions an' two dozen other units. It's not in human nature. Coppinger-Brown swore he was all right when he came here after a job — he produced all sorts of chits from doctors to that effect. And he looked all right, too. But you know how it is, Curzon. You've got to work like a blasted nigger to get anything done with new formations. Otherwise everything's held

[95]

up while everyone's waiting for something else to get done which they think they can't do without. Or else everybody's getting in everybody else's way and'll go on doing it until you come down on 'em. Doesn't matter how good a staff you've got when you're in that kind of muddle. It's only the boss who can put it straight. Nobody gives a hoot for what a staff officer says when they know the general won't take action. But you'll put ginger into them, Curzon, I know."

That had been all very well at the War Office, but it was rather different by the time General Coppinger-Brown had finished the introductions and had shuffled out of the room with his aides-de-camp beside him. Curzon stood and faced his staff — nearly all of them ten or twenty years his senior, and most of them, until a few weeks back, immeasurably his senior in military rank. He felt as awkward and embarrassed as at the time of General Coppinger-Brown's first greeting of him. It was not in him to be conciliatory. His whole instinct in a time of difficulty was to be unbending and expressionless. It was a natural reaction that there should creep into his voice the tone he employed on parade — he felt as if he were on parade for the first time with some new recalcitrant unit.

"Gentlemen," he rasped, and paused. He had not anticipated having to make a speech. He tugged at his moustache until he saw the light; he had felt at a loss at remembering that there was no regimental esprit de corps to which to appeal. But he could at any rate appeal to the spirit of the division. "Gentlemen, it is my responsibility now to prepare the Ninety-First Division in readiness to go to France. We can never have it said that our division, one of the earliest to be raised, was the last to be sent overseas. That would be too bad. We must make up our minds that we are not going to be left behind by the other divisions. We must work hard to catch up on them and pass them. I am quite sure we can."

His expression hardened as he remembered the precariousness of his own temporary rank. It flashed through his mind that the Duchess' elegant friends would sneer delightedly if he were to be unstuck like poor old Coppinger-Brown.

"I am going to see that we do," he added grimly, looking round the group from one to another. Each pair of eyes dropped as they met his, such was the savage force of his glance as he thought of Emily and the urgency of the need to justify himself to her. And the mention of the corporate existence of the Ninety-First Division had served its purpose in starting him off in what he had to say. He was able to wind up his little speech on the note he wanted.

"This is wartime," he said. "A time of great emergency. There will be no mercy at all in this division for officers who are not up to their work."

It was a speech which served its purpose as well as any other might have done and better than some. Some generals might have appealed to their subordinates' loyalty, or might have put new vigour into them by force of personality, but Curzon, if such suggestions had been put forward to him, would have dismissed them as "claptrap" or "idealism." As it was, a subdued and impressed staff crept quietly out of the room all quite decided to work a great deal harder for the new Major General with the scowl on his face and the barely concealed threat in his speech.

The pink-cheeked aide-de-camp came back into the room. General Coppinger-Brown would be very much obliged if General Curzon could spare him a few minutes for the discussion of private business. Curzon followed the aide-de-camp out of the headquarters office and across the tiled hall to the wing of the house which still remained furnished as a private residence. There was an old, old lady sitting in an armchair in the drawing room with Coppinger-Brown standing beside her.

[97]

"Lucy," said Coppinger-Brown. "This is my successor, General Curzon. Curzon, may I introduce my wife?"

Curzon bowed, and the old lady nodded icily to him across the room, while the aide-de-camp retired with the tact expected of aides-de-camp.

"The first thing we wanted to say," said Coppinger-Brown, "was whether we might expect the pleasure of your company at lunch? It is one o'clock now, and lunch can be served at any time to suit you."

"Thank you," said Curzon, "but I have just arranged to lunch in the staff officers' mess."

He forebore from adding that he was itching to start work with his chief of staff and make up for the time lost by Coppinger-Brown, and intended to start as soon as lunch began.

"What a pity," replied Coppinger-Brown. "I hope you can spare us a few minutes, all the same, so that we can settle our private arrangements."

"I am at your service now," said Curzon.

"That's very good of you," said Coppinger-Brown. "Because we are anxious to hear from you how soon we must vacate this house."

Coppinger-Brown and his wife stared at Curzon with an unvoiced appeal in their eyes. The house was one taken over furnished by the War Office; half of it had been adapted as Staff Offices, and the other half was retained as a residence for the Major General commanding the division. The last two months had been a wonderful time for the old couple. It had been an end of retirement; they had turned their backs on the Cheltenham boarding house; there had been a future once more ahead of them; they were back again in the army in which he had served for forty-five years. Now they were being condemned once more to exile, with all the added bitterness of disappointment and consciousness of failure. Until this morning they had felt secure in the pomp and power of their official position. It was a shock for old people to be flung out like this without warning. They were loth to leave the substantial comfort of the Priory; they shrank from the last open acknowledgment of failure implied by their leaving, as they might shrink from an icy bath. With the tenacity of very old people for the good things of life they wanted to spin out their stay here, even for only a few days.

Curzon, unsympathetic though he was, had a glimpse of these emotions, and stopped for a moment to think. The Coppinger-Browns might be considered harmless old folk, and to allow them to remain for a week or two longer at the Priory might be a kindness which would do no one any harm. But he knew he must not; he felt it in his bones. Coppinger-Brown would never be able to resist the temptation to put his nose into the new organization of the division. Young officers could hardly be expected to order off a Major General, under whom they had only recently been serving, even though he was again retired. There would be hitches, perhaps nasty scenes. And for all he knew Mrs. Coppinger-Brown might make trouble among the women — Curzon had all an unmarried man's suspicions of army women's capacity for making trouble. There must be no chance, not the faintest possibility, of trouble in his division. Moreover, it might weaken his authority a little if people assumed that Coppinger-Brown was staying on to see him firmly in the saddle. He was not going to run the least risk of any of these unpleasant contingencies when a little firmness at the start would obviate them.

"I am afraid," he said, slowly, "that I need the house myself. It would be convenient if you could see your way to leaving at the earliest possible moment. Perhaps if I put the divisional motor car at your disposal to-morrow morning you would have your kit and luggage ready?"

[99]

They looked at each other, all three of them.

"Very well, since you insist," said Coppinger-Brown; Curzon had made no show of insisting. "We had better not keep you any longer from your lunch. We shall be ready to leave at ten o'clock to-morrow. Is that all right, Lucy?"

Mrs. Coppinger-Brown nodded; from beginning to end of the interview she had said no word, but even a wooden-headed man like Curzon was conscious of the hatred she felt towards him as the supplanter of her husband, the man who was driving her out once more into the lonely, pitiable exile of the Cheltenham boarding house. Curzon withdrew as quickly as he could, and he comforted himself as he walked back across the hall by telling himself that after all a soldier's wife should be reconciled by now to having to make sudden migrations, while Coppinger-Brown was a doddering old fool who should never have been entrusted with a division. Which was all perfectly true.

Chapter XI

THE Ninety-First Division was composed of troops of a sort Curzon had never even thought of. They were the first flower of England; of a standard of education, enthusiasm, and physique far superior to anything the recruits of the old regiments of the line could show. In the old days for every man who joined the army because he actively wanted to there were ten who did so because they could find nothing better to do; but in the new units of 1914 every single man had joined because he felt it to be his duty. To Curzon and his like (who in the old days had thoroughly appreciated the value of the occasional "born soldier" in the ranks) the merit of the new material should have been obvious. These were no unemployable riff-raff, no uneducable boys, but men who had made some part of their way already in the world, men of some experience and education, quicker-witted, more accustomed to think for themselves, and filled with the desire to avenge Belgium and to give of their best for England — the same stuff as Cromwell (who in an early speech had pointed out its virtues) had employed when he had made of the Ironsides the finest troops in Europe.

But Cromwell had not been a regular soldier, nor — save for the presence of an occasional veteran of the Thirty Years' War — was there any framework of a regular army, any Procrustean bed of tradition, to which the Ironside army was compelled to adapt itself as in 1914. Kitchener's army was organised by a War Office which had already forgotten the Boer War and clung to the ideals of the Peninsula; but that statement is only correct in a very limited degree, because most of the great body of rules and precedents dealt not with the training of an army for war, but with keeping it inexpensive and out of the way in time of peace. The system was, moreover, adapted to the needs of an army recruited from the very young and the very stupid, officered by men of uniform ideas and training; what the system did for the new armies has been told over and over again.

Besides all this, the War Office was found wanting (perhaps not through its own fault) even in the very elementary duties it might have been expected to perform efficiently. The new armies were left unclothed, unhoused, and unarmed. Units rotted through the winter of 1914–15 under canvas on the bleak exposed hills and plains which had been passed as suitable for a summer camp. They shivered in tents pitched in seas of mud; they ate food prepared by inefficient cooks on inefficient apparatus; they were practised in the evolutions of 1870 by sexagenarian non-commissioned officers, and they used make-believe rifles and make-believe guns under the coördination of make-believe staffs.

Of such good stuff, nevertheless, were the new armies that they came through the ordeal successfully, their spirits unimpaired by what had been done to them, and made of themselves, despite the efforts of their commanders, the finest fighting force ever seen, and able to carry that reputation through years of slaughter and mismanagement despite the constant filling up with drafts whose quality steadily and persistently declined as the war continued.

By a fortunate combination of circumstances Curzon was able to prove himself during these months of training one of the best generals appointed to the new armies. He was full of energy, so that the curse of inertia was not allowed to settle down over the Ninety-First Division. He had no preconceived ideas about the employment of infantry in the field. His barrack traditions were confined to cavalry, and in young Frobisher, his Third Grade General Staff Officer, he found an assistant whose desperate laziness had no play under his supervision and who came of a family in which revolutionary ideas were traditional, so that he did not badger the infantrymen with peace-time regulations nearly as much as occurred in some units.

That very first day at Narling Curzon showed the stuff he was made of. He had no personal staff at all — no aides-decamp, no servants, no grooms; until to-morrow he had no home, for that matter. It never occurred to him to attend to the very important business of settling himself in first. He sent his kit to the local hotel, and made Frobisher telephone to the nearest unit to find him a servant. Before this concession to his immediate needs was fulfilled he was calling for the regimental returns, reading the lists of sick and of those found guilty recently of military crime so as to form his first estimate of the quality of the troops under his command, and halfway through the afternoon, finding this office work unsatisfying, he borrowed a horse from Miller and set off with Frobisher riding beside him in the rain in his anxiety to see things for himself.

He dropped like a bolt from the blue into the troops he had been given to command, trotting in over the rolling downs into the camps of the Three Hundred and First Brigade, the rain streaming from his cap brim and the hem of his cape. There was a moment of hesitation when he confronted his work face to face for the first time — when he realised how extraordinarily little he knew about infantry. But he knew something about men in uniform, at least. There were certain things he could

[103]

inspect — six months ago he had been inspecting similar arrangements from a regimental aspect. There were the cookhouses; he went stalking into the battalion cooking huts, to be appalled by their filth and squalor. Frightened cooking staffs stood shivering at attention while he blistered them with his tongue, and startled commanding officers, summoned by flying orderlies, stood scared at his shoulder while he peered into dixies and cauldrons, and sampled the contents.

General Coppinger-Brown had not been seen in a cookhouse since the weather broke six weeks ago; here was the new general inspecting them before even the rumour of his appointment had run round the regimental headquarters. Curzon plodded through the mud down the lines of tents with the icy wind blowing through his burberry — it was that walk which first gave him an insight into the quality of his men, for any regular unit before the war compelled to submit to such conditions would have shown its resentment by going sick in hundreds. Startled soldiers, huddled under blankets, turned out hastily to stare at him. That morning the bugles had blown "no parade," for no soldiers' work could have been done in those dreadful conditions, and they had settled down to another day of shivering idleness. The sight of a Major General come to see how they were getting on was a most welcome break in the day, reviving hope in breasts where hope of anything was fast dying altogether.

Far more was this the case with the wretched special battalion of Fusiliers who were farther out still — moved there when cerebro-spinal meningitis had appeared in their ranks, to endure the life of outcasts during their period of quarantine. The sense of isolation and guilt had been bad for the Fusiliers, huddled in their tents waiting for the spotted fever. Frobisher had ventured to protest when Curzon announced his intention of visiting the Fusiliers, but Curzon was heedless.

"There's no quarantine for generals," said Curzon. He had no intention of being epigrammatic, either.

He got on his horse again and rode furiously along the slippery chalk track over the summit of the downs to where the Fusiliers languished. A spiritless guard, besodden with misery, turned out to present arms to this extraordinary spectacle of a brass hat in the icy rain, and Curzon, without waiting for the arrival of the commanding officer, began his inspection. Three weeks of quarantine, of isolation, of rain and spotted fever, had taken the heart nearly out of the Fusiliers, but it was the sight of Curzon which put it back. Someone raised a faint cheer, even, when he rode out of the entrance afterwards, in the gathering darkness.

And the word passed round the division, from battalion to battalion, that the new general was crazy on the subject of military cookery. Generals, as the army had long ago resigned itself to believe, are always crazy on some point or other. Coppinger-Brown's particular weakness (as far as anyone had been able to guess from the little seen of him) had been bootlaces. Under Coppinger-Brown's régime colonels had chivvied captains, and captains had chivvied sergeants, into seeing that every man had two pairs at least of spare bootlaces, and had quoted Coppinger-Brown's dictum that "a division might be held up any day on the march if a man's bootlace broke." Nowadays it was cookery instead, and no one knew when the General's big nose and moustache might not be seen coming round the cookhouse corner as he demanded to taste whatever indescribable mess was to be found in the dixies. It was a matter which the men in the ranks, after the food they had been enduring for the last two months, could thoroughly appreciate.

There seemed to be no limit to Curzon's abounding energy in those days when he took over the command of the Ninety-First Division. Mason, the soldier servant whom Miller found for him in the infantry, was under orders always to call him at five — and usually found him awake at that time. Officers, sleepy-eyed and weary, crawling into the divisional head-quarters at seven o'clock, found Curzon at his desk running through the pile of returns and states of the kind which previously had been seen by no other eye than theirs. Isolated companies on the downs, practising the open-order advance in alternate rushes which none of them was to live to see employed in action, were surprised to find him riding up to watch them at their work.

After three days of it Curzon had himself whirled up to London in the divisional motor car and had his presence announced to General Mackenzie with an urgent request for an interview. Mackenzie had him sent up, and blenched a little at the comprehensive sequence of demands which Curzon made on behalf of his division.

"My dear fellow," said Mackenzie, "it's not me whom you should ask for all this. It's all the Q.M.G.'s department, most of it, except for this officer question, and I've promised already to see to that for you. Go round and look up the Q.M.G. — I'll give you a chit to the right quarter, if you like."

Curzon shook his head. He knew a great deal about the army method of passing on inconvenient requests to the next man.

"No," he said, "they don't know me there. I wouldn't be able to get anything done. I'd far rather you saw about it; unofficially, for that matter, if you like. You could get it done in no time, even though it's not your department."

Mackenzie began to show some signs of irritation at this upstart young general's behaviour. The fellow was certainly growing too big for his boots. He took a breath preparatory to administering a proper "telling off."

"You see," said Curzon, eyeing him attentively as he made his first essay in diplomatic converse, "I've got a lot to do, and

I could only spare one day away from the division. I've got an appointment to lunch with Lady Cross and one or two other people — newspaper editors or something, I think they are."

"H'm," said Mackenzie. The struggle behind the scenes for power was rising to a climax, and he knew it. "All right, I'll see what I can do."

When Mackenzie said that, Curzon knew that he could expect immediate attention to be paid to the sweeping indents he had sent in — demands for duckboards and all the other things to make life bearable for the Ninety-First Division in the chalky downland mud — huts and stoves and so on, of which the War Office had such a meagre store. Curzon could leave the War Office now with a clear conscience. He was not lunching with Lady Cross, of course. That had been a blank lie just to apply pressure on Mackenzie. It was his Emily, naturally, with whom he had his next appointment. The big Vauxhall car rolled him smoothly round to Bude House, and the butler showed Curzon in to Emily's sitting room.

Curzon's heart was beating fast, for it was ten days since he had last seen Emily, and she might have changed her mind in that long time. He came into the room stiffly and formally, ready to meet his fate if need be, but all doubts were instantly dispelled on his entrance, and it was as though they had never been separated, as Emily came to him with both hands out and a murmur of "My dear, my dear." She came into his arms as if she were no Duke's daughter. With her head on his shoulder she fingered his row of medal ribbons, and he caught her hand and raised it to his lips, pressing his cruel black moustache upon her fingers. Even if Curzon had taken care to give his affections to a suitable person, there was no doubt that he had given them thoroughly enough. He was head over ears in love with her, just as she was with him.

When sanity came back to them, Curzon spoke straight to

[107]

the point, as might be expected of him. To him love was not a thing to be soiled by roundabout ways of approach, or delicate diplomacy.

"Dear," he said, "can we be married on Christmas Eve?"

"Christmas Eve?" Emily's eyes opened a little wider, for Christmas Eve was only five days off.

"Yes," said Curzon. He made no attempt to mask his reasons. "I've had to take this morning away from the division, when I didn't want to. I can't spare another one, except Christmas morning. There won't be a lot to do on that day. I could come up the afternoon before, and we could get married and go down to Narling the same evening. I mustn't be away from the division."

"Of course not, dear," said Emily. She was rather dazed. She had not seen the house she would have to live in; she knew nothing about it, in fact, except that Curzon's brief notes had assured her that it was quite a nice one. She had made no preparations for housekeeping there — in fact she had made no preparations for being married at all. But she knew quite well that there was nobody and nothing in the world as important as the General and the division he commanded.

"We'll do whatever you think we ought to do, dear," said Emily, and Curzon kissed her hard on the lips in a way he had never kissed her before. Her head swam and her knees went weak so that she leaned against him and clung to him trembling, and they kissed again until the trembling passed and her kind eyes were bright with a passion she had never known before. She found — what she had never expected — that when the world obtruded itself upon them again she was able to meet it boldly face to face, encountering her mother and father across the luncheon table as though a quarter of an hour before she had not been in a man's arms and glad to be there.

At lunch they had to talk practical details regarding the servants Emily must find for Narling Priory, housekeeper and cook and parlourmaid and kitchenmaid. Curzon's three soldier servants (the regulation number allotted to a Major General) could be relied upon to do the other work. The Duchess was perturbed when she heard how hurried was the wedding they had decided upon, but she raised no objection. The Duke took on the responsibility of making the arrangements regarding the licence; the Duchess said she would see to it that St. Margaret's was available for the ceremony — it had to be St. Margaret's, of course. In return, Curzon was able to tell the Duke and Duchess that he had applied for the services of Captain Horatio Winter-Willoughby and Mr. Bertram Greven as his aides-de-camp, and that his application had been approved and orders issued for the officers in question to join him. The Duke and Duchess were undoubtedly grateful to him. Horatio Winter-Willoughby was Lord George's son and the ultimate heir to the title, while Greven was a nephew of the Duchess, and somehow no one had as yet made application for their services on the staff. Curzon felt remarkably pleased with himself when he received the thanks of the Duke and the Duchess. Even though they were about to become his parents-in-law it was gratifying to be able to do them favours.

Then when lunch was finished there was only time for one last embrace before Curzon tore himself away to get into the Vauxhall and be driven away through Guildford and Petersfield back to the division. There was this to be said in favour of wartime conditions, that there was no time for shilly-shallying argument.

Chapter XII

SO IT WAS that the next two or three days witnessed a whole sequence of arrivals at Narling Priory. There came the grim under-housekeeper from Bude Hall, Somersetshire — the Duchess had made a present of her to her daughter, and with her the trio of servants selected from the staff of the three ducal houses. It had rather frightened the Duchess to hear that her daughter would have to be lady's-maided by the parlourmaid; it was not so easy for her to reconcile herself to that as one of the necessary sacrifices of wartime, but as the Priory was only a medium-sized house and half of it was occupied by the divisional headquarters there had to be a line drawn somewhere, and this was Emily's own suggestion.

Curzon's soldier servants regarded the arrival of the women with unconcealed interest, but they were disappointed in the reception accorded their advances. Not even the kitchenmaid — at any rate with the cook's eye on her — would allow mere grooms and private soldiers any liberties with one who represented the fifth greatest house in all England. Curzon handed over house and keys to the housekeeper — he was living with the headquarters mess at the moment — and went on with his work for the division.

The two brigadiers for whom he had been clamouring turned up next. One was Challis, who as a battalion commander had lost half a hand at Mons and had miraculously escaped capture during the retreat; the other was Daunt, brought home from some South African colony, Nigeria or somewhere. Curzon looked them over and was pleased with them both, although he deferred final judgment. Men had to be good before he could be assured of their suitability for the Ninety-First Division. He was not nearly so satisfied with his two aides-de-camp, who turned up unfeignedly glad at having been released by this miracle from the rigours of service in the Guards' Brigade in France. Winter-Willoughby was nearly as bald as his father Lord George, and nearly as fat. Despite the fact that he was indebted to Curzon for this staff appointment he was inclined to be a little resentful and patronising towards the bounder who was marrying his cousin. And Greven had no forehead and no chin and wore riding breeches whose khaki dye carried the particular admixture of pink which was growing fashionable among the younger officers and for which Curzon had a peculiar dislike. Curzon began to see that there were some special disadvantages about marrying into a ducal family.

He disliked his two aides-de-camp at sight the afternoon on which they reported themselves, and the very next day they deepened his prejudice further still, for they were both of them ten minutes late, on the very first morning on which they were on duty. Curzon had to sit fretting in his office while the horses were being walked up and down outside. Curzon told them off furiously as he got into the saddle, and they sulked as they cantered through the rain over the downs to where there was an artillery brigade to be inspected.

Curzon was a little more at home inspecting artillery than infantry. An infantry battalion's horse lines were so small and insignificant that one could not in decency spend much time over them, but it was different with artillery. Horses were as important as gunners, and Curzon felt justified in devoting most of his attention to the horses, which he knew something about, rather than to the artillery technicalities, about which he knew nothing at all. The inspection was long and meticulous, and Curzon found fault with everything he saw. The battery commanders wilted under the lash of his tongue, the sergeant majors flinched, the veterinary surgeons trembled. When Curzon rode away the rumour was ready to circulate through the division that "Curzon was just as mad about horse lines as about cookhouses." Yet nobody knew the reason of this savage bad temper which he had displayed — those who were in the secret of the General's private life were inclined to attribute it to the fact that he was being married that afternoon, but they were wrong. A letter had come to Curzon that morning, in a cheap shabby envelope, addressed originally to the regimental depôt, and readdressed three times before it had reached him. Curzon had read it while he ate his breakfast, and the sight of it had spoiled his day.

117, Shoesmith St.
Brixton.
16th December, 1914.

My dear Bertie,

I suppose I must call you that still although you are a General now and going to marry a great Lady. We are all of us here very pleased to see how well you are getting on. Your Uncle Stanley reads the papers a great deal and has shown us lots about you in them. He did not approve of the war at first but when we heard about what the Germans did in Belgium he feels differently about it now. Maud has just got married too to a gentleman in a very good way of business as a tailor. It seems only like yesterday since she was a little girl like when you saw her last. Gertie is in a government office and doing very well, and our Dick has just made up his mind that he must do his bit and he is going to join the army as soon as Christmas is over. Your Uncle Stanley is very well considering although his chest troubles him a lot, and of course I am all right as usual except for my leg. This is just a line to wish

you much joy and happiness in your new life with your bride and
to say that if ever you are in Brixton again we shall be glad the
same as ever, although you are so grand now, if you would pop
in and see us just for a minute.

Your loving
Aunt Kate.

P.S. We saw your photograph in the paper and you look just the
same as ever which is why I wrote to you dear.

That was a very disturbing letter for a man about to marry
a Duke's daughter to receive on his wedding morning. Curzon's flesh had crept as he read it. He had been perfectly sincere when he told Emily and the Duchess that he had not a
relation in the world — he had forgotten all about the Coles of
Brixton, honestly and sincerely forgotten all about them. It
was a shock to be reminded of their existence. If any word
about them should reach the Duchess's ears it would make her
into his deadly enemy, for she would never forgive him the
deception. Even now she was hardly a benevolent neutral. Any
revelation would turn the scale. It would lose him Emily's
good opinion and regard. Probably it would ruin his life and
his career as well and that was an important although a minor
consideration. Curzon felt slightly sick like a man with no
head for heights looking over the edge of a precipice. Why in
the world had Aunt Kate married beneath her station, instead
of above it as his own mother had very sensibly seen fit to do?

He had plenty of time to think about it during the long
motor journey up to London. There had been no time for
lunch after the artillery inspection, and he and Horatio Winter-
Willoughby and Greven ate sandwiches in the stuffy saloon car
as they raced along past the Devil's Punchbowl and on to
Guildford. They were cumbered with their greatcoats and
swords. Curzon actually found himself thankful that he had
been compelled to put aside the Duchess's suggestion that he

should be married in all the glory of his Lancer full dress. He simply had not been able to make allowance in the day's time-table for that change of clothing, and he was glad now, swaying about in the motor car, feeling slightly sick, what with the motion, and the sandwiches, and the imminence of marriage, and that letter from Aunt Kate. From Guildford onwards he was looking at his watch. It was going to be a near-run thing. There were only a few minutes left when they ran through Esher, and he called on the driver for yet more speed. Kingston — Putney Bridge — King's Road, crowded with people shopping industriously on this, the first Christmas Eve of the war.

Big Ben showed one minute to two as they swung out of Victoria Street. The paragraphs in the newspapers about the romantic war wedding of a Duke's daughter and the sight of the carpet and awning outside St. Margaret's, had called to-gether a big crowd on the pavement. The Vauxhall stopped at the end of the awning, and Curzon and his two aides got out while the crowd surged under the control of the police. They had hardly sat down up by the chancel rails when the organ changed its tune and up the aisle came Emily in her bridal white, her bridesmaids and her pages behind her, and the Duke in support.

As the Duchess had said, the fact that Emily was marrying a General was a very adequate excuse for so much ceremony at the wedding, when otherwise it might not be quite good taste in wartime. The Bishop (he was a Winter-Willoughby, too; by common report the only one with any brains, and he had too many) went through the service, while Curzon rasped out the responses and Emily whispered them. Then the sign-ing of the register, and the march out through the church, while the guests stood up on their seats to catch a better glimpse of the bride and the beribboned bridegroom.

While Curzon was waiting for Emily, encumbered with train and veil, to get into the motor car, the crowd surged more violently than ever. He looked round. Between two policemen, and waving violently, was Aunt Kate — there was no mistaking her; and the two women beside her were presumably Maud and Gertie. It was only for a second that their eyes met. Aunt Kate had the decency and the common sense not to call out "Bertie!" although for an idiotic second Curzon was filled with fear in case she should say something about her sore leg. He had not time to betray recognition, as he had to climb in at once beside Emily. Next instant they were off, with Curzon sitting shaken beside Emily, who for some woman's reason or other had tears on her face.

So on the way to Bude House Curzon had time to reflect that there were some relatives of his at his wedding. The church had been crammed with Winter-Willoughbys and Grevens, hordes of them. There had not been more than half a dozen people invited at Curzon's request — three or four members of the Cavalry Club, and Mackenzie, who (perhaps for reasons of his own) had intimated that he might be able to get away from his duties at the War Office for an hour. Curzon had not even been able to find a friend close enough to be asked to be groom's man — the one or two possibles were in France, which was why the egregious Horatio had had to fulfill that duty.

There was an hour's torment in Bude House, where even those colossal rooms were not big enough to shelter all the seething horde without crushing. The sparse khaki amidst the morning coats and the elaborate dresses would have been significant to an attentive observer. Those uniforms were like the secret seeds of decay in the midst of an apparently healthy body. They were significant of the end of a great era. The decline had already set in, although those most intimately concerned (despite the fact that they already were talking sorrowfully about the good old days, and lamenting the changes all about them) obstinately refused to recognise it. In ten years' time the world would have no room for Bude House. It would be torn to pieces; the British public would be blackmailed into buying its paintings by the threat of selling them to America; its Adam fireplaces would be sold with less advertisement to the same country; and the people who thronged its rooms would be stockbroking on half commission or opening little hat shops in side streets.

But nobody cared to think about all this at the moment, least of all Curzon, the most significant figure present, with his hand nervously resting on his sword hilt and the letter from Aunt Kate in his pocket. He greeted starchily the people who came up to wish him happiness and to look him over covertly; he did not feel in the least complimented when he overheard withered little Mr. Anstey whispering to an aged female crony, "Most romantic. A real cloak and sword wedding, just like Napoleon's"; he had not even found any real pleasure in the contemplation of the inkstand which was a present from the King. The longer the reception lasted, the stiffer and more formal he became, and the attempts at boisterousness made by the few younger people (among whom should be reckoned his two aides-de-camp) irritated him unbearably.

By the time Emily appeared again in a sober travelling costume, and still in unaccountable tears, his nerves were on edge —although Curzon would have indignantly denied the possession of any nerves at all if anyone had been rash enough to impute them to him. The premature evening had already fallen as he climbed after Emily into the big Vauxhall. They slid through the darkened streets (the A.S.C. driver keeping his eyes rigidly to the front) and Curzon still sat cold and formal in his corner, while Emily drooped from her stiff uprightness in hers. From the darkness that surrounded her there came at intervals something suspiciously like a sniff — unbelievable though it might be that a Duke's daughter, and one moreover of her Spartan upbringing, should ever sniff.

Curzon was not given to self-contemplation. He would have seen nothing incongruous in the spectacle of the Major General, who that morning had reduced an artillery brigade to a condition of gibbering terror, caressing his bride on their bridal journey. Why he held aloof from her during that first hour was merely because he did not feel like doing otherwise. The events of the day had left him unfitted for love. Emily was like a stranger to him at present.

Later on, as the headlights tore lanes through the darkness, and the car weaved its way precariously round the curves at Hindhead, he put his hand out and groped for hers. He touched it, and she leaped in panic. Her nerves were in as bad a state as his, and for all this hour she had been expecting and dreading this contact. She was consumed with misgivings regarding the unbelievable things that men do to women when they are married to them, and to which the woman has to submit — the half-knowledge she had gained of these matters during her cloistered existence made the future absolutely terrifying to her. It was five days since she had last had the comfort and stimulus of Curzon's presence, and during those five days she had lapsed from her mood of reckless passion into one more consonant with an upbringing dating from the 'eighties. She was brooding darkly over the prospect of "that kind of thing"; and this new, wordless, reserved, cold, formal Curzon beside her was of no help to her. From the way she jumped at his touch one might have guessed that she feared lest he should begin at once.

There was no fear of that, nor of the least resemblance to it. When Curzon felt the gloved hand snatched away from him he withdrew further into himself than ever. They sat stiffly silent, one in each corner, while the Vauxhall nosed its way through Petersfield, out into the main road beyond, and then swung aside into the by-roads which led to Narling Priory. The servants came out to welcome them — the grim housekeeper, and the prim elderly parlourmaid, and Curzon's groom and soldier servant. The A.S.C. driver was left to unstrap the trunks from the grid at the back, while the housekeeper walked up the stairs to the bridal chamber with the bride, while Curzon trailed behind. They found themselves alone together at last in her bedroom. Emily looked round for comfort, and found none in the unpleasant furniture which the War Office had taken over at a thumping rental along with the house. She saw Curzon standing waiting, with his predatory nose and cruel moustache.

"I — I want to lie down," she said wildly. "I — I'm tired."

The arrival of the parlourmaid and servant with the trunks eased the situation for a moment. As the servant withdrew the parlourmaid addressed herself with decision to the business of unpacking. Curzon was glad that in the circumstances he could be expected to say nothing beyond pure formalities.

"I shall see you at dinner, then," he said, backing away with his spurs clinking.

Dinner was an ordeal, too, with the elderly parlourmaid breathing discretion at every pore. They looked at each other across the little table and tried to make conversation, but it was not easy. Both of them would have been interested if they had told each other the stories of their lives, for they were still extraordinarily ignorant of each other's past, but it hardly became a husband and wife to tell facts about themselves to the other. In the absence of that resource, and after the inevitable comments about the dreariness of the weather, conversation

[118]

came to a standstill. Lady Emily looked with bewilderment at the spruce dinner-jacketed man with the red face whom she had married. She told herself that he did not look in the least like the man she had fallen in love with. And Curzon looked at Emily, a little drawn and haggard, and marvelled to himself at the contrariness of women, and felt ill at ease because on other occasions when he had dined with a woman previous to sleeping with her the circumstances had not been in the least like these.

As soon as dinner was over Emily withdrew to the drawing room, leaving Curzon alone to his port and his brandy, and when Curzon came into the drawing room she shrank down nervously in her chair and fluttered the weekly newspaper she had been pretending to read. Curzon sat on the edge of his chair and tugged at his moustache; the clock ticked away inexorably on the mantelpiece while he stared into the fire. Emily kept her eyes on the page before her although she could read no word of its print; she was making an effort now at this late hour to rally her self-control as became one of her blue blood and to go stoically through the ordeal before her without a sign of weakness, like a French aristocrat on the way to the guillotine. It was not easy, all the same.

She put down her paper and got to her feet.

"I think I shall go to bed now," she said; only the acutest. ear could have caught the quaver in her voice.

"Yes," said Curzon. He could not help drawling on occasions like the present of extreme nervous tension. "You've had a tiring day, m'dear."

By an effort of rigid self-control Emily kept her upper lip from trembling. Curzon's face was blank and expressionless, like a block of wood, as though he were playing at poker, and when he looked at her he looked right through her — he could

[119]

not help it; it was only a natural reaction to his shyness. He opened the door for her, and she cast one more glance at that wooden countenance before she fled up the stairs.

Curzon went back beside the fire and drew deeply on a fresh cigar. He stared again into the fire. Somehow his thoughts were jumbled. He tried to think about the division, that hotch-potch of jarring personalities which he had to straighten out, but he could not think about it for long. For some reason other mental pictures obtruded themselves. For the first time for years he found himself thinking about Manningtree-Field, his Captain at Volkslaagte, lying in a mess of blood and brains at his feet. Then his thoughts leaped back a dozen years more, until he was a small boy coming home from prep school, being met at Victoria Station by his mother. He thought of Mac-kenzie with his pink face and sandy hair. He thought of Miss Cissie Barnes, the lady with whom he had spent many joyful evenings. Miss Barnes wore decorative garters whose clasps were miniature five-barred gates with "trespassers will be pros-ecuted" engraved upon them. Curzon remembered vividly how they had looked encircling the black-stockinged leg with the luscious white thigh showing above the stocking. Curzon flung the cigar into the fire and strode twice up and down the room. Then he went out, up the stairs, to the upper landing. On the right was the door into his small bedroom and dressing room. On the left was the door into Emily's room — there was a con-necting door between the two, but he did not consider that. He stood still for a moment before he knocked on the door on the left and entered abruptly.

Emily stood by the fire. There were candles alight on the dressing table, on the mantelpiece, beside the wardrobe, so that the room was brightly illuminated. Emily's clothes, save for her evening frock, lay neatly on the chair where the maid had placed them; the long formidable corset was on the top, with the suspenders hanging down. Emily was wearing a night-dress of the kind considered by orthodox people in 1914 as the most frivolous possible (the kind of nightdress worn by sub-urban housewives twenty years later was at that time only worn by prostitutes) and she stood there by the fire with a cataract of lace falling over her breast and her long hair in a rope down her back.

She saw him come in, his face a little flushed, the cruel mouth and the big nose much in evidence, and she saw him shut and lock the door.

"Bertie," she said, and she wanted to add, "be kind to me," but she could say no more than the one word, because pride on the one hand and passion on the other dried up her throat. Curzon came slowly over to her, his face wearing the expression of stony calm which always characterised it at tense moments. He put out his hands to her, and she came towards him, fascinated.

Chapter XIII

PERHAPS it was Emily's stoic upbringing which made that marriage a success. Certainly she knew more misery in the opening few weeks of her married life than she had ever known before — the misery of loneliness, and the misery of doubt. But she had long been taught to bear her troubles uncomplainingly, along with the doctrine, comforting in its fatalism, that the ways of mankind (as compared with those of womankind) are inscrutable. Thanks to her patience and powers of endurance they learned after a short interval to live together as happy as two people of their limited capacity for happiness could expect to be.

Miss Cissie Barnes had much to answer for. The memory of joyous unrepressed evenings with her influenced Curzon profoundly. He could not dream of treating his wife in the same way as he had once treated Cissie Barnes, with the unfortunate result that he made love to Emily with a stern aloofness that could raise no response in her virginal body. As Emily never expected anything else, however, not so much harm was done as might have been the case. Emily went through that part of the business as her necessary duty, like opening Girl Guides' displays or going to church. It was her duty, something it was incumbent upon her to do, so she did it with the best grace possible, short of taking an active interest in it — women were not supposed to do that.

For the rest, she was everything a General's wife should be. On Christmas morning, the very day after her wedding, she breakfasted with him with every appearance of cheerfulness, and saw him off on his tour of inspection with a wave of her hand that told the inquisitive world that they were absolutely happy. There were not many generals of division in England who spent that Christmas Day with the troops, but Curzon was one of them. He managed to visit every one of the twenty units under his command. For nearly all the men it was their first Christmas in the army; for a great number of them it would also be their last, but no one — certainly not Curzon and not even Emily — stopped to think about that. Curzon had not the time to visit the men in the ranks, but he called in to every officer's mess, and the surprise and delight of the regimental officers at this condescension on the part of high authority filtered in the end down to the men in the ranks and did its part in tuning up the Ninety-First Division to the pitch of excellence which it eventually displayed.

It did Curzon no harm that everyone knew he was newly married, nor that regimental wits were busy producing obscene jokes about him and his wife. It made him known, gave him a personality for the private soldiers, just as did his acquisition of the nickname of "Bertie" — which reached the troops of the line from the Staff, who had heard Lady Emily address him by that name. Neither Emily nor Curzon saw anything comic or undignified about the name of "Bertie," and to the army the irony of the name's suggestion of weak good fellowship as contrasted with his reputation for savage energy and discipline appealed to the wry sense of humour of the sufferers, making a deeper impression still. The catch-word "Bertie's the boy" was current in the Ninety-First Division long before it spread among the troops in France.

Everyone knew that Bertie would tolerate no inefficiency or

slackness. The whole army was aware of the reasons why Lieutenant Colonel Ringer of the Fusiliers was removed from his command and sent into retirement, and of the energy of Bertie's representations to the War Office which brought this about. Yet not so many people knew that the leakage of gossip regarding this affair was the cause of the return of Captain Horatio Winter-Willoughby to regimental duty. The information regarding the leakage reached Curzon through Emily. Emily had plunged in duty bound into the business of leading army society locally — most of the senior officers of the division had brought down their wives to be near them, and installed them at exorbitant prices in hotels and cottages roundabout. Sooner or later someone told her how much they knew about the Ringer scandal, and what was the source of the information.

Emily told Curzon in all innocence — she had not yet learned what a crime gossip was in Curzon's eyes. Curzon struck at once. That same day a report went into the War Office saying that Major General Curzon much regretted being under the necessity of informing the Director General of Staff Personnel that Captain Horatio Winter-Willoughby had been found unsuitable for work on the staff, and of requesting that he be ordered to return to his unit. There was a wail of despair from Horatio when the news reached him — a wail expressed in indignant letters to London, which brought down the Duchess of Bude and Lady Constance Winter-Willoughby, simply seething with indignation.

The Duchess was angry largely because this upstart son-in-law of hers was betraying the family which had condescended to admit him into its circle. What was the good of having a General in the family if he did not find places on the staff for the nephews? And the suggestion that a Winter-Willoughby was not up to his work was perfectly preposterous — more preposterous still, because the Duchess could never imagine that it mattered a rap which man did which work as long as she had a finger in the pie. There was the question of the succession to the title, too. If Horatio was sent back into the Guards as a result of this ridiculous notion of Curzon's it was possible that he might be killed — not likely, of course, because Winter-Willoughbys were not killed, but possible — and that would make the continued existence of the title almost precarious.

"So you see," said the Duchess, putting down her teacup, "you simply can't go on with this wicked idea. You must write to the War Office *at once* — or it would be better to telephone to them perhaps — and tell them that you have made a mistake and you want Horatio to stay here with you."

Curzon would have found it difficult to have answered politely if he had cast about for words with which to tell his mother-in-law that he was not going to do what she said. But as it was he did not stop to try to be polite. He was not going to have the efficiency of his division interfered with by anyone not in authority, least of all a woman.

"I'm not going to do anything of the sort," he said, briefly.

"Bertie!" said the Duchess, scandalised.

"No," said Curzon. "This isn't the first time I've had to find fault with Horatio. I'm sorry he's no good, but I can't have him on my Staff. I hope he will find regimental duty more — more congenial."

"Do you mean," said the Duchess, "that you're not going to do what I ask — what the Family ask you to do?"

"I'm not going to keep him as my A.D.C.," said Curzon, sturdily.

"I think," said Lady Constance, "that is perfectly horrible of you."

Lady Constance happened to be more moved by anxiety for her son than by Curzon's blasphemous denial of the family.

[125]

"I'm sorry," said Curzon, "but I can't help it. I have the division to think about."

"Division fiddlesticks!" said the Duchess, which made Curzon exceedingly angry. Lady Constance saw the look in his eye, and did her best to soothe him.

"Perhaps Horatio was a little indiscreet," she said, "but he's only young. I think he will have learned his lesson after this. Don't you think you might give him another chance?"

Lady Constance made play with all her beauty and all her elegance as she spoke. Curzon would certainly have wavered if it had not been the concern of the division. He was suddenly able to visualise with appalling clarity Horatio, lazy, casual, and unpunctual, confronted suddenly with a crisis like any one of the fifty which had occurred during the eleven days at Ypres. If the existence of the division should at any time depend on Horatio, which was perfectly possible, the division would cease to exist. It was unthinkable that Horatio should continue in a position of potential responsibility.

"No," said Curzon. "I can't have him."

Lady Constance and the Duchess looked at each other, and with one accord they turned to Emily, who had been sitting mute beside the tea things.

"Emily," said Lady Constance. "Can't you persuade him?"

"Horatio is your first cousin," said the Duchess. "He's the future Duke of Bude."

Emily looked in distress, first at her mother and her aunt, and then at her husband in his khaki and red tabs beside the fire. Anyone — even a woman only three weeks married to him — could see by his stiff attitude that the matter was very near to his heart, that his mind was made up, and that his temper was growing short. In the last two months the Family had declined in importance in her eyes; it was her husband who mattered. Yet it was frightening that they should be debating

[126]

a matter on which Horatio's very life might depend — it was that thought which distressed her more than the need to oppose her mother.

"Don't ask me," she said. "I can't interfere with the division. I don't think you ought to ask me."

The Duchess snapped her handbag shut with a vicious click, and rose to her feet.

"It appears to me," she said, "as if we were unwelcome even in my daughter's house."

She rose superbly to her feet, carrying Lady Constance along with her by sheer force of personality.

"I can see no profit," she went on, "in continuing this subject. Perhaps, Bertie, you will be good enough to send and have my car brought round?"

Curzon tugged at the bellrope and gave the order to the parlourmaid; it is just possible that the Duchess had not expected to be taken quite so readily at her word. At any rate, Lady Constance made a last appeal.

"I don't want to have to part in anger like this," she said. "Can't something be arranged, Emily — Bertie?"

"Something will doubtless be arranged," said the Duchess, with a venomous glance at her daughter and son-in-law. "Please do not be too distressed, Constance."

Curzon and Emily walked out to the door with them, but the Duchess so far forgot her good manners as to climb into the car without saying good-bye. Enough had happened that afternoon to make her angry; that a Winter-Willoughby should be denied something apparently desirable, and that a Duchess of Bude should be forced to plead with an upstart little General and then be refused was a state of affairs calculated to make her perfectly furious.

The sequel followed promptly, materialising in the arrival of the Duke the next day, preceded by a telegram. Curzon talked with him alone, at his special request, Emily withdrawing after receiving his fatherly greetings. They sat one each side of the fire and pulled at their cigars in silence for several minutes until the Duke began on the inevitable subject.

"You've made my wife a bit annoyed over this business of young Horatio, Curzon, you know," said the Duke. "As a matter of fact I've never seen her so angry before in my life."

The tone of the Duke's voice suggested that he had frequently seen her fairly angry.

"I'm sorry," said Curzon.

"Trouble is, with women," went on the Duke, "they never know when to stop. And they don't draw any distinctions between a man's private life and his official one — they don't render unto Caesar the things that are Caesar's, you know. My wife's determined to put the screw on you somehow or other — you know what women are like. You can guess what she made me do last night — first shot in the campaign, so to speak?"

"No," said Curzon.

"She made me sit down there and then, with dinner half an hour late already, and write an order to Coutt's. Dash it all, you can guess what that was about, can't you?"

"I suppose so," said Curzon.

"It was to countermand my previous order to pay one-seventy a month into your account. Women never know what's good form, and what isn't."

Curzon said nothing. The prospect of losing the Duke's two thousand a year was disturbing; it would mean altering the whole scale of his domestic arrangements, but it did absolutely nothing towards making him incline again in the direction of retaining Horatio's services.

"I suppose," said the Duke, nervously, "there isn't any chance of your changing your mind about Horatio?"

[128]

"Not the least," snapped Curzon. "And I don't think we had better discuss the subject."

"Quite right," said the Duke. "I was sure you would say that. Dam' good thing you didn't kick me out of the house the minute I said what I did. Of course, I wrote another order to Coutt's this morning, saying that they were to continue paying that one-seventy. But I'd rather you didn't let the Duchess know, all the same."

"Thank you," said Curzon.

"Now," said the Duke, with enormous relief, "is there any way out of this mess? Can you think of any job Horatio could do?"

"He might make a good regimental officer," said Curzon. Most of the regimental officers he had known had not been much more distinguished for capacity than Horatio. The Duke nodded.

"I suppose so," he said. "There aren't many brains in us Winters, when all is said and done. Fact is, I don't think we'd be very important people if the first Winter hadn't married William of Orange's lady friend. But it's not much good telling the Duchess that. I've got to do something about it."

The Duke looked quite pathetic.

"There are some staff positions," said Curzon, "where he couldn't do much harm."

Curzon was quite incapable of expressing that awkward truth any less awkwardly.

"M'm," said the Duke. "And none of them in your gift, I suppose?"

"No."

"It's awkward," said the Duke. "But I'll have to see what I can do up in town. I suppose you know that I'll be in office again soon?"

"No," said Curzon. Despite the revelations of the last few

[129]

weeks he was still abysmally ignorant of the behind-the-scenes moves in politics.

"Yes," said the Duke. "I don't think it matters if I tell you. The Radicals won't be able to keep us out much longer. Then I may be able to do a bit more for Horatio and satisfy the Duchess. There's a good many points I want your advice about, too. What's this man Mackenzie like? Any good?"

"First rate," said Curzon without any hesitation. Had not Mackenzie been instrumental in promoting him to Major General, in giving him the Ninety-First Division, and in supplying that division with material far beyond its quota? Quite apart from that, it would have needed a very serious deficiency indeed to induce Curzon not to give the simple loyalty which he in turn expected from his subordinates.

"You really mean that?" asked the Duke anxiously.

"Of course," said Curzon. "He's one of the best soldiers we've got. Works like a nigger and plenty of brains."

"M'm," said the Duke meditatively, pulling at his long fleshy chin. "You see — well, it doesn't matter. If you think he's satisfactory and you ought to know, I don't think I ought — anyway, that's all right."

Having made this cryptic speech the Duke fell silent again, transferring his attentions from his chin to his cigar, while Curzon smoked opposite to him, silent also, for the adequate enough reason that he had nothing more to say. Finally the Duke got to his feet.

"Well," he said. "There's going to be a hot reception awaiting me when I get back to London again, but it's no use putting it off. I'll start back now, I think. No, thank you very much, I won't stay to dinner. It won't be very late by the time I'm home. Good-bye, Curzon. Don't be too gloomy."

Captain Horatio Winter-Willoughby did not serve his

country at the risk of his life despite Curzon's adverse report upon him. It only needed the War Office's attention to be seriously drawn to the reference to him in the Peerage for him to be found a safe position on the staff of the military attaché to a neutral government — the War Office was quite well aware of the importance of safeguarding the ultimate heir to a dukedom, just as when the threat of air raids became more than a threat they sent the masterpieces of the National Gallery into safe storage in Wales.

Yet in one respect the Duke's conversation bore fruit. The inevitable spy who tries to serve both sides was able to report a discussion which had been held among the prospective Ins, and his report had come to the knowledge of General Mackenzie. The spy had had a respectable education, and he was able to compare that discussion with the famous debate among the Triumvirate in *Julius Caesar,* when they prick off the prospective victims.

"No," the Duke had said. "I can't say I agree with you about this fellow Mackenzie. My son-in-law, who's in command of a division — I've told you about him before, haven't I? — well, he says that Mackenzie's all right. Swears by him, in fact. And my son-in-law's got his head screwed on the right way. He wouldn't say a thing like that if he didn't think it was true, either. I don't think Mackenzie ought to go. Hang it, someone's got to do the brainwork."

That was why — and Mackenzie knew it — when the Liberal government at last yielded to the overwhelming pressure and admitted some of the Opposition to the sweets of office, while men in high position fell right and left, General Mackenzie remained Director General of Tactical Services. Others greater than he — among them the greatest Minister of War that England ever had — were flung out of office, but Mackenzie remained despite his very unsound attitude in the Ulster crisis. Perhaps that is the most important contribution Curzon ever made to the history of England.

In addition, as a born intriguer, Mackenzie could not possibly credit Curzon with ordinary honesty, but considered him as just a fellow intriguer, an ally worth having and especially a potential enemy worth placating.

Chapter XIV

THE training of the Ninety-First Division proceeded apace, even though every day added to the total amount to be learned. A good many wounded and convalescent officers rejoined its ranks, and regarded with quiet amusement the parade movements and formal battle tactics which the division was slowly learning to perform. Their recent experience of Flanders mud, and barbed wire, and German machine guns had deprived them of their faith in rigid attacking movements.

Besides these informal ambassadors, the War Office began to send instructors with more explicit credentials — trench warfare experts, barbed-wire maniacs, bombing officers, machine gun enthusiasts, and — after the second battle of Ypres — gas warfare specialists. These men were attached to Curzon's staff with orders to teach the Ninety-First Division all they knew, and every one of them was quite convinced that his particular speciality was the vital necessity in the new kind of warfare which was being waged, and clamoured for wider and wider powers to be given them.

Curzon had to listen to them patiently and arbitrate among them; sometimes, under the urging of express orders from the War Office, he had to acquiesce in the teaching of doctrines which to him were only a shade less than heretical. He had no sooner made arrangements for an intensive instruction in bayonet fighting than he had to coerce his colonels into submitting to an enlargement of the battalion machine gun establishments which would diminish very seriously the number of bayonets that could be put in line. He had to see to it that the artillery brigades received instruction regarding the new but already highly technical business of spotting from the air. He had to let the sappers have their way and try to make every infantryman an expert in matters which before the war had been strictly left to the engineers.

Curzon himself had small belief still in the theories of a long war to be conducted exclusively in trenches. That would leave such small scope for the kind of soldiering he appreciated that he simply could not believe in it. Even in the spring of 1915, when the line in France reeled under the blow dealt it at Ypres, he was in a fever of apprehension lest the Allied victory should come too quickly, before the Ninety-First Division could arrive to take its share of the glory. In March the first reports of the battle of Neuve Chapelle were construed by him as indicating a great victory, the first step in the advance to Berlin, and he was left puzzled, even after the circulation of the War Office confidential memoranda on the battle, by the subsequent inactivity.

He threw himself more ardently than ever into his duty of preparing the Ninety-First Division for active service. His brigadiers — Daunt and Challis and Webb — needed no goading. They were prepared to work until they dropped. The main part of Curzon's work consisted of coördinating the activities of all the officers under him. It would have called for a Solomon to adjudicate between the conflicting claims put before him. Curzon was able to keep the pace not by the ingenuity or justice of his decisions, but solely by the strictness of the discipline maintained. There was no one who dared to dispute or evade his orders. He was the terror of the shirkers and of the wrigglers. His reputation as a relentless disciplinarian stood him in good stead, and after he had made an example of Colonel Ringer he had no more trouble with his subordinates.

The paper work which all this involved was a sore trial to him. Despite the growth of the headquarters Staff, of the introduction of clerks, of the multiplication of specialist officers, the office work which he personally had to attend to increased inordinately. His anxiety regarding his division prevented him from delegating more of his authority than he was compelled to, and early morning and late night found him patiently reading court martial records and confidential reports on junior officers. He signed no indents or statements which he had not read; he set himself painfully to learn all about the idiosyncrasies and strengths and weaknesses of every officer and unit with which he came in contact. He exercised his mind over the Rifles' regrettable tendency to absence without leave, and the proneness of the Seventh (Service) Battalion of the Cumberland Light Infantry to acquire sore feet on route marches.

It was his duty to make the division efficient; that was why he slaved and toiled over the business. His desire for his own professional advancement, his anxiety to stand well in Emily's eyes and in those of her family, were undoubtedly acute, but they were not the motives which guided him. He had been given a job of work to do, and he did it to the best of his ability, although the desk work made him thin and irritable and spoilt his digestion and his eyesight, and although he could never find time now to have all the exercise for which he craved.

He usually had to leave Lady Emily to hunt by herself, or under the escort of either Greven or Follett, his aides-de-camp — there was a good deal of fox-hunting to be enjoyed, because various patriotic people had decided that hunting must go on, so that when the boys returned from the trenches they would find this essential characteristic of England still flourishing, while officers in England should be provided with sport; nor might foxes be allowed to diminish the food supply of England; nor might the breed of English horses, so essential in wartime, be allowed to decline; nor might the hunt servants be thrown out of employment — there were dozens of reasons put forward for the maintenance of fox-hunting besides the real one that the hunters did not believe a war to be nearly as serious as the suspension of fox-hunting. It was highly convenient for all concerned that their patriotic feelings should run so closely parallel to their own desires.

Yet it is possible that fox-hunting played its part in welding the Ninety-First Division into a living, active whole, for every officer did his best to hunt, and the friendships formed in the hunting field may have influenced subsequent events in No Man's Land. At any rate, the Major General commanding the division gave his approval and his blessing to fox-hunting, and when the season came to an end at the approach of summer he condoled with his wife on the subject. Emily looked at him a little queerly — they were dining at the time, alone for once in the absence of any guests from the division, but the parlour-maid was in the room and her presence caused Lady Emily not to say immediately what she was going to say. Later on, when they sat in the drawing room with their coffee beside them, Emily reverted to the subject, nervously.

"You were saying I must be sorry that hunting was coming to an end, Bertie," said Emily.

"That's right," said Curzon. "I always think it's a pity."

"Well," said Emily, "it doesn't matter to me now. I couldn't go on hunting in any case."

Curzon looked across at Emily with surprise in his face. He had naturally, like any sane newly married man, thought occasionally of the possibility of his wife having a child, but now

that she was trying to tell him about it that was the last idea
to occur to him.

"Why, m'dear," he asked, "is anything the matter?"

"Not really the *matter*," said Emily. Her eyes were wide and
she made herself meet Curzon's glance without flinching.

"But — but — " said Curzon. "What is it, then?"

Emily went on looking at him without speaking, and yet
still he would not jump to the right conclusion. For a moment
he was honestly worried lest Emily should have decided that
fox-hunting was unpatriotic or cruel. And Emily was not at all
deterred at the thought of saying she was pregnant (although
that was not the word she would use). What was holding her
back was the thought that after that announcement she would
have to tell her husband her reasons for thinking herself to be
in that condition, and that would involve discussion of matters she had never mentioned to any man at all, not even (as
yet) to a doctor. Curzon and she had skated safely (only those
of Victorian upbringing can guess how) during three months
of married life over the thin ice of feminine weaknesses without crashing through into revelations.

"But, my good girl," protested Curzon, and then the truth
dawned upon him.

"God bless my soul," said Curzon, his coffee cup clattering
into its saucer. He grinned with surprised delight; already, in
this his early middle age, there was just noticeable the old-
maidish quality about his smile which was later to become so
pronounced.

For some unaccountable reason Emily found tears in her
eyes; they were soon rolling down her cheeks.

"Oh my dear, my darling," said Curzon, hurrying across the
room to her. Words of endearment did not come too easily to
him; in part that was because of lurking memories of having
used them to Cissie Barnes. He patted her on the shoulder, and

[137]

then, as that did not avail, he knelt in stiff dinner-jacketed awkwardness beside her in her low chair. Emily wiped her eyes and smiled at him, tear-dazzled.

"You're — you're not sorry, m'dear, are you?" said Curzon.

"No," replied Emily, boldly. "I'm glad. I'm glad."

"So am I," endorsed Curzon, and his imagination awoke. "My son. I shall have a son," he said. Mental pictures were streaming through his mind like a cinematograph — he thought of the boy at school; later on in Sandhurst uniform; he could picture all the triumphs which would come the boy's way and which he would enjoy vicariously. As a young man he had envied the representatives of military families, with a long record of service from generation to generation. His son would be one of a military family now, General Curzon's eldest boy, and after him there would be a long unbroken succession of military Curzons. It was as good to be an ancestor as to have ancestors.

"He'll be a fine little chap," said Curzon, gazing into the future.

Emily was able to smile at the light in his face even though she had no intention of bringing a son into the world — her wish was for a daughter to whom she had already promised a childhood far happier than ever she had enjoyed.

"Darling," she said to Curzon, taking the lapels of his coat in her hands.

"Darling," said Curzon to her, his face empurpling as he craned over his stiff collar to kiss her hands. He toppled forward against her, and her arms went round him, and his about her, and they kissed, and Emily's cheek was wet against his, and Curzon's eyes did not remain absolutely dry. Curzon went to bed that night without having read through the Deputy Judge Advocate General's comments on the conflicting evidence in the court martial on Sergeant Major Robinson, accused of having been drunk on parade. But he got up early next morning to read them, all the same.

The news brought the Duke and Duchess swooping down upon the Priory despite the fact that the crisis in the cabinet was at its height. Curzon found that his mother-in-law, while almost ignoring him as a mere male in this exclusively feminine business, had practically forgiven him for his obstinacy with regard to Horatio Winter-Willoughby — time, the finding of a new appointment for the young man, and Emily's pregnancy had between them taken the sting out of her enmity. Yet she irritated Curzon inexpressibly by the way in which she took charge of Emily. Emily must leave this old-fashioned house *at once,* and come to London where the finest professional advice was to be obtained. She had already retained the services of Sir Trevor Choape for the event. Bude House would of course be open to Emily all this summer, Sir Trevor had recommended a nurse to whom she had written that very day. The child must have all the care a Winter deserved.

At that even the Duke ventured a mild protest.

"Hang it all, my dear," he said. "The child's a Curzon, not a Winter, when all is said and done."

The Duchess only shot a glance of freezing contempt at him.

"The child will be my grandchild, and yours," she said — but what she left unspoken about the infant's other grandparents was far more weighty. The Duchess went on to declare, either expressly or by implication, her distrust of Curzon in a crisis of this sort, her doubts as to the suitability of Hampshire as a prenatal environment, and her certainty of the undesirability of Narling Priory as the home for a pregnant woman. She made such skilful play with the most obvious points of her argument that it was difficult to pick up the weak ones. Narling Priory was a hideously old-fashioned house; it was lit by oil lamps and candles; it had only two bathrooms, and its hot water system was a mid-Victorian relic in the last stages of senility. The Duchess did not say that it was indecent for a woman to be pregnant in a house half of which was occupied by a horde of staff officers, but she implied it. The nearest doctor of any reputation was at Petersfield or Southampton, miles away — the Duchess brushed aside Curzon's tentative reminder that there were fifty regimental doctors within five miles.

The Duchess had taken it for granted that they would take Emily back to London with them that very day, leaving Curzon to revert to his primitive bachelorhood; she was quite surprised when both Emily and Curzon protested against this separation. In the end they compromised on a decision that Emily was to return to London with them so as to keep the appointment with Sir Trevor, but was to come back to Narling Priory for as long as Sir Trevor gave permission.

"As a matter of fact," said the Duke to Curzon, when Lady Emily and the Duchess had left them to themselves while they retired to discuss women's secrets, "as a matter of fact, I suppose neither of us will be much surprised if Emily has to be put in the charge of the Duchess and me quite soon."

He looked across at Curzon significantly, and Curzon was instantly all attention.

"You haven't heard anything about going to France?" went on the Duke.

"No," said Curzon. "Nothing more than rumours."

"I don't know what's been settled about your division," went on the Duke, "even although I am in office again I don't hear everything, you know."

"Have any new formations gone to France already then?" demanded Curzon, sick at heart.

"Yes," said the Duke. "Two divisions went this week. There's no harm in your knowing, after all. There are two more earmarked for the Mediterranean, too — I don't know which. The news will be public property in a week."

Curzon sat tugging at his moustache. He knew how rapidly the army had expanded. There were fifteen divisions in England which had been created after the Ninety-First. In France the expansion, thanks to the arrival of the Indian Corps and other units, had been such that a new sub-division of a nature never previously contemplated had been devised — the Expeditionary Force was divided into three armies now, each comprising several army corps. After his flying start he was being left behind again in the race for promotion. He was shocked to hear that other new divisions had preceded his to France. He had not the least wish to be ordered to the Mediterranean — and in that he displayed intuition, even though the Dardanelles landing had not yet taken place. The whole opinion of the army, expressed in all the discussions in which he had taken part, was emphatically that France was the decisive area. It was in France that glory and promotion, therefore, were to be won. It was essential to his career that the Ninety-First Division should be despatched to France, and quickly.

"There's a good deal of talk," went on the Duke, "about a big offensive soon. One that will win the war at a blow. They've got to accumulate a big reserve of munitions, and have all the available troops to hand first, of course, but I don't think it will be long. Everybody's talking about it in London, especially the women, though God knows how these things leak out."

This final speech made up Curzon's mind for him, definitely. The Ninety-First Division must take part in this knockout blow. Something very decided must be done to ensure that.

"Do you know," said Curzon, meditatively, "I think I'll come back to town with you to-night, as well? You don't mind, do you?"

"Of course not, my dear fellow," said the Duke. "Of course, we shall have to be starting soon."

"I shall be ready when you are," said Curzon, getting out of his chair with astonishing rapidity. His mind was already racing through the programme he had planned with his staff for the morrow, and devising means whereby it could be carried through without his presence.

"I'll just go through and give orders to my staff, if you will excuse me," said Curzon.

"Of course," said the Duke once more, and, left alone, he gazed into the fire and called up memories of his own prospective fatherhood, and how jumpy he had been, and how unwilling he would have been to allow his wife out of his sight for twenty-four hours. It did not occur to the Duke that Curzon's decision to travel to London was not influenced by his wife's condition, but was simply caused by the gossip he had been retailing about the military situation.

Chapter XV

A DEFERENTIAL staff captain came quietly into Major
General Mackenzie's room at the War Office — there
was a notice on the door saying "Don't knock."

"It's General Curzon speaking on the telephone, sir," said
the captain. "He says he would be glad if you could spare
the time to see him for a few minutes to-day."

"Oh hell," said Mackenzie, irritably. "Tell him I'm just off
to York on a tour of inspection."

Two minutes later the captain was back again.

"General Curzon says it is a matter of great importance, and
he would be very much obliged if you could see him before
you go to York."

"Blast the man," said Mackenzie.

"He said that he was only in town for to-day, and must
return to his division to-night, sir. But he asked me to tell you
that he was lunching with the Duke of Bude and that it would
be more convenient if he could see you first."

"Damn his eyes," said Mackenzie. "Oh, all right. Tell him
to come round now. Have him sent straight in."

Despite the language Mackenzie had used about him, there
was cordiality in his reception of Curzon, in his offering of a
chair and a cigar. Curzon smoked and waited for Mackenzie
to open the conversation.

"Well," said Mackenzie, "what do you want this time?"

Curzon pulled at his cigar. He was doing his best to keep himself calm and well in hand while playing this unaccustomed game of diplomacy.

"I want," he said eventually, "orders for France."

"For France?"

"Yes, for me and my division."

"The hell you do," said Mackenzie. "Who's been talking?"

Curzon said nothing in reply to that; he judged that in his case silence would be more effective than speech.

"It's blasted impertinence on your part," said Mackenzie "to come in like this asking for the earth. You're a temporary Major General, but you're a substantive Major. It wouldn't be hard to gazette you back to your substantive rank."

Curzon had faced this possibility; he was well aware of the risk he was running, but the prize before him was worth the risk. He pulled at his cigar while weighing his words.

"I daresay," he said, "but I was hoping you wouldn't do that."

Curzon's mind was seething with memories, despite his outward calm. He remembered Mackenzie's words on his appointment to his division — "The closer you and I stay by each other, the better it will be for both of us." That necessarily implied that Mackenzie credited him with the ability to do him harm if he wanted to. There was that question the Duke had asked only a short time ago, about whether Mackenzie was "any good." That had been more than a hint that the Duke could influence Mackenzie's dismissal from office. There had been Mackenzie's pliability with regard to special issues for the Ninety-First Division in the early winter days. That had not been a matter of any great importance, but it constituted good confirmatory evidence.

"You're asking for trouble, you know," said Mackenzie, with a warning note in his voice.

[144]

"What, in asking to go to France?" said Curzon.

"Your division's told off to join Hamilton's command in the Mediterranean, and you know it," said Mackenzie. Curzon judged it best not to say he did not know it. "How it's got out I can't imagine. These bloody women, I suppose. Of course you don't want to go there. Of course you want to go to France. So does everybody else. D'you think I'm going to listen to every little poop of a temporary major general who doesn't want to do what he's told? You'd have had your orders next week, and you'd have been out of England in three shakes of a duck's tail where you couldn't have made this fuss. Somebody's got to go, haven't they? Don't you start thinking I'm in love with this Constantinople idea, because I'm not. It hurts me just as much to have to find troops for it as it does you to go. But I've got my duty to do, the same as the rest of us."

"There are other divisions besides the Ninety-First," said Curzon. This was the first he had ever heard about any venture being made against Constantinople, and his opinion was against it from the start. It appeared to him to involve an unmilitary dispersal of force, and now he was more anxious than ever for his division to go to France where the real fighting was to be had.

"Yes," admitted Mackenzie. "There *are* other divisions. But yours was the one I had selected as the most suitable."

"On what grounds?" asked Curzon, and his interest nearly betrayed his ignorance.

There was a struggle on Mackenzie's face as he looked back at the variety of motives which had influenced his choice, some military, some not. Curzon's lack of seniority as a major general had played its part, as making it easy to fit him into the hierarchy of a small army; so had the fact that Miller, his G.S.O.1, had had experience in Egypt and Cyprus. But also there was the wish to get someone who might be a dangerous

[145]

enemy and had served most of his purpose as a friend well away from London. Incidentally, there were other generals commanding divisions who also had influential connections in need of propitiation. Mackenzie much regretted the failure of his original plan to order Curzon off without leaving him time to protest. He would have to send someone else now — a decision which would cause him further trouble but which must be adhered to, he was afraid. A man whose father-in-law held office with the certain prospect of a seat in the cabinet, and who was hand in glove with the Bude House women, must not be offended, the more so because Mackenzie had sure and certain knowledge that Curzon had saved him once from annihilation.

"It's too long a story for me to tell you now," said Mackenzie. "Anyway, since you're so damned keen about it, I'll see what I can do about France for you."

Mackenzie allowed no indication to creep into his tone of his fervent wish that as soon as the Ninety-First Division arrived in France some bomb or shell would relieve him of this Old Man of the Sea who was clinging so tightly to his shoulders.

"Thank you very much," said Curzon. "I'm very much obliged to you. And I'd better not take up any more of your time. Good-bye."

"Good-bye," said Mackenzie, resignedly.

Curzon ran down the War Office stairs like a schoolboy, without waiting for the lift. The Bath chair on Bournemouth promenade had been brought appreciably nearer by that interview, but no thought of Bath chairs had ever crossed his mind. He walked briskly back across wartime London; his red tabs and his row of ribbons brought him the salutes of every uniform he passed. At Bude House the butler opened the door for him with all the reverence to be accorded to one who was nearly a son of the house and who had the additional merit of being a General. He sat down and fidgeted as he re-read *The Times* and waited for Emily to return with her mother from her visit to Sir Trevor Choape.

The women came back soon enough, and the moment Curzon heard the subdued noise of their arrival in the hall he hastened down to greet them. Emily put off her furs with a little gesture of weariness; she had vomited badly that morning and still felt slightly upset and Sir Trevor's brusque treatment of her had not helped to make her more comfortable.

"Well?" said Curzon, smiling at her, but for the moment Emily could only nod to him as a sign that her suspicions had been confirmed — there were too many servants about, relieving her and the Duchess of their coats, for her to say more at present. And later the Duchess was still very much in charge of her daughter. It was she who told Curzon about what Sir Trevor had said.

"Everything's quite all right, Bertie," said the Duchess. "Sir Trevor agrees with me that it will be about the end of October. He says we must take care of her, of course."

"What about this sickness?" asked Curzon, consumed with the anxiety which was only natural to him as an inexperienced prospective father.

"Oh, that's only to be expected," said the Duchess, echoing Sir Trevor's bluff words — Sir Trevor was one of the old school who took it for granted that a pregnant woman must always vomit her heart out every morning.

"I suppose so," said Curzon, feebly. From the little he had heard about pregnancy he found it easy to believe the same, although some instinct or intuition inspired him with tiny doubts which he naturally put aside.

"At the same time, Bertie," said the Duchess, clearing for action, "I think it would be *most unwise* for Emily to make the journey to Narling to-day, as I believe you were intending."

The Duchess clearly anticipated violent opposition to this suggestion.

"I certainly must get back," said Curzon. "I can't be away from the division any longer."

He glanced at Emily, lying back lax in her chair.

"I should like to come too," said Emily, "but — but I think I'm going to be sick again."

There was an immediate bustle and upheaval.

"I'll have that nurse here to-day or know the reason why," said the Duchess, decisively, when the excitement passed. "You see it's impossible for Emily to come with you, Bertie."

Curzon could only agree, weakly.

"At the same time — " he began, hesitantly, and paused, looking first at Emily and then at the Duchess, wondering whether he ought to continue.

"Well?" said the Duchess. Now that she had gained her point she had little more attention to spare for this mere man. "Speak up, and don't dither like that. You'll upset Emily again."

The fact that a man like Curzon should dither ought to have made her believe that he had something important to say, but it did not.

"I expect I shall be receiving orders for France very shortly," Curzon managed to blurt out in the end.

"Indeed?" said the Duchess. She did not feel that her son-in-law's prospective re-entry into active service was a tiny bit as important as her daughter's pregnancy.

"Oh, Bertie," said Emily. She was feeling too limp to say more.

But Emily had known for months that Curzon's greatest wish was to command a division in France; she was glad that his ambition was going to be gratified so soon. And she felt little fear for him. The war had not yet lasted long enough for the fear of death to their best loved to have crept into every heart, and she had so much confidence in him that she felt it to be impossible for him to come to any harm — and, beyond all these considerations there was the fact that he was a general. No one, not even a loving wife, can be quite as afraid for a general as for a subaltern. She would miss him sadly, but not so much now that her mother was reasserting her old dominion over her. There might perhaps even be the slightest suspicion of pique in her attitude, that he should be going off on his own concerns and leave her to bear her troubles alone.

"When do you think you will be going?" asked the Duchess, as a concession to politeness.

Curzon came as near to a shrug of his shoulders as a man of his upbringing can.

"I don't know for certain," he said. "Next week, perhaps. Any time."

"Then," said the Duchess, "Emily need not worry any more about this house of yours. I suppose you will have to give it back to the War Office when you go?"

"Yes."

"That's all right then. You can trust Thompson, my dear, to settle about the inventories and so on, of course. Perhaps you will be good enough, Bertie, when you reach Narling, to instruct Hammett to return to us here and bring Emily's clothes with her?"

For a moment Curzon was on the verge of acquiescence. The domineering woman who was addressing him seemed to exert a spell on all who came into contact with her, by virtue of her calm assumption that no one could deny her. And then Curzon braced himself up. He was nettled that his announcement that he was shortly going to risk his life for King and Country should be received as calmly as if he had said he was going shooting in Scotland. He wanted to have his wife with him for his last few days in England.

"No," he said. "I don't think I want to do that."

"I beg your pardon?" said the Duchess, in a tone which left a doubt as to whether she did anything of the kind.

"I should like Emily to come back to Narling as soon as she's well enough to travel. I think to-morrow she might be, easily."

The Duchess turned on Emily.

"I think so too," said Emily. "That's what we settled yesterday, wasn't it, mother?"

Curzon had only to speak to bring Emily back to his side again, and the Duchess had the perspicacity to see it.

"Just as you like," she said, washing her hands of them. "I have already expressed my opinion, and if you two wish to act in a manner contrary to it I cannot say more."

So that although Curzon dined that night in the headquarters mess, the next afternoon as he sat discussing with Hill the newest instructions from France regarding liaison between infantry and artillery, there was a sound of wheels on the gravel outside, and Curzon just had time to see the ducal motor car come slowly past the window with Emily inside. It was typical of Curzon that after glancing up he was able, despite the throb of excitement in his breast, to go on in an even tone with what he was saying. Curzon had the feeling that it would be harmful to discipline if a major general were to admit to his subordinates that he had human attributes — that he was capable of making a woman pregnant, or of being anxious about her afterwards. He prided himself on the way in which he brought the discussion to an end without apparently cutting it short, and on the unhurried and disinterested manner in which he said good-bye to Hill and walked calmly out of the office towards the private half of the house.

He might have been disconcerted if he had seen the quiet wink which Hill exchanged with Runcorn the C.R.E.—in a headquarters which buzzed with rumours like a hive of bees no one could hope to have any private life at all. Headquarters knew of Emily's little secret already—although it would be difficult to discover how. Any private in the Ninety-First Division who might be interested would know of it before a week was out, but as Curzon would not know he knew there was no harm in it.

Curzon ran with clinking spurs up the stairs to Emily's bedroom, reaching the door just as Hammett, the parlourmaid and lady's maid, was coming out. Inside Emily, without her frock, was lying down on the ugly Victorian bed. She smiled with pleasure at sight of him.

"All safe and sound?" asked Curzon, bluffly.

"Yes, dear," said Emily, and then she stretched out her thin arms to him and drew him to her. That brought about the new miracle, whereby Curzon forgot his self-consciousness and the formality acquired during forty years of bachelorhood, and felt surging up within him the wave of hot passion which submerged his cold manner so that he kissed his wife with an ardour which otherwise he would have felt to sit incongruously upon a major general.

In this fashion there began a second instalment of their honeymoon, in which in a few days they managed to cram in as much happiness as they had succeeded in finding in the previous three months—and this despite the handicaps under which they laboured, of Curzon's increasing work and the wretchedness which Emily experienced each morning when sickness overtook her. It might have been the fault of the long

[151]

formidable corset which Emily had worn since her childhood, or it may have been the result of a faulty heredity, but Emily's pregnancy was highly uncomfortable to her, and Curzon found himself tortured with apprehension and remorse even while he rejoiced in the coming of that son for whom he was making such lofty plans.

Not very long after the last interview with Mackenzie there came a large official envelope for Major General H. Curzon, C.B., D.S.O., and Curzon read its contents with a grimly neutral expression. They were his orders for France. Curzon was instructed temporarily to hand over the command of the Ninety-First Division to Brigadier General J. Webb, D.S.O., and proceed with his personal staff and Colonel Miller to the headquarters of the Forty-Second Corps, Lieutenant General Sir Charles Wayland-Leigh, K.C.M.G., D.S.O. His division was to follow in accordance with the orders enclosed.

Emily felt a sudden pang when Curzon told her the news, and brought her face to face with the reality instead of merely the possibility. In that first spring of the war the passing of every month altered the attitude of the civilians towards it. It was growing usual now for families who in 1914 had no military connections whatever to have relations killed. Even in the last month Emily had developed a fear lest Curzon, although he was her invulnerable husband and a general to boot, might soon be lost to her for more than just a few weeks.

"Now that the boy's on his way, m'dear," said Curzon, "it almost makes me wish I wasn't going. But there it is. And with any luck the war'll be won and I'll be back with you before he's born."

Curzon's pathetic faith in the sex of the child to be born raised a wan smile on Emily's face — she had never yet had the courage to break the news to him of her perfect certainty that she was going to bear a daughter.

"I hope you will," she said bravely, and then, her tone altering, "I *do* hope you will, dear."

"Why, are you going to miss me?" said Curzon.

"Yes."

No one had ever said that to Curzon before in his life. It gave him a sudden thrill; it brought reality to his statement that he almost wished that he had not been ordered to France. He kissed her desperately.

But there was small time for love-making for a general anxious about his professional success, who was shortly due to lose sight-of his division completely until he next saw it under conditions of active service. Curzon spent his last few days reassuring himself about his division. Time and again the sweating battalions, plodding along the dusty roads on the route marches which were getting them finally into condition, received the order "March at attention. Eyes left" and gazed with interest at the stiffly erect figure at the roadside who controlled their destinies. The red and gold on his cap and the ribbons on his breast marked him off as one far different from themselves, and to those amateur soldiers, who never yet had experienced the muddle and slaughter of battle, a general was an object of interest, about whom they felt curiosity but little else.

During those glorious spring days of 1915 the Hampshire lanes echoed with the music of bands (Curzon had laboured long and hard to see that every battalion had its band) as the finest division in the finest army England had ever raised put a final polish on its training under the anxious eyes of its general. Strangely, he, a cavalry man, had come to love the long ordered ranks of infantry. He could thrill to the squeal of the fifes and the roar of the side drums where once the sweetest music to his ears had been kettle-drums and trumpets. He loved this division of his now, with the love the singleminded and the simple-minded can give so readily to what they have laboured over. He could not feel the least doubt but that these big battalions of weatherbeaten men would crash their way almost unimpeded through the German line. He looked forward with confidence now to riding with them across the Rhine to Berlin.

The thought of his wonderful division sustained him when he kissed Emily good-bye, which was as well, for the parting was an even bigger wrench than he had feared. He had no doubt about himself; but there was the coming of the child, and Emily's constant sickness (about which his fears were steadily increasing) and his apprehension lest his mother-in-law should succeed in alienating his wife from him.

"Look after yourself, dear," he said, his old-time brusqueness concealing his anxiety as he patted her on the shoulder with the gesture which seems universal among departing husbands.

"You must do the same," said Emily, trying to smile, and he tore himself away and climbed into the waiting Vauxhall where his chief of staff and his two aides-de-camp (the latter perched uncomfortably on the stools of repentance with their backs to the driver) sat waiting for him. The tyres tore up the gravel, and they had started, for Southampton and France.

Two days later the party, four officers, eight horses, and eight grooms and servants, reached St. Cérisy, the headquarters of the Forty-Second Corps, and Curzon reported his arrival to Lieutenant General Sir Charles Wayland-Leigh. The Lieutenant General was a huge man with a face the colour of mahogany and a tendency to corpulence.

"Glad to see you, Curzon," he said, although he showed no signs of it at all and made no attempt to shake hands. He ran his eyes up and down Curzon from his military crop to his glittering field boots, sizing up with cold green eyes the new

[154]

subordinate upon whose capacity depended in part his own reputation.

Curzon felt no inclination to resent his manner, for Wayland-Leigh was a much more eminent general than he was himself — he had been a general in the original expeditionary force of 1914. He stood stiffly to attention and submitted to scrutiny.

"Ha" said Wayland-Leigh, abruptly and without committing himself — or he might even have been merely clearing his throat. "Here, Norton. This is Norton, my B.G.G.S. I expect you'll know him better quite soon. Major General Curzon."

The Brigadier General, General Staff — chief staff officer of the Corps — was dark and pale, but his face was stamped with the same truculent and imperious expression as his chief's, as befitted a man whose word swayed the destinies of forty thousand men. There was the same cold eye, the same slight scowl between the eyebrows, the same thrust-forward jaw and cruel mouth. Yet despite Curzon's more modest attitude as a newcomer, his face had just the same trade marks, curiously enough. He met the stare of the two Generals without flinching. No observer could have witnessed that encounter without thinking of the proverb about the meeting of Greek with Greek.

"What's your division like?" said Wayland-Leigh suddenly.

"All right," said Curzon, and then, throwing traditional modesty to the winds, "first rate. As good as anyone could hope for."

"Let's hope you're right," said Wayland-Leigh. "Don't think much of these new army divisions myself. We've seen a couple of 'em, haven't we, Norton?"

"Mine's good stuff," persisted Curzon, refusing to be browbeaten.

"We'll see for ourselves soon enough," said Wayland-Leigh

[155]

brutally. "And look here, Curzon, we may as well begin as we mean to go on. There are certain standing orders in this corps which you'd better hear about now — they're not written orders. In this corps there are no excuses. A man who's got to find excuses — goes, just like that."

His thick hand cut the air with an abrupt gesture.

"Yes, sir," said Curzon.

"This corps does not retire," went on Wayland-Leigh. "It never gives up ground. And in the same way if it is given an objective to reach, it reaches it. You understand?"

"Yes, sir."

"We don't have any bloody weak-kneed hanky-panky. You've never commanded a division in action, have you, Curzon?"

"No, sir."

"Well, you'll find that the commanders of units are always looking out for a chance to dodge the dirty work and pass it on to someone else — anxious to spare their own men, and all that. Take my advice and don't listen to 'em. It'll be a dam' sight better for you, believe me."

"Yes, sir."

"Most of the officers in this army want *driving,* God knows why — the army's changed since I was a regimental officer. You drive 'em, and you're all right. *I'*ll back you up. And if you don't — I'll have to find someone who will."

"I understand."

"I hope you do. What about a drink before dinner? Norton, you can look after him. I'll see you at dinner, Curzon."

Dinner at Corps Headquarters was a stiffly military function. It was served at a long table in what had once been the state bedroom of the jewel-like little château. There were silver candlesticks on the table, and a fair show of other silver — somehow St. Cérisy had escaped being looted by any of the

[156]

three armies which had fought in its streets. The Lieutenant General sat at the head of the table, huge and silent, with Curzon as the newest arrived guest on his right. Looking down the table Curzon saw a long double row of red-tabbed officers whose rank dwindled in accordance with their distance from him as though in perspective — generals and colonels at the head, and aides-de-camp and signal officers at the foot. There was small attempt at conversation at the far end. The brooding immobility of the Lieutenant General seemed to crush the young men into awed silence. Even their requests to the mess waiters were couched in half-whispers.

On Curzon's right was another Major General commanding a division. Bewly, his name was, and he reminded Curzon of Coppinger-Brown, his predecessor in command of the Ninety-First Division. Bewly was able to talk despite the presence of his corps commander; he spent dinner time complaining unnecessarily to Curzon about the lack of social position of the officers of the new army.

"I should have thought," said Bewly, "that they would have drawn the line *somewhere,* but they haven't. There's a battalion of my old regiment in my division. The subalterns come from *anywhere,* literally *anywhere.* I suppose we had to have stockbrokers and schoolmasters. But there are *clerks* in the regiment now, no better than office boys. And that's not all. There's a *linen draper!* It's enough to make one weep. What was your regiment?"

Curzon told him.

"Ah!" said Bewly, and there crept into his voice the slight deference which Curzon was accustomed to hear from infantrymen. "I don't expect it has happened in your regiment? You can keep that kind of thing out of the cavalry."

"I suppose so," said Curzon. He was not much interested in this question of the introduction of the lower orders into the commissioned ranks of the infantry. Partly that may have been because he was a cavalry man, but partly it must have been because he was conscious of his own Mincing Lane parentage. As regards his own division he would have wished for no change in its present constitution, and being without blue blood himself he failed to see the necessity of blue blood as a qualification for leadership.

At the same time he found himself wondering vaguely how long Bewly would last under Wayland-Leigh's command, and he guessed it would not be long. Bewly's division was a New Army formation which had been in France for three weeks. The other two divisions in the corps besides the Ninety-First were of an older pedigree, although as Bewly pessimistically informed Curzon they had lost so many men and had been filled up so often with drafts that they retained precious little likeness to their originals.

The dinner was admirable and the service more efficient than that of any mess Curzon had ever known. This was due — Bewly was his informant again, speaking with dropped voice and with nods and winks at Curzon's left-hand neighbour — to the fact that Wayland-Leigh systematically combed his corps for ex-waiters and ex-cooks. The mess sergeant was lately a maître d'hôtel; the cook had been an assistant chef in a famous restaurant.

"Trust the Buffalo to have the best of everything," murmured Bewly, and Curzon suddenly remembered that far back in the old Indian Army days Wayland-Leigh had been nicknamed "the Buffalo." The original reason for the name had long been forgotten, but the name remained, distinguished by its appropriateness.

As soon as dinner was over the Buffalo rose abruptly from his chair without a glance either to left or to right, and strode away from the table to vanish through an inconspicuous door behind him. A second later Curzon heard another door slam in the farther depths of the house.

"He's settled for the night, thank God," said Bewly, heaving a sigh of relief. Curzon was reminded (until he put the similarity out of his mind as ludicrous) of the attitude of a small boy at school at the disappearance of a dreaded master.

Chapter XVI

NEXT morning Curzon formed one of a select party sent round a section of the front line to be initiated into the new developments of trench warfare. Their guide was a tall lean Captain named Hodge, who occupied some ill-defined position on the Corps Headquarters staff, and who wore not merely the blue and red ribbon of the Distinguished Service Order but the purple and white one of the newfangled Military Cross. More noticeable than his ribbons was his air of weary lackadaisical tolerance towards his seniors, even major generals. His uninterested apathy made a bad impression on Curzon, but Bewly took no notice of it, and with Bewly present and senior to him he could not pull him up for it. Life seemed to hold no more secrets and no more attraction for Captain Hodge, who lounged in front of the party along the winding trenches with a weary indifference in striking contrast with the keen interest of the newcomers.

Motor cars had brought them to a cross-roads close behind the line; on the journey up Captain Hodge condescended to point out to them all sorts of things which were new to Curzon, in the way of ammunition dumps (tiny ones, the mere microcosm of their successors, but an innovation as far as Curzon was concerned) and rest billets for troops out of the line, and all the other unheard-of accessories of static warfare.

At the cross-roads Hodge actually was sufficiently awake to say "Dangerous place for shelling here" and to display some sign of haste as he walked across with the staff officers scuttling behind him. But the sky was blue and peace seemed to have settled down upon the tortured landscape. There was hardly a sound of firing to be heard. The armies of both sides seemed to be basking like lizards in the unwonted sunshine. A tiny breath of wind fanned Curzon's face, and brought with it the stink of the front line trenches, compounded of carrion and mud and latrines ripened by the present warmth. When Curzon had last quitted the trenches after the First Battle of Ypres that stink had been in its immaturity, only just beginning, but the present whiff called up a torrent of memories of those wild days, of the peril and the fatigue and the excitement. Curzon felt vaguely irritated by the prevailing tranquillity. First Ypres had been real fighting; this was nothing of the sort.

The road they were on had ceased to be a road at the cross-roads, where the red-hatted military policeman had stopped the cars. A vague indication of a trench had grown up around them as they progressed, and soon it was quite definitely a trench, floored with mud, in which they sank ankle deep — the warm weather had not dried it — crumbling and slipshod in appearance for lack of revetting. They floundered in single file along the trench. Twice Hodge turned and said, "Keep low here. They've got a fixed rifle on this point." Hodge made no bones at all at bending himself double, despite his lackadaisical air, as he made his way round the dangerous bay. Curzon stooped, but could not bring himself to adopt Hodge's cowardly and undignified attitude. He heard a sharp *zzick* and felt the breath of a bullet past the back of his neck.

"Better be careful," said Hodge.

A little later they had to crowd themselves against the side of the trench to allow a stretcher to go by; the stretcher bearers were breathing deeply, and on the stretcher lay a soldier deadly pale, his boots protruding beyond the blanket which covered him. That was all the traffic they met in the communication trench.

They reached the support line and went along it. There were soldiers here, lounging about, sleeping in the sun, making tea over little smokeless flames of solid methylated spirit. They came up to attention not very promptly at sight of the string of brass hats making their way along the trench. Battalion headquarters was established in a dugout burrowed into the front of the trench; not a very good dugout, a mere rabbit scrape compared with the dugouts of the future, but the first Curzon had seen. A worn-looking Colonel greeted them, and offered them drinks, which all of them except Curzon drank thirstily; Curzon had no desire at all to drink whisky and water at ten in the morning. The battalion runners were waiting on duty in a smaller dugout still, next door; in the headquarters dugout was the telephone which linked precariously the battalion to brigade, and thence through division and corps and army to G.H.Q.

They went on by a muddy communication trench to the front line. Here there was the same idleness, the same lack of promptitude in acknowledging the Generals' presence. There were men asleep squatting on the firestep who had to be wakened for discipline's sake. There were certain concessions made to active service conditions; the sentries peering into the periscopes were rigidly attentive and stirred not at all at the bustle passing them by; the shell cases hung inverted in every bay to act as gongs for a gas warning should gas come over.

Curzon took a periscope and gazed eagerly over the parapet. He saw a few strands of barbed wire with a tattered dead man — a sort of parody of a corpse — hanging on the farthest one. Then there was a strip of mud pocked with shell craters, more barbed wire beyond, and then the enemy's front line, whose sand-bagged parapet, although neater and more substantial than the British, showed no more sign of life. It was hard to believe that a wave of disciplined men could not sweep across that frail barrier, and as Curzon began to think of that he found himself believing that it would be better even that they should try and fail than moulder here in unsoldierly idleness — it would be the more appropriate, the more correct thing.

The other Generals, and Captain Hodge, waited patiently while he peered and stared, twisting the periscope this way and that — it was not easy to form a military estimate of a landscape while using a periscope for the first time — and were clearly relieved when at last his curiosity was satisfied and he handed back the periscope to the platoon officer from whom he had taken it.

"We shall be late for lunch if we don't hurry on our way back, Hodge," said Bewly.

"Yes, sir," said Hodge. "I'll try and get you back in time."

Bewly's anxiety about lunch irritated Curzon — there was a good deal about Bewly which had begun to irritate him. He almost sympathised with Hodge in his attitude of scarcely concealed contempt for Bewly, even though it was reprehensible in a junior officer. They pushed on along the front line trench, round bays and traverses innumerable; one bit of trench was very like another, and everywhere the men seemed half asleep, as might have been expected of soldiers who had spent five nights in the trenches — except by Curzon, who could not imagine the physical and still less the moral effects of experiences he had not shared and which were not noticed in the military textbooks.

The sparseness of the garrison of the trenches made a profound effect on him; it was a continual source of surprise to him to see how few men there were in each sector. He had long known, of course, the length of line allotted on the average to a division, and he had laboriously worked out sums giving the number of rifles per yard of trench from the data issued by the War Office (Most Secret: For the information of Officers Commanding Divisions Only) but he was not gifted with the power of visualising in actual pictures the results obtained. Now that he could see for himself he marvelled; presumably the German trenches over there were as scantily manned — it seemed to him impossible that such a frail force could withstand a heavy artillery preparation and then a brisk attack with overwhelming numbers.

He already itched with the desire to make the attempt to head a fierce offensive which would end this slovenly, unmilitary, unnatural kind of warfare once and for all. There must have been mismanagement at Festubert and Neuve Chapelle, or bad leadership, or bad troops. Nothing else could account for their failure to put an end to a situation against which all Curzon's training caused him to revolt with loathing. His feverish feeling made him reply very shortly indeed to Bewly's droned platitudes on the way back to corps headquarters and at lunch, and later, when Miller and he were called in to discuss with Wayland-Leigh and Norton what they had seen, his sincerity lent a touch of eloquence to his unready tongue.

He spoke vehemently against the effect on the troops of life in the trenches, and of this system of petty ambuscades and sniping and dirt and idleness. And, with his experience of improvised attacks and defence to help him, he was able to say how advantageous it must be to be allowed ample time to mount and prepare a careful attack in which nothing could go wrong and overwhelming force could be brought upon the decisive point. Curzon checked himself at last when he suddenly realised how fluently he was talking. It was un-English and lawyerlike to be eloquent, and his little speech ended lamely as he looked in embarrassment from Wayland-Leigh to Norton and back again.

But Wayland-Leigh apparently was too pleased with the sentiments Curzon had expressed to be suspicious of his eloquence. There was a gleam of appreciation in his green eyes. He exchanged glances with Norton.

"That's the stuff, Curzon," he said. "That's different from what I've been hearing lately from these can't-be-doners and better-notters and leave-it-to-youers that the army's crowded with nowadays. What about you, Miller?"

Miller, dark, saturnine, silent, had said nothing so far, and now, after a Lieutenant General and a Major General had expressed themselves so enthusiastically it could not be expected of a mere Colonel to go against their opinions — not a Colonel, at any rate, who placed the least value on his professional career.

"I think there's a lot in it, sir," said Miller, striving to keep the caution out of his voice and to meet Wayland-Leigh's sharp glance imperturbably.

"Right," said Wayland-Leigh. "Norton's got a lot of trench maps and appreciations and skeleton schemes for local offensives. I want you to start going through them with him. We all know that the real big push can't come for a month or two while these bloody politicians are muddling about with munitions and conscription and all the rest of it — why in hell they can't put a soldier in to show them how to run the affair properly I can't imagine. Your division's due to arrive in two days. We'll give 'em a couple of turns in the front line to shake 'em together, and then we'll start in and get something done. Your lot and Hope's Seventy-Ninth are the people I'm relying on."

Curzon ate his dinner with enjoyment that night — it was enough to give any man pleasure in his food to be told that the

Buffalo relied upon him. There was a letter from Emily, too — full of the shy half declarations of love which were as far as Emily could be expected to write and as far as Curzon wished. Burning phrases in black and white would have made Curzon uncomfortable; he was well satisfied with Emily's saying that she missed him and hoped he would soon be back again with her, and with the timid "dears," three in all, interpolated in the halting sentences. Emily was at Bude House, which the Duke had decided to keep open all the summer, but she would soon be going for a few weeks to Bude Manor in Somerset. She was still being a little sick — Curzon fidgeted with a premonition which he told himself to be unfounded when he read that. The last paragraph but one brought a grin to his lips, both because of its contents and its embarrassed phrasing. The grim gaunt housekeeper who had ruled Narling Priory under their nominal control had been found to be with child after forty-one years of frozen virginity, and obstinately refused to name her partner beyond saying he was a soldier. As Emily said, the war was changing a lot of things.

Curzon wrote back the next day, bluffly as usual. The only "dear" he was able to put into his letter was the one that came in "my dear wife," and the only sentiment appeared in the bits addressed in reply to Emily's statement that she missed him. He devoted three or four lines to the excellent weather prevailing, and he committed himself to a cautiously optimistic sentence or two regarding the future of the war. He bit the end of his pen in the effort of trying to think of something more to say, but found inspiration slow in coming, and ended the letter with a brief recommendation that Emily should take great care of herself, and a note of amused surprise at the fall of the housekeeper.

He did not think the letter inadequate (nor did Emily when she received it) but it was a relief to turn aside from these barren literary labours and to plunge once more into the living business of the army. The division arrived, and Curzon rode over to join it with all the thrill and anticipation of a lover — he had been separated from it for more than a week, and it was with delight that he sat his horse at the side of the road watching the big bronzed battalions stream past him. He gave a meticulous salute in reply to each salute he received, and his eyes scanned the dusty ranks with penetrating keenness. He heard an ejaculation from the ranks — "Gawd, there's old Bertie again," and he looked on with grim approval while a sergeant took the offender's name — not because he objected to being called Bertie, but because the battalion was marching at attention and so to call out in that fashion was a grave breach of discipline.

It was an indication, all the same, of the high spirits of the men, who were bubbling over with the excitement of the journey and with the prospect of action. They took a childlike interest in everything — in French farming methods, in the aeroplanes overhead with the white puffs of anti-aircraft shells about them, in the queer French words written over shop windows, in the uncanny ability of even the youngest children to talk French, in the distant nocturnal firework display that indicated the front line.

They showed a decided tendency to let their high spirits grow too much for them, all the same. The arrival of the division coincided with a large increase in the military crimes in which the British soldier never ceases to indulge. They stole fruit (horrible unripe apples) and poultry and eggs. Their inappeasable yearning for fuel led them to steal every bit of wood, from fence rails and doors to military stores, which they could lay their hands on. They drank far too much of the French wine and beer even while they expressed their contempt for it, and sometimes they conducted themselves familiarly

[167]

towards Frenchwomen who were not ready to appreciate the compliment.

Curzon read the statistics of regimental crime with growing indignation. All this gross indiscipline must be checked at once. He circulated a scathing divisional order, and strengthened the hands of the military police, and saw to it that a score of offenders received exemplary punishments. The effect was immediate and gratifying, because the amount of crime decreased abruptly — as soon as the men had grown accustomed to the new conditions and to the methods of those in authority, so that they could evade detection; for no disciplinary methods on earth could keep British soldiers from wine, women, and wood.

The Ninety-First Division took its place in the line without any great flourish of trumpets. Norton chose a quiet section for them, and the ten days went by with nothing special to report. There were a hundred casualties — the steady drain of losses to be expected in trench warfare — and a general court martial on a man caught asleep while on sentry duty, from which the culprit was lucky enough to escape with his life. Curzon fretted a little at the conditions under which he had to command his men. It went against his conscience to a certain extent to spend his time, while his men were in the line, in a comfortable house. He could eat good dinners, he could ride as much as he wanted, he could sleep safely in a good bed; and it was not easy to reconcile all this with his memory of First Ypres. He chafed against the feeling of impotence which he experienced at having to command his division by telephone. He was still imbued with the regimental ideal of sharing on active service the dangers and discomforts of his men.

During the division's turns of duty in the trenches his anxiety drove him repeatedly up into the front line to see that all was well. He plodded about along the trenches trying to

[168]

ignore fatigue — for a journey of a dozen miles through the mud, stooping and scrambling, was the most exhausting way of spending a day he had ever known. His aide-de-camp Greven bewailed his fate to unsympathetic audiences; the other one, Follett, was more hardy — but then Curzon had selected him with care and without regard to family connections, on the recommendation that Follett had once ridden in the Grand National and completed the course. Follett endured the mud and the weariness and the danger without complaint.

There was inconvenience in making these trench tours. Miller had to be left in charge at headquarters, and however capable Miller might be, the ultimate responsibility — as Curzon well appreciated — was Curzon's own. During the dozen hours of Curzon's absence orders might come by telephone or by motor cycle despatch rider calling for instant decision. While Curzon was in the trenches he found himself to be just as anxious about what was happening at headquarters as he was about the front line when he was at headquarters. It took all the soothing blandishments which Greven could devise with the aid of Curzon's personal servants to keep him from making an unbearable nuisance of himself, and quite a little while elapsed before he was able to reconcile himself to this business of leading by telephone.

On the division's third turn in the front line Curzon was allowed by Wayland-Leigh to put into practice some of the principles he had been forming. Curzon came to believe, in the event, that it was more harassing to sit by a telephone looking at his watch waiting for news, than to take part in the operations which he had ordered. The first one was the merest trifle, a matter of a raid made by no more than a company, but two o'clock in the morning — the hour fixed — found Curzon and all his staff fully dressed in the office and consumed with anxiety. It was a battalion of a Minden regiment which was making the raid — the Colonel had begged the honour for his unit because it was Minden day without realising that this was a tactless argument to employ to a cavalry man — and Curzon spent an anxious half hour wondering whether he had been wise in his selection. The buzz of the telephone made them all start when at last it came. Frobisher answered it while Curzon tugged at his moustache.

"Yes," said Frobisher. "Yes. Right you are. Yes."

The studied neutrality of his tone enabled Curzon to guess nothing of the import of the message until Frobisher looked up from the telephone.

"It's all right, sir," he said. "They rushed the post quite easily. Seven prisoners. Bombed the other bit of trench and heard a lot of groans. The party's back now, sir. We won't get their casualty return until the morning."

"All right," said Curzon. His first independent operation had been crowned with success.

He got up from the table and walked out to the front door, and stood in the porch looking towards the line, his staff following. There was far more commotion there than usually. The sky was lighted by the coloured lights which were being sent up, and the ground shook with the fire of the guns whose flashes made a dancing line of pin points of light on the horizon. The raid had put the line on the alert, and the attitude of expectancy had led to the inevitable "wind-up" until ten thousand rifles and two hundred guns were all blazing away together — and killing a man or two here and there, while wiring parties and patrols, caught in No Man's Land by the unexpected activity, crouched in shell holes and cursed the unknown fool who had started the trouble.

That glare in the sky which indicated unusual nocturnal activity was to be seen frequently after that over the sector occupied by the Ninety-First Division. There were all sorts of little local operations awaiting their attention — small salients to be pinched out and exposed listening posts to be raided — and the Ninety-First Division engaged in them wholeheartedly.

Moreover, as Curzon had suspected, a certain amount of a live-and-let-live convention had grown up in the line. Each side had inclined to refrain from inflicting casualties on the other side at moments when retaliation would cause casualties to themselves — ration parties were being mutually spared, and certain dangerous localities received reciprocal consideration. Curzon would have none of this. It seemed to him to be a most dangerous and unsoldierly state of affairs; if a soldier whose duty it was to kill the enemy refrained from doing so he was clearly not doing his duty and it might lead to untold damage to discipline. Drastic divisional orders put a stop to this. The keenness of the new troops and the energy of their commander brought renewed activity into the line; the number of snipers was increased, and places where the enemy had been inclined to be careless were regularly sprayed with machine gun fire, with, as far as headquarters could tell, a most gratifying increase in German casualties.

Naturally, the enemy retaliated. British divisions accustomed to a peaceful turn of duty were annoyed and surprised, when they relieved the Ninety-First, to find that localities hitherto regarded as safe were now highly dangerous, and that sniping had vastly increased, and that the Germans had developed a system of sudden bombing raids which made life in the trenches a continual strain on the nerves. This was especially noticeable because, as the Germans had the advantage of direct observation from the low heights which they occupied, and did not trouble themselves nearly as much as the British about holding on to dangerous salients, and worked far harder at making their trenches safe and habitable, they could make things far more uncomfortable for the British than the British could for them.

Both officers and men of the other divisions complained of the new state of affairs to their fellows of the Ninety-First, but they found small satisfaction in doing so. The Ninety-First Division pleaded the direct orders of their commander. "Bertie's the boy" they said, half proud, and half rueful, and the daily drain of casualties increased — Curzon was already making application for drafts and new officers for his battalions.

The new system met with one protest from an unexpected quarter. Young Captain Frobisher, the general staff officer, third grade, found an opportunity while he and Miller and Curzon, sitting at the table littered with trench maps, were drafting the orders for fresh activity. The weak points of the German line in their sector had by now been blotted out, and Curzon casually admitted in conversation that it was not easy now to find suitable objects for attention.

"Perhaps," said Frobisher, "it might be wise to quiet down for a bit, sir?"

"No, it's not good for the men," replied Curzon.

"Casualties are getting a bit high," said Frobisher.

"You can't make war without casualties," said Curzon. He had been a casualty himself, once, and he had freely exposed himself to the chance of its occurring again.

"Wellington tried to keep 'em down, sir," said Frobisher, suddenly bold.

"What on earth do you mean, boy?" asked Curzon.

"Wellington always discouraged sniping and outpost fighting and that sort of thing."

"Good God!" said Curzon. "Wellington lived a hundred years ago."

"Human nature's the same now, though, sir."

"Human nature? What in hell are you talking about? Anyone would think you were a poet or one of these beastly intellectuals. I don't like this, Frobisher."

Curzon was definitely angry. There was a frosty gleam in his eyes and a deep line between his brows. It was not so much because a Captain was venturing to argue with him, a Major General, as that the Captain was putting forward suggestions of a suspicious theoretical nature in direct opposition to the creed of the army, that the side which does not attack is bound to lose.

"Frobisher's had too much history and not enough practical experience, yet, sir," said Miller. He put his word in hastily, because he did not want to lose the services of the best G.S.O.S. he could hope to get hold of.

"So I should think," said Curzon, still staring indignantly at the delinquent, but somewhat appeased. He had grown fond of young Frobisher after six months of work with him, and had been pained as well as shocked at his heresy, just as if his son (supposing he had one) had announced his intention of marrying a tobacconist's daughter. His fondness for Frobisher even led him into defending his own actions by argument.

"We're giving the Germans hell, aren't we?" said Curzon.

"Yes, sir," said Frobisher with dropped eyes. A word from Curzon would take him from his staff position where he could think even though his mouth remained shut and put him into an infantry battalion where he would not be able to think at all.

"Well, don't let me hear any more of this nonsense. Pass me that map and let's get down to business."

Chapter XVII

THE next time that the Ninety-First Division came out of the line Curzon was summoned to attend a conference at Corps Headquarters. Wayland-Leigh and Norton were jubilant. The Big Push was being planned at last — the great offensive which was to bring with it the decisive victory and the march to Berlin. There were nine divisions available, about three times as many Englishmen — as Curzon jovially pointed out to Frobisher on his return — as Wellington had commanded at Waterloo. There were more field guns ready for use in the preliminary bombardment than the entire British army had owned in 1914, and there was a stock of ammunition accumulated for them sufficient for fifty hours of continuous steady firing — a longer bombardment than had ever been known in the field before. Besides all this, they were going to take a leaf out of the Germans' book and employ poison gas, but on a far larger scale than the Germans' timorous attempt at Ypres. There were mountainous dumps already formed of cylinders of chlorine, and every ship that crossed the Channel was bringing further supplies.

But the great cause for rejoicing was that the Forty-Second Corps had been selected to take part in the attack — the Buffalo was to be turned loose to crash through the gap made by the leading divisions. The maps were brought out — not the finicking little trench maps on which Curzon had planned his petty little offensives, but big maps, covering all North Eastern France. The French were to attack at Vimy, storm the ridge, push forward; the British were to strike at Loos, break the German line, and join hands with the French behind Lens, which was to fall as the first ripe fruit of victory into the Allies' hands unassailed. At this stage of the battle the Forty-Second Corps would be in the van, with open country before them, and nothing to stop them.

"It's a pity in a way," said Norton, "that we've had to wait until autumn for this attack. It makes it just possible that the Huns will be able to hold us up for a winter campaign on the Rhine."

Before this campaign on the Rhine could be begun, there was more work to be done. The Ninety-First Division had to take another turn of duty in the front line trenches, working like beavers over the preparations for the great attack. One morning Frobisher brought the divisional orders for Curzon to sign, and Curzon, as ever, read them carefully through before assuming responsibility for them.

"Here, what's this, boy?" he said suddenly. "Two men to carry up each gas cylinder? We've only been using one for the empty ones."

"Yes, sir," said Frobisher. "These are full, and they're heavier in consequence."

"Nonsense," said Curzon. He was glad to be able to find something he was quite certain he was right about while Frobisher was wrong, even though he bore him no ill will. "Everyone knows that gas makes things lighter. They put it in balloons and things."

"That's coal gas, sir," said Frobisher with deference. "This is chlorine, and highly compressed."

"You mean I'm talking nonsense?" demanded Curzon.

"No, sir," said Frobisher, treading as warily as he could over this dangerous ground, "but we've never had to deal with full cylinders before."

Curzon glared at this persistent young captain, and decided that his victory would be more crushing still if he gained it without recourse to his hierarchical authority.

"Well, if you don't believe *me*," he said, with all the dignity he could summon, "you'd better ring up the gas officer at Corps Headquarters and see what *he* says. You may believe him, if he's had the advantage of an education at Camberley, too, as well as you."

"Yes, sir," said Frobisher.

It took Frobisher ten minutes to make his call and get his answer, and he was decidedly nervous on his return.

"Well?" said Curzon.

"The gas officer says that the full cylinders are fifty pounds heavier than the empty ones, sir," said Frobisher.

Curzon looked very sharply at him, but Frobisher's face was immobile. Without a word Curzon drew the orders to him, dashed off his signature, and handed them back. It must be recorded to Curzon's credit that he never afterwards allowed that incident to prejudice him against Frobisher — and it is significant of his reputation for fairness that Frobisher had no real fear that he would.

By the time the Ninety-First Division came out of the line preparations for the attack were nearly complete. The ammunition dumps were gorged. There were drafts to fill the ranks of the waiting divisions up to their full establishment, and further drafts ready at the base to make up for the inevitable casualties of the initial fighting. There were hospitals, and prisoners' cages, and three divisions of cavalry ready to pursue the flying enemy.

Curzon's heart went out to these latter when he saw them.

For a moment he regretted his infantry command. He felt he would gladly give up his general officer's rank just to hear the roar of the hoofs behind him as he led the Lancers in the charge again. He rode over to their billets, and visited the Twenty-Second, to be rapturously received by those men in the ranks who had survived First Ypres. Browning, in command, was not quite so delighted to see him — he had unhappy memories of their previous contacts, when Curzon had been to no trouble to conceal his contempt for his indecision and loss of nerve in the climax of the battle. The officers' mess was full of strange faces, and familiar ones were missing — Borthwick, for instance, when he had recovered from his wounds, had been transferred to the Staff and was organising some piratical new formation of machine gunners with the rank of Colonel. The fact that Borthwick should ever be a Colonel when he had never properly learned to ride a horse was sufficient proof of what a topsy-turvy war this was, as Curzon and his contemporaries agreed over a drink in the mess.

Curzon bade the Twenty-Second a sorrowful good-bye at the end of the day. He could not stay to dinner, as he had an invitation to Corps Headquarters. As he stood shaking hands with his friends they heard the roar of the bombardment — in its third day now — which was opening the battle of Loos.

"They're getting hell over there," said a subaltern, and everyone agreed.

"You'll be having your chance in less than a week," said Curzon, and regret surged up in him again as he mounted his horse. He had gained nothing in forsaking a regiment for a division. He would never know now the rapture of pursuit; all there was for him to do now was to make the way smooth for the cavalry.

There were high spirits at Corps Headquarters, all the same, to counter his sentimental depression. Wayland-Leigh had provided champagne for this great occasion, and in an unwontedly expansive moment he turned to Curzon with his lifted glass.

"Well, here's to the Big Push, Curzon," he said. His green eyes were aflame with excitement.

"Here's to it, sir," said Curzon, fervently.

"It's like that bit of Shakespeare," said Wayland-Leigh — and the fact that Wayland-Leigh should quote Shakespeare was a sufficient indication of the greatness of the occasion. "'When shall we three meet again?' Or rather we five, I ought to say."

He looked round at his four divisional generals.

"On the Rhine, sir," said Hope of the Seventy-Ninth.

"Please God," said Wayland-Leigh.

The horizon that night was all sparkling with the flashes of the guns as Curzon rode back to his headquarters; the bombardment was reaching it culminating point, and the gentle west wind — Curzon wetted his finger and held it up to make sure — was still blowing. It would waft the poison gas beautifully towards the German lines, and those devils would have a chance of finding out what it was like.

At dawn next morning Curzon was waiting in his headquarters for orders and news. The horses of the staff were waiting saddled outside; within half a mile's radius the battalions and batteries of the division were on parade ready to march. Neither orders nor news came for some time, while Curzon restlessly told himself that he was a fool to expect anything so early. Nothing could come through for seven or eight hours. But Frobisher looked out at the divisional flag drooping on its staff, and he went outside and held up a wet finger, and came in again gloomily. There was no wind, or almost none. In fact Frobisher had a suspicion that what little there was came from the east. There could be small hope today for a successful use of gas.

"We can win battles without gas, gentlemen," said Curzon, looking round at his staff.

As time went on Curzon grew seriously alarmed. They were fifteen miles from the line, and if orders to move did not come soon they might be too late to exploit the initial advantage. Curzon knew that the Forty-Second Corps was being held directly under the command of General Headquarters, so that he could try to quiet his fears by telling himself that there was no question of a muddle in the command; G.H.Q. must know more than he did. The orders came in the end some time after noon, brought by a goggled motor cyclist. He and Miller ran through them rapidly; all they said was that the division was to move up the road at once — it was not more than a quarter of an hour after the motor cyclist's arrival that Curzon had his leading battalion stepping out briskly towards the battle.

By the time the division was on the march there was news of sorts to be picked up on the road as the débris of the battle drifted back. Ambulance drivers and lorry drivers and wounded contributed their quota, and the tales told brought the deepest depression and revived the wildest hope alternately. A Light Infantry officer told of disastrous failure, of the ruin of his division amid a tangle of uncut wire. An ambulance load of wounded Scots reported a triumphant advance, the overrunning of miles of German trenches, and desperate fighting still in progress. From a Seventh Division Major Curzon learned of the failure of the gas, and how it was released in some sectors and not in others, and how it had drifted over the German lines, or had stayed stagnant in No Man's Land, or had blown sideways over the advancing British troops as if moved by a spirit of murderous mischief. Then on the other hand there came the news that the British had reached Hill 70 and Hulluch, that the German line was definitely broken, and that the enemy was fighting desperately hard to stave off disaster.

A big motor car with the flag of the Forty-Second Corps fluttering at the bonnet came bouncing up the road. Inside could be caught glimpses of scarlet and gold — it was Way-land-Leigh and his staff. The car stopped where Curzon's horse pranced upon the *pavé,* and Curzon dismounted, gave his reins to Greven, and hurried to the door.

"Keep your men stepping out, Curzon," said Wayland-Leigh, leaning forward in his seat and speaking in a hoarse whisper.

"Yes, sir," answered Curzon. "Can — can you give me any news?"

"I don't know any myself," said Wayland-Leigh, grimly. "G.H.Q. has hashed it all up, as far as I can see. Your division's ten miles back from where it ought to be. We broke through this morning, and hadn't the reserves to make a clean thing of it. You'll have to break through again to-morrow, Curzon. And I know you'll do it. Good luck."

The motor car jolted on along the road, while Curzon swung himself back into the saddle. His division might be late, but he would see to it that it made up for some of the lost time. All down the five-mile-long column the pace quickened as his orders reached each unit to lengthen the pace. Then the head of the column came to a halt, and as Curzon was spurring furiously forward to ascertain the cause of the delay word came back that the road was jammed with broken-down transport. So it was, as Curzon saw when he reached there five minutes later, but it did not remain so long. His blazing anger goaded the transport drivers into a final effort to clear the road. An empty lorry was heaved bodily clear into the ditch, where it lay with its wheels in the air. A distracted officer was bullied into organising a party to empty the lorry with the broken wheel of the ammunition in it so that the same could be done with that, but before the party had even set to work the Ninety-First Division was pouring through the gap Curzon had contrived.

They marched on while darkness fell and the battle flamed and flickered before them. Long ago the men had lost their brisk stride and air of eager anticipation; now they were merely staggering along under the burden of their packs. No one sang, and the weary sergeants snapped at the exhausted men as they blundered on the slippery *pavé*. At midnight they reached what billets were available — half the division slept in wet bivouacs at the roadside, while Curzon slept in his boots and clothes in an armchair in the back room of the *estaminet* which became his temporary headquarters.

The orders he had been waiting for came during the night. The division was given an objective and a sector and a time in to-morrow's attack. Miller and Curzon compared the orders with the maps spread on the marble-topped tables. Miller made his measurements, looked involuntarily at his watch, and said, "It can't be done."

"It's got to be done," said Curzon, with a rasp in his voice.

"Dawn's at six-fifteen," said Miller. "We'll have two hours of daylight for seven miles, on these roads."

"Can't help that," snapped Curzon. "The division'll have to move at five. We'll have to get the orders for the brigades out now. Here, Frobisher —"

A weary staff wrote out the orders, and weary orderlies took them to brigade headquarters, where tired brigadiers were roused from sleep to read them and to curse the higher command which forced their men to go into action with no more than four hours' rest — and those, for most of them, passed in muddy bivouacs.

In the half light the division formed up on the road, trying to loosen its stiff joints. The march began long before dawn, and they toiled forward up the road to the summons of grumbling guns. Dawn had hardly come when there was another hitch ahead. Curzon was almost beside himself with rage as he rode forward, and what he found made him boil over completely. The road was crammed with cavalry, two whole brigades of it, a forest of leaden-hued lance points. Their transport was all over the road, apparently in the process of being moved from one end of the column to the other. What miracles of staff work had brought that cavalry there at that time and in that place and in that condition Curzon did not stop to inquire.

He turned his horse off the road and galloped madly along the side of the column over the muddy fields; not even Follett could pace with him. Curzon's quick eye caught sight of a cluster of red cap bands. He leaped his horse over the low bank again, risking a nasty fall on the greasy *pavé,* and addressed himself to the General of a cavalry division.

"Get your men off this road at once, sir!" he blared. "You're stopping the march of my division. Orders? I don't care a damn what your orders are. Clear the road this minute! No, sir, I will *not* be careful what I say to you. I've got my duty to do."

The two Major Generals glared fiercely at each other for a moment, before the cavalry man turned to his staff and said, "Better see to it."

Curzon was tapping with impatience on his saddlebow with his crop during the slow process of moving the cavalry with their lances and their forage nets and their impedimenta over the bank into the fields, but it was done at last; soon Curzon saw his leading battalion come plodding up the road, a few staunch spirits singing "Hullo, Hullo, Who's your lady friend?" with intervals for jeers and boos for the disgruntled cavalry watching them go by.

A precious quarter of an hour had been wasted; it seemed

almost certain that the division would be late at the rendez-vous appointed for it. Soon afterwards it became quite certain, for the narrow road, only just wide enough for two vehicles side by side, was utterly jammed with transport. There was a road junction just ahead, and no military police in the world could have combated successfully with the confusion there, where every vehicle in nine divisions seemed to have converged from all four directions.

Frobisher and Follett galloped hither and thither to find someone in authority who could compel the way to be cleared for the Ninety-First Division, but it was Curzon who achieved it in the end, riding his maddened horse into the thick of the turmoil, and using the weight of his authority and the urge of his blazing anger to hold up the traffic.

It was not for Curzon to decide whether the state of the battle made it desirable that the division should have precedence; that was for the General Staff, but as the General Staff was seemingly making no effort to tackle the problem he had to deal with it himself — and as his division was an hour late his decision was a natural one. For Curzon was not to know that German counter attacks launched in the early morning had completely stultified the orders he had received that night, and that the task before the Ninety-First Division was not now to exploit a success, but to endeavour to hold on to precarious gains.

They were nearing the line now. There were battery positions beside the road, firing away with a desperate rapidity which indicated the severity of the fighting ahead. Curzon rode on through the drifting flotsam of the battle to the house which his orders had laid down should be established as his headquarters. There was a signal section already there, as Curzon saw with satisfaction. Telephonic communication with the new front line had at last been established, and headquarters would not have to rest content with the news dribbled out an hour too late by scribbled messages borne by runners.

Curzon had no intention of staying in these headquarters of his. He was determined upon going forward with his division. Miller could be trusted with the task of communicating with Corps Headquarters. Curzon knew the value of a commander on the spot in a confused battle; as Curzon saw it, a divisional general among his men even if they were occupying a mile of tangled front was of more use than a divisional general two miles behind.

The division came on up the road — it was hardly a road by now. The artillery branched off, rocking and swaying over the drab shell-torn fields to take up the position assigned them. Webb and Challis rode up for their final orders, and then the division began to plunge forward into action, while Curzon waited, with Daunt's brigade still in hand, in case new orders should come during this period of deployment.

New orders came, right enough. Frobisher came running out of the headquarters to where Curzon stood chatting with Daunt and staring forward at the battle he could not see.

"Please, sir," said Frobisher, breaking into the conversation, and discarding prefixes and circumlocutions with the urgency of the situation. "Miller wants you. Quickly, sir. Buffalo's on the 'phone."

When Curzon arrived indoors Miller was listening at the telephone, writing hard with his free hand. He waved Curzon impatiently into silence at his noisy entrance.

"Yes," said Miller. "Yes. All right. Hold on now while I repeat."

Miller ran slowly through a list of map references and cryptic sentences about units of the division.

"All correct? Then General Curzon is here if General Way-land-Leigh would care to speak to him."

He handed the instrument to Curzon. A moment later Wayland-Leigh's voice came through.

"Hullo, Curzon. You've got your new orders?"

"Miller has."

"Right. I've nothing to add, except to remind you of the standing orders of this corps. But I can trust you, Curzon. There's all hell let loose, but as far as I can see it's just a last effort on the part of the Huns. You've got to hold on until I can persuade G.H.Q. to reinforce you. Sorry to break up your division. Good-bye."

Curzon turned to Miller, appalled at these last words. Miller was already engaged in writing orders in a bold, careful hand.

"What's all this about?" demanded Curzon, and Miller told him, briefly.

There was no intention now of sending the Ninety-First Division in to break through an attenuated line. The German reserves had arrived and were counter-attacking everywhere. So difficult had been communication with troops a mile forward that only now was the higher command able to form an approximately correct picture of the situation of units far forward with their flanks exposed, and other units beating themselves to pieces against strong positions, units in retreat and units holding on desperately in face of superior numbers. The Ninety-First Division was to be used piecemeal to sustain the reeling line. The new orders prescribed that two battalions should be sent in here, and another employed in a counter attack there, a brigade held in reserve at this point, and support given at that.

"Christ damn and blast it all!" said Curzon, as the situation was explained.

He had had enough experience in South Africa as well as elsewhere of the confusion which follows countermanded orders in the heat of action. His artillery were already getting into action; two brigades of infantry were in movement on points quite different from the new objectives. He tore at his moustache while Miller went on steadily writing, and then mastered his fury.

"All right," he said. "There's nothing for it. Show me these orders of yours."

So the Ninety-First Division, after a morning of interminable delays on the road, was now subjected to all the heartbreaking checks which were inevitable with the change of scheme. The bewildered rank and file, marched apparently aimlessly first here and then there, cursed the staff which heaped this confusion upon them. They were short of sleep and short of food. They came under fire unexpectedly; they came under the fire of British artillery who had been left in the dark regarding the fluctuations in the line; and then, when that mistake had been set right, they remained under the fire of shells from British artillery — shells bought in Japan and America, the trajectory and time of flight of ten per cent of which were quite unpredictable.

Curzon had perforce to fight his battle from headquarters. Wayland-Leigh, besieged by requests for help and by orders to give help, coming from all quarters, was persistent in his demands upon the Ninety-First. Challis with a fraction of his 302nd Brigade reported that he had stormed the redoubt whose enfilade fire had caused such losses in the Guards' division, but an hour later was appealing for permission to use another of his battalions to consolidate his position. Daunt in another part of the line sent back a warning that a counter attack was being organised in front of him apparently of such strength that he doubted whether he would be able to stop it. From every hand came appeals for artillery support, at moments when Colonel Hill was warning Curzon that he must persuade Corps Headquarters to send up yet more ammunition.

To reconcile all these conflicting claims, to induce Corps Headquarters to abate something of their exacting demands, and to try and find out from the hasty reports sent in which patch of the line might be left unreinforced and in which part a renewed attack was absolutely necessary, constituted a task which Curzon could leave to no one else. All through the evening of September 26th, and on through the night, Curzon had to deal with reports and orders brought in by runner, by telephone and by motor cyclist. There was no possible chance of his being in line with his men — there was no chance either of guessing in which part of the line his presence would do most good. Miller and Frobisher, Greven and Follett, slept in turns on the floor of the next room, but Curzon stayed awake through the night, dealing with each crisis as it came.

He was red-eyed and weary by the morning, but in the morning there were fresh counter attacks to be beaten back. All through the night German divisions had been marching to the point of danger, and now they were let loose upon the unstable British line. The nine British divisions had been prodigal of their blood and strength. The mile or half mile of shell-torn ground behind them impeded communications and supply; the inexperienced artillery seemed to take an interminable time to register upon fresh targets. It was all a nightmare. Units which had lost their sense of direction and position in the wild landscape reported points strongly held by the enemy which other units at the same moment were reporting as being in their possession.

Wayland-Leigh's voice on the telephone carried a hint of anxiety with it. General Headquarters, dealing with the conflicting reports sent in by two Armies and an Army Corps, had changed its mood from one of wild optimism to one of equally wild despair. They had begun to fear that where they had planned a break through, the enemy instead would effect a breach, and they were dealing out threats on all sides in search of a possible scapegoat.

"Somebody's going to be for it," said Wayland-Leigh. "You've got to hold on."

Curzon was not in need of that spur. He would hold on without being told. He held on through that day and the next, while the bloody confusion of the battle gradually sorted itself out. General Headquarters had found one last belated division with which to reinforce the weak line, and its arrival enabled Curzon at last to bring Daunt's brigade into line with Challis's and have his division a little more concentrated — although, as Miller grimly pointed out, the two brigades together did not contain as many men as either of them before the battle. The front was growing stabilised now, as parapets were being built in the new trenches, and carrying parties toiled through the night to bring up the barbed wire which meant security.

Curzon could actually sleep, now, and he was not specially perturbed when a new increase in the din of the bombardment presaged a fresh flood of reports from the trenches to the effect that the German attacks were being renewed. But once more the situation grew serious. The German command was throwing away lives now as freely as the British in a last effort to recover important strategic points. Fosse 8 and the quarries were lost again; the British line was bending, even if it would not break. Webb's 300th Brigade, in the very process of transfer to the side of its two fellows, was caught up by imperative orders from Wayland-Leigh and flung back into the battle — Curzon had to disregard a wail of protest from Webb regarding the fatigue of his men. Later in the same day Curzon, coming into the headquarters office, found Miller speaking urgently on the telephone.

"Here's the General come back," he said, breaking off the conversation. "You'd better speak to him personally."

He handed over the instrument.

"It's Webb," he explained, *sotto voce.* "Usual sort of grouse."

Curzon frowned as he took the receiver. Webb had been making difficulties all through the battle.

"Curzon speaking."

"Oh, this is Webb here, sir. I want to withdraw my line a bit. P.3–8. It's a nasty bit of salient — "

Webb went on with voluble explanations of the difficulty of his position and the losses the retention of the line would involve. Curzon looked at the map which Miller held out to him while Webb's voice went on droning in the receiver. As far as he could see by the map Webb's brigade was undoubtedly in an awkward salient. But that was no argument in favour of withdrawal. The line as at present constituted had been reported to Corps Headquarters, and the alteration would have to be explained to Wayland-Leigh — not that Curzon would flinch from daring the Buffalo's wrath if he thought it necessary. But he did not think so; it never once crossed his mind to authorise Webb to withdraw from the salient. Retreat was un-English, an admission of failure, something not to be thought of. There had never been any suggestion of retreat at First Ypres, and retreat there would indubitably have spelt disaster. Curzon did not stop to debate the pros and cons in this way — he dismissed the suggestion as impossible the moment he heard it.

"You must hold on where you are," he said, harshly, breaking into Webb's voluble explanations.

"But that's absurd," said Webb. "The other line would be far safer. Why should — "

"Did you hear what I said?" asked Curzon.

"Yes, but — but — " Webb had sufficient sense to hesitate

[189]

before taking the plunge, but not enough to refrain from doing so altogether. "I'm on the spot, and you're not. I'm within my rights if I make the withdrawal without your permission."

"You think you are?" said Curzon. He was tired of Webb and his complaints, and he certainly was not going to have his express orders questioned in this way. After that last speech of Webb's he could not trust him, however definitely he laid down his orders. "Well, you're not going to have the chance. You will terminate your command of your brigade from this moment. You will leave your headquarters and report here on your way down the line at once. No, I'm not going to argue about it. Call your Brigade Major and have him speak to me. At once, please. Is that Captain Home? General Webb has ceased to command the brigade. You will be in charge of your headquarters until Colonel Meredith can be informed and arrives to take command. Understand? Right. Send the message to Colonel Meredith immediately, and ask him to report to me on his arrival."

So Brigadier General Webb was unstuck and sent home, and lost his chance of ever commanding a division. The last Curzon saw of him was when he left divisional headquarters. There was actually a tear — a ridiculous tear — on one cheek just below his blue eye as he went away, but Curzon felt neither pity for him nor dislike. He had been found wanting, as men of that type were bound to be sooner or later. Curzon would have no man in the Ninety-First Division whom he could not trust.

And as Webb left the headquarters the divisional mail arrived. There were letters for each unit in the division, sorted with the efficiency the Army Postal Service always managed to display. They would go up with the rations that night, but the letters for the headquarters personnel could be delivered at once. For the General, besides bills and circulars and the half dozen obviously unimportant official ones there was one letter in a heavy cream envelope addressed to him in a sprawling writing which he recognised as the Duke's. He hesitated a moment when Greven gave it to him, but he could not refrain from opening it there and then. He read the letter through, and the big sprawling writing became suddenly vague and ill defined as he did so. The wording of the letter escaped him completely; it was only its import which was borne in upon him.

That vomiting of Emily's, about which he had always felt a premonition, had actually been a serious symptom. There had been a disaster. Young Herbert Winter Greven Curzon (Curzon had determined on those names long ago) would never open his eyes to the wonder of the day. He was dead — he had never lived; and Emily had nearly followed him. She was out of the wood now, the Duke wrote, doing his best to soften the blow, but Sir Trevor Choape had laid it down very definitely that she must never again try to have a child. If she did, Sir Trevor could not answer for the consequences.

Curzon turned a little pale as he stood holding the letter, and he sat down rather heavily in the chair beside his telephone.

"Not bad news, sir, I hope?" said Greven.

"Nothing that matters," answered Curzon stoically, stuffing the letter into his pocket.

"Colonel Runcorn would like to speak to you, sir," said Follett, appearing at the door.

"Send him in," said Curzon. He had no time to weep for Herbert Winter Greven Curzon, just as Napoleon at Marengo had no time to weep for Desaix.

Chapter XVIII

THE battle of Loos had come to an end, and at last the Ninety-First Division was relieved and could march out to its billets. It was not the division which had gone into action. Curzon stood by the road to see them march by, as he had so often done in Hampshire and France, and they took far less time to pass him. Each brigade bulked no larger on the road than a battalion had done before the battle; each battalion was no larger than a company. The artillery had suffered as badly; there were woefully few men with the guns, and to many of the guns there were only four horses, and to many of the waggons there were only two mules. Curzon's heart sank a little as he returned the salute of the skeleton units. Even with the drafts which were awaiting them they would not be up to establishment; it would be a long time before the Ninety-First Division would be built up again into the fine fighting unit it had been a fortnight ago.

He did not attempt to conceal from himself that Loos had been a disaster for the British army; he could only comfort himself with the thought that it had been a disaster for the German Army as well. The next attack to be made would have to be planned very differently. The bombardment had been insufficient. Then they must have a bombardment which would make certain of it — fifty days, instead of fifty hours, if the ammunition supply could be built up to bear the strain. There must be reserves at hand, instead of seventeen miles back, to exploit the success. The Flying Corps must intensify its operations so that maps of the German second line could be ready in the utmost detail, to enable the artillery to register on fresh targets from new positions without delay. Equally important, there must be none of the muddle and confusion behind the line which had caused so much harm at Loos.

Curzon, despite his red tabs and the oak leaves on his cap peak, could still feel the fighting man's wrath against the staffs that were responsible for that muddle. It was their business to prevent muddle, and they had failed. Curzon was quite well aware of his own incapacity to do that sort of staff officer's work. He was not too reliable in the matter of addition and multiplication and division; the mathematical problems involved in the arrangement of supply and transport and of march time tables would certainly be too much for him. But it was not his job to solve them; it was the responsibility of the men at Army Headquarters and G.H.Q., and they had not been equal to it. Curzon felt that if he were in chief command he would make a clean sweep of the gilded young men who had made such a hash of the time tables and replace them by efficient mathematicians. Hang it, he would put civilians on the Staff for that matter, if they could do the job better — and for Curzon to permit himself even for a moment to be guilty of a heresy of that sort showed how strongly he felt about it.

There were others of the same opinion, as Curzon discovered when he reported himself at Corps Headquarters. Over the whole personnel there lay a brooding sense of disaster both past and to come. Someone would have to bear the responsibility of failure. It would not be long before heads began to fly. Some were gone already — Bewly had been sent home by

Wayland-Leigh just as Webb had been sent back by Curzon. Hope of the Seventy-Ninth was in hospital, dying of his wounds — rumour said he had gone up to the line to seek death, and death was not so hard to find in the front line trenches. No one in that gloomy assembly dared to think of the brave words at the last Headquarters dinner, and the brave anticipations of an immediate advance to the Rhine.

Wayland-Leigh, bulky yet restless, sat at the head of the conference table and looked round with his sidelong green eyes. Everyone knew that it would be touch and go with him. He might be selected as the scapegoat, and deprived of his command and packed off at any moment, if G.H.Q. should decide that such a sacrifice would be acceptable to the strange gods of Downing Street. He was conscious of the trembling of his throne even while he presided at this meeting to discuss what suggestions should be put forward regarding future operations.

Curzon was inevitably called upon for his opinion. He spoke hesitatingly, as might be expected of him; as he told himself, he was no hand at these infernal board-meetings, and speech-making was the bane of his life. He was conscious of the eyes upon him, and he kept his own on the table, and fumbled with pen and pencil as he spoke. Yet he had something very definite to say, and no man with that advantage can speak without point. He briefly described what he thought must be considered essentials for the next battle. More men. More guns. More ammunition. More artillery preparation. More energy. He fumbled with his pencil more wildly than ever when he had to pass on from these, to his mind the obvious things, to the other less tangible desiderata. The arrangements behind the lines had been disgraceful. There must be an efficient staff created which would handle them properly. Someone must work out an effective method of bringing fresh troops into the front line at the decisive moments. Someone must see to it that reserves should be ready in the right place at the right time.

Curzon was surprised by the little murmur of applause which went round the table when he had finished. More than one of the subsequent speakers alluded in complimentary terms to General Curzon's suggestions. The whole opinion of the assembly was with him. The attack at Loos had been correct enough in theory. There had only been a failure in practical details and an insufficiency of men and materials. It could all be made good. A staff that could handle half a million men in action could be found. So could the half million men. So could the guns and ammunition for a really adequate artillery preparation.

Quite noticeably the spirits of the gathering rose; within a very few minutes they were discussing the ideal battle, with forty divisions to draw upon, and elaborate time tables, and a preliminary bombardment which would transcend anything the most vaulting imagination could depict, and a steady methodical advance which nothing could stop — in a word, they were drawing up designs to be put forward before higher authority for the battle of the Somme. With visions like this before them, they could hardly be blamed for ignoring the minor details of machine guns and barbed wire. Minor details vanished into insignificance when compared with the enormous power they pictured at their disposal.

Wayland-Leigh sat in his chair and writhed his bulk about, grinning like an ogre as the suggestions assumed more and more concrete form, while Norton beside him took industrious notes to form the skeleton of the long reports he would have to send in to Army Headquarters and to G.H.Q. In some ways it was like the debate of a group of savages as to how to extract a screw from a piece of wood. Accustomed only to nails, they had made one effort to pull out the screw by main force, and now that it had failed they were devising methods of applying more force still, of obtaining more efficient pincers, of using levers and fulcrums so that more men could bring their strength to bear. They could hardly be blamed for not guessing that by rotating the screw it would come out after the exertion of far less effort; it would be a notion so different from anything they had ever encountered that they would laugh at the man who suggested it.

The Generals round the table were not men who were easily discouraged — men of that sort did not last long in command in France. Now that the first shock of disappointment had been faced they were prepared to make a fresh effort, and to go on making those efforts as long as their strength lasted. Wayland-Leigh was pleased with their attitude; indeed, so apparent was his pleasure that Curzon had no hesitation in asking him, after the conference, for special leave to England for urgent private affairs. Curzon was able to point out (if it had not been the case he would never have dreamed of making the application, despite the urgency of his desire to see Emily) that the division would not be fit to go into the line for some time, and that the knocking into shape of the new drafts could safely be left to the regimental officers.

"Oh, yes, you can go all right," said Wayland-Leigh. "You've earned it, anyway. We can spare you for a bit."

"Thank you, sir," said Curzon.

"But whether you'll find me here when you come back is quite another matter."

"I don't understand," said Curzon. He had heard rumours, of course, but he judged it to be tactless to admit it.

"I've got half an idea I'm going to be unstuck. Sent home because those bloody poops at G.H.Q. have got to find someone to blame besides themselves."

"I hope not, sir," said Curzon.

Wayland-Leigh's huge face writhed into an expression of resignation.

"Can't be helped if I am," he said. "I've done nothing to be ashamed of, and people will know it sometime, even if they don't now. I'm sorry for your sake, though."

"For me, sir?"

"Yes. I was hoping they'd give you one of the new corps which are being formed. I've written recommending it in the strongest terms. I wanted Hope to have one, too, but he'll never be fit for active service again even if he lives. But what my recommendation's good for is more than I can say. Probably do you more harm than good, as things are."

"Thank you, sir. But I don't care about myself. It's you that matters."

Curzon meant what he said.

"Very good of you to say so, Curzon. We'll see what happens. G.H.Q. have got their eye on you anyway, one way or the other. I've had a hell of a lot of bother with 'em about your unsticking that beggar Webb, you know."

"Sorry about that, sir."

"Oh, I didn't mind. I backed you up, of course. And I sent your report on him in to G.H.Q. with 'concur' written on it as big as I could make it. Push off, now. Tell Norton you've, got my permission. If you drive like hell to Boulogne you'll catch the leave boat all right."

In reply to Curzon's telegram the Duke's big motor car was at Victoria Station to meet the train, and in it was Emily, very wan and pale. She was thinner than usual, and in the front of her neck the sterno-mastoid muscles had assumed the prominence they were permanently to retain. She smiled at Curzon, and waved through the window to attract his attention although she did not stand up.

"It was splendid to have your telegram, Bertie," she said,

as the car slid through the sombre streets of war-time London. "Mother's been wanting to move me off to Somerset ever since the air raids started to get so bad. But I wouldn't go, not after your letter saying you might be home any minute. We want every hour together we can possibly have, don't we, Bertie?"

They squeezed hands, and went on squeezing them all the short time it took the car to reach Bude House.

The Duke and Duchess welcomed Curzon hospitably, the latter almost effusively. Yet to Curzon's mind there was something incongruous about the Duchess' volubility about the hardships civilians were going through. If it were not for the supplies they could draw from the model farm and dairy in Somerset, the family and servants might almost be going short of food, and if it were not for the Duke's official position petrol and tyres for the motor cars would be nearly unobtainable. That Ducal servants should be given margarine instead of butter seemed to the Duchess to be far more unthinkable than it did to Curzon, although he had the wit not to say so; and it gave the Duchess an uneasy sense of outraged convention that aeroplane bombs should slay those in high places as readily as those in low. She described the horrors of air raids to Curzon as though he had never seen a bombardment.

The Duke's sense of proportion was less warped than his wife's, although naturally he was inclined to attribute undue importance to his activities under the new government. Between Curzon's anxiety for Emily, and the Duchess's desire to tell him much and to hear a little from him, it was some time before Curzon and the Duke were able to converse privately and at leisure, but when they did the conversation was a momentous one. The Duke was an anxious as all his other colleagues in the government to receive an unbiased account of what was really happening on the Western Front, freed from official verbiage and told by someone without a cause to plead. Out of Curzon's brief sentences — for the conversation was of the fashion of small talk, in which the state of military affairs usurped the time honoured preëminence of the weather as a topic of conversation — the Duke was able to form a clearer picture than even before of the bloody confusion which had been the battle of Loos. He stroked his chin and said "H'm" a great many times, but he was able to keep the conversational ball rolling by the aid of a few conjunctive phrases.

"You say it wasn't this chap Wayland-Leigh's fault?" he asked.

"Good God, no. He wouldn't stand anything like that for a moment. It'll be a crime if they unstick him."

"Why, is there any talk about it?"

"Yes. You see someone's got to go, after all that was said beforehand."

"I see. H'm."

The Duke was aware that anxiety in the Cabinet was reaching a maximum. The decline of Russian power, the alliance of Bulgaria with the Central Powers, the crushing of Serbia, the failure at Gallipoli, Townshend's difficulties in Mesopotamia, and now the fiasco at Loos had been a succession of blows which might well shake anyone's nerve. Yet there were three million Allied troops in France opposed to only two million Germans. That superiority at the decisive point about which the military were so insistent seemed to be attained, and yet nothing was being done. The Duke knew as well as any soldier that a crushing victory in France would make all troubles and difficulties vanish like ghosts, and he yearned and hungered for that victory.

"H'm," he said again, rousing himself from his reverie. "Then there's this business about conscription, too."

Curzon's views on the matter of conscription were easily ascertained. When forty divisions began their great attack in

France the need for drafts would become insistent. However decisive the victory they won, the volunteer divisions would need to be brought promptly up to strength. Not all the recruiting songs and propaganda — not even the shooting of Nurse Cavell — would ensure an inflow of recruits as reliable as a drastic conscription law like that of the French. In Curzon's opinion, too, this was a golden opportunity for bringing in a measure which he had always favoured, even before the war.

"It is every man's duty to serve his country," said Curzon, remembering fragments of what Lord Roberts had said in peace time.

"It won't be easy to do," said the Duke, visualising a harassed Cabinet striving to avoid disruption while being dragged in every direction by conflicting forces.

"Drafts have got to be found, all the same," said Curzon. He thought of the effect it would have on his own attitude if he were warned that the supply of recruits was uncertain and dwindling. It would mean caution; it would mean an encroachment upon his liberty to attack; it would mean thinking twice about every offensive movement, and an inevitable inclination towards a defensive attitude; it might conceivably come to mean the breaking up of some of the units which had been built up with such care — the Ninety-First Division, even.

He was filled with genuine horror at such a prospect — a horror that made him almost voluble. He laid down as stiffly and as definitely as he possibly could the extreme urgency of a lavish supply of recruits. He thumped his knee with his hand to make himself quite clear on the subject. The Duke could not help but be impressed by Curzon's animation and obvious sincerity — they were bound to be impressive to a man who had had experience of Curzon's usual tongue-tied formality of manner.

Chapter XIX

CURZON found his leave as bewilderingly short as any young subaltern home from France. It seemed to him as though he had scarcely reached England before he was back again in the steamer at Folkestone; and when he had rejoined the flood of khaki pouring across the Channel, and heard once more the old military talk, and received the salutes of soldiers stiffened into awed attention by the sight of his brass hat and medal ribbons, he experienced the old sensation known to every returning soldier — as if his leave had never happened, as if it had been someone else, and not himself, who had revelled in the delights of London and received the embraces of his wife.

Curzon had to think very hard about Emily, about her last brave smile, and her waving handkerchief, before he could make the events of the last week lose their veneer of unreality. He had to make himself remember Emily stroking his hair, and speaking soberly about the amount of grey to be seen in it. Emily had held his head to her breast, kissing his forehead and eyes, that time when they had at last brought themselves to mention the brief sojourn in this world of Herbert Winter Greven Curzon. She had offered herself up to him again, a mute voluntary sacrifice, and he had declined like a gentleman; like a gentleman who in the year of grace 1915 had only the vaguest hearsay knowledge of birth control methods and did not want to extend it. There would never be a Herbert Winter Greven Curzon now. He was the last of his line. He blew his nose, harshly, with a military sort of noise, and made himself forget Emily and England again while he turned back to the problems of his profession and his duty.

Miller had thoughtfully sent a motor car to meet him at Boulogne — not for him the jolting, uncomfortable, endless journey by train. He sat back in the car fingering his moustache as the well-remembered countryside sped by. There were French troops on the roads, and French Territorials guarding bridges. Then the British zone; grooms exercising chargers; villages full of British soldiers in shirt sleeves with their braces hanging down by their thighs; aeroplanes overhead. Divisional headquarters; Challis ready to hand over the command, Greven and Follet with polite questions about how he had enjoyed his leave; piles of states and returns awaiting his examination.

And there was something new about the atmosphere of headquarters, too. Miller and Frobisher bore themselves towards him with a slight difference in their manner. Curzon, none too susceptible to atmosphere, was only aware of the difference and could not account for it. He could only tell that they had heard some rumour about him; whether good news or bad he could not tell. The General Staff, as he bitterly told himself, were as thick as thieves with one another, and passed rumours from mouth to mouth and telephone to telephone, so that these men, his juniors and assistants, were always aware of things long before they reached his ears, because he was not one of the blood brotherhood of Camberley.

He asked Miller tentatively about news, and Miller was ready with a vast amount of divisional information, but nothing that would in the least account for the new atmosphere. In the end he ordered out his motor car again, without even waiting to go round the stables and see how his horses had been looked after during his leave, and had himself driven over to Corps Headquarters at St. Cérisy. He had to report his return to Wayland-Leigh, and he felt that if he did so in person he might discover what this new unannounced development was.

But at St. Cérisy the affair only became more portentous and no less mysterious. Wayland-Leigh and Norton were both of them away. Stanwell, the senior staff officer in charge, told Curzon that they were at G.H.Q. He conveyed this piece of information in a manner which gave full weight to it, and when he went on to suggest that General Curzon should stay to dinner at the Headquarters mess, he did so in such a manner, likewise, as to leave Curzon in no doubt at all that he would be glad later that he had done so. The atmosphere of Corps headquarters was yet more tensely charged with expectancy even than divisional headquarters had been. Fortunately it was the hour before dinner, and Curzon was able to fall back upon gin-and-angostura to help him through the trying wait. He actually had four drinks before dinner, although it was rare for him to exceed two. Then at last the anteroom door opened, and Wayland-Leigh came in, followed by Norton, and one glance at their faces told everyone that the news they brought was good.

The news was historic, as well as good. There had been complete upheaval at General Headquarters. The Field Marshal Commanding-in-Chief had fallen; the new cabinet at home had decided they would prefer to risk their reputations upon someone different. His exit was to be made as dignified as possible — a Peerage, the Commandership in Chief of the Home Forces, Grand Crosses and ribbons and stars were to be given him, but no one present at the headquarters of the Forty-Second Corps cared a rap about this aspect of his fate. It was far more important to them to know that his successor was to be a man after their own heart, an Army commander, a cavalry man, a man of the most steadfast determination of purpose. Under his leadership they could look forward to a relentless, methodical, unremitting pressure upon the enemy; nothing fluky, nothing temperamental; something Scottish instead of Irish. Curzon remembered how he had come riding up to his brigade headquarters at First Ypres, and his unmoved calm in the face of the most desperate danger.

But there was a personal aspect as well as a general one. One Army Commander had been promoted; one had gone home; the creation of a new army made a vacancy for a third. Three Army Corps commanders would receive promotion to the full rank of General and the command of an Army — and Wayland-Leigh was to be one of them. He was a man cast in the same mould as the new Commander-in-Chief; where the previous one would have cast him down, the new one had raised him higher yet. It meant promotion, power, and new opportunities for distinction for all the officers of his staff.

Next there was the question of the lower ranks still. Three Army Corps commanders were being promoted to Armies; three divisional commanders would be promoted to take their places. And ten new divisions had now reached France, or were on their way. Three new Army Corps would have to be formed to control these, so that altogether six Major Generals could expect promotion to Lieutenant General. Wayland-Leigh did not know yet all their names, but he knew that Curzon had been selected. He clapped Curzon on the shoulder as he told him, with extraordinary bon-homie. Curzon flushed with pleasure as he received the congratulations of those present. He was destined for the command of four divisions, for the control of something like a hundred thousand men in battle — as many as Wellington or Marlborough ever commanded. He was destined, too, to the Bath chair on

Bournemouth promenade, but Bournemouth and Bath chairs were far from his thoughts as he sat, a little shy, his cheeks red and his eyes on his plate, contemplating his future.

The personality of the new Commander-in-Chief was already noticeable in his selection of his subordinates, and so through them to the holders of the lesser commands. The men who were wanted were men without fear of responsibility, men of ceaseless energy and of iron will, who could be relied upon to carry out their part in a plan of battle as far as flesh and blood — their own and their men's — would permit. Men without imagination were necessary to execute a military policy devoid of imagination, devised by a man without imagination. Anything resembling freakishness or originality was suspect in view of the plan of campaign. Every general desired as subordinates officers who would meticulously obey orders undaunted by difficulties or losses or fears for the future; every general knew what would be expected of him (and approved of it) and took care to have under him generals of whom he could expect the same. When brute force was to be systematically applied only men who could fit into the system without allowance having to be made for them were wanted. Curzon had deprived Brigadier General Webb of his command for this very reason.

In point of fact, Curzon's report on this matter had been the factor which had turned the scale and won him his promotion against the rival influences of seniority and influence. Read with painstaking care by those highest in authority, the sentiments expressed in it had so exactly suited the mood of the moment that Wayland-Leigh had been allowed to have his way in the matter of Curzon's promotion.

Curzon himself did not trouble to analyse the possible reason for his promotion. If some intimate had ventured to ask him what it was likely to be, he would have answered, as convention dictated, that it must have been merely good luck. Right far within himself, in that innermost sanctuary of his soul where convention ceased to rule, would have dwelt the admission that his rise was due to his own merit, and that admission would not have indicated hollow pride. It was his possession of the qualities which he most admired, and which he strove most to ingrain into himself, and which he thought were the necessary characteristics of true greatness, which had won for him the distinction of being almost the youngest Lieutenant General in the British Army.

The conversation round the mess table was light-hearted. The shadow of calamity had been lifted, for if Wayland-Leigh had been removed from his command the careers of all the staff officers under him would have been gravely checked. As it was, Norton, Brigadier General, General Staff, would now become Major General and Chief of Staff of an Army; Commanding Officers of Artillery and Engineers could confidently look forward to a new step in rank, and so on down to the most junior G.S.O.'s. Everybody drank champagne and became a little noisier than was usual at dinner at headquarters messes, while Wayland-Leigh at the head of the table allowed his big face to wrinkle into an expression of massive good humour. Soldiers had once drunk to "a bloody war and sickly season"; the bloody war had come, and an expansion of the army far beyond the calculation of the wildest imagination was bringing with it promotion more rapid than any sickly season could have done.

Curzon drove back to his headquarters with his brain whirling with something more than champagne. He was trying to build up in his mind his conception of the perfect Army Corps, the sort of Army Corps he really wanted. He would have little say in the choice of the divisions under his command, for individual divisions came under and out of Army Corps control according to the needs of the moment. All he could do in that connection was to see that his Major Generals knew what he expected of them — in the darkness of the motor car Curzon's expression hardened and his lips tightened; he did not anticipate much trouble from Major Generals.

It was not in the matter of subordination that his mind chiefly exercised itself. He was preoccupied with the less obvious and more detailed aspect of high command. He had seen something of muddled staff work, and he still retained much of the fighting man's suspicion of the ability of staff officers to handle simple problems of space and time. There was going to be no muddling in *his* corps. Everything was going to be exact, systematic, perfect — to Curzon the adjective "systematic" implied a supremely desirable quality. If his officers could not attain to such a standard then he would replace them by others who would.

Curzon made all this abundantly clear to Miller and Frobisher next morning, when he summoned them to hear his news and his decisions. He would retain Miller as his chief staff officer, putting him forward, as would be necessary, for promotion to Brigadier General, General Staff. He would advance Frobisher from third to second grade, always provided, of course, that the War Office consented. He would listen to their suggestions in the selection of their assistants — the more readily because he knew very little still about the relative merits of the men of the General Staff.

But Miller and Frobisher in return must pick the best men who could be got, and must remain uninfluenced by fear or favour. They must work for him with a wholehearted devotion, and the standard of their work would be judged necessarily by results. Curzon could tell as easily as anyone else whether arrangements were working smoothly or not, and if they did not then Miller and Frobisher would feel the whole weight of his displeasure.

Curzon darted frosty glances at his staff when he said this. Ever since he had passed out from Sandhurst he had been unable to do tricky problems of the type of — "If A can do a piece of work in four days, and B can do it in five days, how long will they take working together?" and he knew it, and knew that his staff knew it. Curzon now would be responsible for the correct solution of problems of the same order but far more complicated, dealing with the traffic-capacity of roads, and divisional march time tables, and artillery barrages, and even with railway management — for railways came to a certain extent under corps control. If things went wrong he would have to bear the blame, and he was not going to trust his military reputation to incompetents.

"You've got to find blokes I can rely on," said Curzon. "Some of these University wallahs, or those railway men and engineer fellows who carry slide rules about with them. They make bloody bad soldiers, I know, but I don't care about that. *I'll* do the soldiering."

Curzon's experience of his brother officers left him in no doubt at all that in the ranks of what was left of the old professional army there were not nearly men enough to go round capable of dealing with these semi-military problems, and as the last comer and the junior Lieutenant General he would never have a chance of getting any of them. In these circumstances Curzon had no scruple in making use of the services of civilians in uniform. He could rely upon himself to see that they had no opportunity given them for dangerous theorising or for interfering in the real management and direction of the army.

So in this fashion the staff of Curzon's Forty-Fourth Corps came to include a collection of characters whom a year ago Curzon would not have expected to see as soldiers, far less in the brass hats of field officers and the red tabs of the staff. The

Gas Officer was a University of London chemist, Milward, who was blessed with a Cockney accent that would have upset Curzon every time he heard it had he allowed it to. Spiller, who had been a Second Wrangler, was a Deputy Assistant Quartermaster General, and Colquhoun, whose Lancashire accent was as noticeable as Milward's Cockney, was another — he had had several years' experience in railway management. Runcorn (who had been Curzon's commanding engineer in the Ninety-First Division, and had come on to the Forty-Fourth Corps in the same capacity) had as his assistants a Major who had built bridges in India and a Captain who had built cathedrals in America.

There was no love lost between the Regulars and the others who gayly styled themselves Irregulars. After a short trial it was found impossible for the two sections to mingle without friction in the social life of the Headquarters mess, and by an unspoken agreement the staff fell into two separate cliques, only coming together for the purpose of work. It would have been a vicious arrangement had it not been for the authority of Curzon. He wanted the work done, and under his pressure the work was well done — he wanted no theorising or highfalutin suggestions; all he asked was technical efficiency, and that he got.

The Forty-Fourth Corps began to make a name for itself, just as the Ninety-First Division had done. The sector of the front line which it held was always an area of great liveliness. Divisional generals were encouraged or coerced — the former usually, as no lieutenant general had any use for a major general in need of coercion — to plan and execute local operations of a vigour and enterprise which called forth German retaliation of extreme intensity. Disciplinary measures, carried out with all the severity which Curzon could wring from courts martial, kept the Corps freer than its neighbours of the plagues of trench feet and trench fever which afflicted the British Army during that miserable winter.

It became noticeable that in the Forty-Fourth Corps area there were fewer lorries ditched while taking up supplies to the line at night. A ditched lorry meant that the driver was saved for that night from undergoing personal danger, whatever privations were caused to the men in the line. Curzon knew nothing of lorry driving, but he saw to it that a driver who was ditched suffered so severely that no one else was encouraged to follow his example. Motor transport drivers remained influenced by the fear of a sentence of imprisonment to an extent far greater than in the infantry (the time was at hand when plenty of infantry men would have welcomed a sentence of imprisonment which took them out of the line) and the savage sentences which Curzon obtained for delinquents made the chicken-hearted use their headlights at the risk of drawing fire, and to go on across dangerous cross-roads however easily they could have staged a breakdown.

Chapter XX

EMILY was able to eke out the meagreness of her letters with occasional press cuttings. The notice in the *Gazette* —"Major (temp. Major General) Herbert Curzon, C.B., D.S.O., to be temp. Lieut. General, 4th Dec. 1915" had attracted the attention of the press. They printed paragraphs about his phenomenal rise, and in the absence of the details which the censorship prohibited they fell back upon the old information that he was the husband of Lady Emily Winter-Willoughby, only daughter of the Duke of Bude, Minister of Steel, and that he was connected (they did not say how) with the family of Lord Curzon of Kedleston, leader of the House of Lords and member of the War Cabinet.

Not much was known about generals in the present war — a contrast with the Boer War, when people wore in their button-holes portraits of Buller or White or Baden-Powell. Generals in 1914–15 had ignored the value to them of publicity, and were only just beginning to realise how foolish it had been to do so. Few people could list off-hand the names of Haig's Army commanders; and yet the public desire for news about generals was quite definite although unsatisfied. In consequence the newspapers grasped eagerly at the opportunity of saying something about Curzon, and he became far better known than, say, Plumer or Horne.

Curzon read the paragraphs about "this brilliant young general" and "the satisfaction the public must feel about the promotion of such a young officer" in the privacy of his room with an odd smile on his face. They gave him a feeling of satisfaction without a doubt; he liked publicity, as simple-minded people often do — even though his satisfaction was diminished by the thought that he was indebted for it to "these newspaper fellows," for whom he had decided contempt. It did not occur to him that the publicity was of priceless value to him, and established him more firmly in his new rank than any military virtue could have done. It was left for the army to discover much later that publicity may so strengthen a general's hand that even a cabinet would risk its own destruction if it should hint at incapacity in the general who was nominally their servant.

Probably it was those paragraphs which brought Curzon the rewards which he was able to write to Emily about. Foreign decorations flowed in to him — G.H.Q. were generous in apportioning his share. He received the Legion of Honour (submitting stoically to the accolade of the French general who invested him with it) and the Italian Order of St. Maurice and St. Lazarus, and the Russian Order of St. George, and the Portuguese Order of St. Benedict of Aviz, so that there were three rows of gay ribbons now on his breast. It was not much to write about to Emily, but it was at least something; Curzon could not bring himself to write "I love you," and by the time he had said "I wish I was with you" (which was only partly true, but could be allowed to stand) and remarked on the weather, the page was still only half full. He did not discuss military topics — not so much because of the need for secrecy but because it was difficult to describe trench raids and local offensives without maps — and he doubted whether Emily could read a trench map.

Emily was fortunate in finding plenty to say. She told how

her father had given up the hopeless task of keeping Bude House properly heated and staffed in war time, and had solved his difficulties by lending the place to the Government as office. She described her rural life in Somersetshire, and the patriotic efforts she was making to increase the national food supply. She dwelt in happy reminiscence on Curzon's last leave, and told how much she was looking forward to his next, although she appreciated how difficult it was for a man in his position to get away. In fact Emily chattered away in her letters with a spirit and freedom only to be explained by her delight in having a confidant for the first time in her life.

As the winter ended and the summer began, a new topic crept into Emily's letters. Her mother (whose work on committees caused her to spend half her time in London) was full of the news that a battle was about to be fought which was to end the war. The Duchess said that July 1st was the date fixed. Emily hoped it was true, because at that rate she would have her husband home with her in time for the beginning of the hunting season.

Curzon boiled with anger as he read the artless words — not anger with his wife, but with the thoughtless civilians who were gossiping about matters of the utmost military importance. He was absolutely certain that no soldier could have made the disclosure. It must be the fault of the politicians and the women. Curzon knew well enough that the Germans must be aware of the prospect of an offensive on the Somme. The huge ammunition dumps, the accumulation of gun positions, the new roads and the light railways, for much of which his own staff was responsible, must have given that away long ago. But that the very date should be known was an appalling thought. He wrote with fury to the Duke, and the Duke replied more moderately. It was not he who had told the Duchess — he had learned not to entrust her with secrets of state — but the fact was common gossip in politico-social circles in London. He would be more ready to blame the staff in France than the politicians in England.

That was poor comfort to Curzon, who could only set his teeth and urge on his staff to further efforts to ensure certain success on the great day. In the conferences at army head-quarters statistics were brought forward to show how certain success would be. For every division employed at Loos there would be five on the Somme. For every gun, twenty. For every shell, two hundred. It was inconceivable that an effort on such a scale should fail; there had never been such an accumulation of force in the history of the world. It was doubtful, bearing in mind the heavy loss the Germans had been experiencing at Verdun, whether it was all quite necessary, but as the Chief of Staff of the Sixth Army pointed out, no one ever yet lost a battle by being too strong.

The divisions were slowly moving up into place. The elaborate time tables for the reinforcement and relief of units in the heat of action were settled to the last minute. Then with a crash the bombardment opened. Curzon went up the line to watch the effect. It seemed quite impossible for anything to live a moment under that hell of fire. The German trenches were blotted out by the smoke and the débris. And that bombardment extended for miles back from the front line, and was to endure for a hundred and sixty-eight hours. He had signed orders drawn up by his Commanding Officer of Artillery which had cunningly distributed the fire of the mass of guns at his disposal over every important point in the German defences on his sector — and five other lieutenant generals had signed similar orders.

A week of expectation followed, a week during which the bombardment raved louder than the loudest brief thunder-storm anyone had ever heard; the biggest noise which had shaken the world since it had settled down into its present shape, louder than avalanches, louder than the crackling of icefloes or the explosion of volcanoes. The preparations continued without a hitch. Ingenious people solved the problem of finding drinking water for half a million men on that bare chalk plain; ammunition flowed in steadily from rail heads to dumps, from dumps to guns; divisions packed themselves neatly into the camps and bivouacs awaiting them. There were no last-minute difficulties, no sudden emergencies. Curzon drove and rode hither and thither through his area and was satisfied. He had done good work for England.

He was stern and unmoved on the morning of July 1st. He shaved himself with a steady hand, long before dawn; he drank his coffee and ate his eggs and bacon (he experienced a momentary distaste for them at first sight, but he fought that down) while the bombardment rose to its maximum pitch. With a calm that was only partly assumed he stalked into the inner headquarters office where Miller and Frobisher, Spiller and Runcorn, Follett and Greven, and a dozen other officers were waiting, drumming on the green baize tables with their fingers and looking at their watches. Colquhoun was biting his nails. Curzon lit his cigar with care; as he struck the match, under the furtive gaze of his staff, came the moment for the lifting of the barrage. There was a moment's appalling silence, followed by a crash which seemed louder than it was in consequence of the silence which had preceded it. Curzon held the flame to the cigar with steady fingers, drawing slowly until the cigar was lit as well as a good cigar deserved to be lit. As the tobacco flared a hundred and twenty thousand Englishmen were rising up from the shelter of their trenches and exposing their bodies to the lash of the German machine guns hastily dragged from the dugouts; but that was no reason for an English general to show un-English emotion.

Even now, despite all the elaborate precautions which had been taken to ensure the prompt passage of messages, despite telephones and buzzers and runners and pigeons and aeroplanes and despatch riders, there must necessarily be a long wait before the reports came in. Runcorn rose and paced about the cramped space between the tables, to Curzon's unspoken irritation. Greven blew his nose. Colquhoun dealt with a couple of messages whose arrival made everyone stir expectantly but proved to be no more than railway routine matters.

Then, in a flood, the reports began to pour in. Divisional commanders were reporting progress. The Army command telephoned, demanding news, describing the result of the attacks on the flanks of the Forty-Fourth Corps, issuing hasty orders to meet the new situation. Irascible messages came in from the corps headquarters on each side. Miller sat with Curzon, the maps before them, and a tray of coloured pins with which to indicate the situation. Despite the rush and the bustle, there was a strange lack of force about the general tenor of the reports, considered in sum. One unit or other seemed to be always behind the rest with its news, and that gave unreality to the situation. Terry's division had found the wire in their front uncut over wide sectors; it was only in places that they had reached the enemy's front line, and heavy fighting was in progress. Franklin reported that his division was still progressing, but he reported heavy losses — fifty per cent was his estimate, at which Curzon tugged at his moustache with annoyance. The man must be unnerved to say a thing like that. He would have small enough means of knowing yet, and no division could possibly suffer fifty per cent of losses in an hour's attack on an enemy who had just been subjected to seven days' bombardment. Similarly Terry must be exaggerating the amount of uncut wire.

What about Green? Follett brought the message from

[216]

Green. His men were all back in their trenches again, such as survived. They had made no progress at all. On that instant Hobday of the Forty-First Corps on the right telephoned. The failure of the Forty-Fourth Corps to push forward their right wing — Green's division, in other words — had left their flank exposed. Curzon spoke to Green personally on the telephone. His division must be roused up and sent forward again. The positions in front of it must be stormed at all costs. At all costs, said Curzon with emphasis. No officer could plead ignorance of what that implied, or find excuses for disobedience. Curzon called for Deane, commanding his artillery, and ordered further artillery support for Green. Deane tended to demur; he pleaded the rigours of a set time table and the disorder which would follow counter order, but Curzon overrode him.

Sixth Army were on the telephone, demanding amplification of the meagre report Frobisher was doling out to them. Curzon dealt with them. He could not amplify the news yet. He was sending stringent orders to his divisional commanders for more details. But what was coming through was positive enough. As he rang off a glance at the clock surprised him. Time was racing by. According to plan his advance should be a mile deep in the German line by now, yet half his forces had not advanced at all and the other half were fighting desperately to retain meagre gains. Halleck and the reserve division should be on the move now to reinforce the advance. That must be countermanded, and Halleck thrown in to complete Green's work for him and clear Hobday's flank. Curzon saw confusion ahead; he telephoned for Halleck to come over in person and have his orders explained to him; it would take hours to switch the division across and mount a new attack. Spiller would have to improvise a route with the help of the I.G.C.

Curzon could hardly believe that things could have gone

so wrong. He got through to Sixth Army again for more news. The Tenth Corps and the Third Corps had failed worse than his. Only towards the Somme was definite progress being made. For a moment Curzon felt comforted, because other lieutenant generals were worse off than he. But that feeling vanished at once. The failure of the attack meant the failure of the method of colossal bombardment, and Curzon could see no alternative to that method. Stalemate lay ahead — a hideous, unthinkable prospect. In savage desperation he sent the harshest orders he could devise to Terry and to Franklin to attack once more, and to snatch success where failure threatened. He knew he would be obeyed.

In the first few hours on the Somme the British Army lost three times as many men as the Boer War, with all its resounding defeats, had cost altogether. Little by little, as confirmation trickled in throughout the day, Curzon came to realise the truth. The result of the day, despite the capture of Mametz and Montauban and the advance of the French on the right, had been a decided setback to British arms. The afternoon brought gloom; the night, while the fighting still continued, black depression. It was not because of the losses. They could be borne and made up again. It was because the method for breaking through the trench line had failed — a method devised according to the very soundest military ideas. Napoleon had said that artillery preparation was necessary for attack — they had employed an artillery preparation greater than the world had ever seen. Careful planning beforehand was desirable — the plans had worked perfectly, without a hitch, up to the moment of proof. Ample reserves — there had been ample reserves in hand. It would have only needed for Curzon that night to have discussed the tactical problems with some hard-bitten infantry subaltern for him to have become convinced that the invention of machine-guns and barbed wire, which Napoleon had never heard of, called for a departure from Napoleon's tactical methods, and if Curzon had once been convinced it would have been hard to unconvince him.

But comfort came in the end, and from higher authority than an infantry subaltern. Hudson, the Sixth Army Chief of Staff, came down in person to explain to Curzon. The examination of prisoners which had been hastily proceeding through the night had revealed the fact that the German losses during the attack and the bombardment had been heavy. Several German units had been ruined. After their Verdun losses the Germans would not be able to stand a prolonged draining of their strength. If the pressure should be kept up long enough the German Army would break completely. Systematic bombardment and attack, relentlessly maintained, would wear them down.

"Their losses are bigger than ours," said Hudson. "And if they're only equal to ours we're bound to win in the end."

Hudson paused to sip at the drink at his side, before he brought in carelessly the blessed word which had occurred to someone at G.H.Q. with a more than military vocabulary.

"The keynote of the next series of operations," said Hudson, "is attrition."

"Attrition," said Curzon, thoughtfully, and then he brightened as he realised the implications of the word. There would be no need for an unmilitary abandonment of the offensive; more than that, there would be a plan and a scheme to work to, and a future to look forward to. A general without these was a most unhappy creature, as Curzon's sleepless night had demonstrated to him.

"Yes," said Curzon. "I see what you mean, of course."

"It's like this —" said Hudson, going on to expand his original thesis.

[219]

There was excuse to be found for them, and for G.H.Q., too. Anyone could realise the terrifying effects of a bombardment, but no one who had not lurked in a dugout through one, emerging alive at the end — shaken, frightened, exhausted, perhaps, but alive and still capable of pressing the double button of a machine gun — could appreciate the possibility of survival.

Two-thirds of yesterday's attack had failed, but there were considerable lengths of the German front line in British hands, where the Forty-Fourth Corps and the Seventeenth and the Third had won footholds. From these points the pressure was to be maintained, bombardment and advance alternating. The Germans would go on losing men, and the advance would slowly progress. Something would give way in the end. The German strength would dwindle, their morale would break down under the ceaselesss strain of the defensive, and, as a further possibility, the advance would in the end climb up to the top of the rolling crest ahead, and something would simply have to happen then.

Hudson's estimate of the enemy's losses was fantastic — he had selected the highest estimate put forward by the Intelligence section, simply because anything less seemed fantastic to him. A month or two of losses on that scale would reduce the German Army to a wreck. There would be corresponding losses on the British side, but the British Army could bear them as long as the leaders kept their nerve — and that was the point which Hudson specially wanted to make with Curzon. Not all corps commanders could be trusted as Curzon could be, to push attacks home relentlessly, applying ceaseless pressure to divisional generals.

So that Curzon was to be maintained in charge of his present sector of the front. He would be supplied with new divisions as fast as they could be brought up to replace his exhausted ones, and he must see to it that the attacks were maintained with all the intensity the situation demanded. It was a high compliment which was being paid to Curzon (or at least both Hudson and Curzon saw it as one). He flushed with pleasure and with renewed hope; he had work to do, a plan to carry out, a goal in front of him, and he was one of the five lieutenant generals who were charged with the execution of the offensive on which England was pinning her whole trust.

After Hudson's departure Curzon called his staff together. He outlined the work before them, and he quoted the figures of the German losses which Hudson had given him. He looked round at them. Miller, dark, sombre, and reliable, nodded approval; the others, even if they did not approve, had learned by now to keep their faces expressionless in the face of schemes they could not oppose.

"Our old Ninety-First Division is coming up into our sector," concluded Curzon. "We know what they can do. What do you suggest, Miller? Hadn't they — "

In this fashion began the orgy of bloodshed which is now looked upon as the second phase of the battle of the Somme, three agonising months during which divisions, "fattened up" in back areas on quiet sectors, were brought up into the line to dissipate in one wild day the strength built up during the previous months. They went into action ten thousand infantry strong; they won a few yards of shell-torn ground, a few trees of a shattered wood, or the cellars of a few houses, and they came out four thousand strong, to be filled up with recruits and made ready for the next ordeal. Kitchener's Army found its grave on the Somme just as the old regular army had done at Ypres.

Curzon worked with grim determination during those three months. There was always pressure to be applied to someone — transport officers who said that a thing could not be done, major generals who flinched from exposing their divisions to some fresh ordeal, artillery colonels who pleaded that their men were on the point of exhaustion. He did his duty with all his nerve and all his strength, as was his way, while the higher command looked on him with growing approval; he was a man after their own heart, who allowed no consideration to impede him in the execution of his orders.

Chapter XXI

O NE morning there was a private letter (it was marked "private" on the envelope) for Curzon, and the sight of it gave Curzon an unpleasant sensation of disquietude. It was addressed to "General Herbert Curzon," care of the regimental depôt of the Twenty-Second Lancers, and had been sent on to him via the War Office — and it was from Aunt Kate. He hesitated before he opened it; he did not want to open it; it was only by an effort of will that he forced himself to open it and read it.

DEAR BERTIE,

Just a line to wish you all success and to ask you if you will do favour for your aunt, because I have not asked you ever for one before. Our Dick has got to go out to the Front again. He was wounded and came back to the hospital, but now he is better and he is going back next week. Bertie, he does not want to go. He does not say so, but I know. He has done his bit because he has been wounded and has got the Military Medal. I showed him something about you that I saw in the paper, and he said joking that he wished you would give him a job. He said he would rather clean out your stables than go over the top at Ginchy again. He said it as if he didn't mean it but I know. Bertie, would you do that for me. You have only got to ask for him. Corporal R. Cole, 1/29 London Regiment, Duke of Connaught's Own. I swear that he won't say he is your cousin to your friends. Because he is your cousin, Bertie. He is my only son and I want him to come back to me safe. Please, Bertie, do this for me because I am only an old woman now. He doesn't know I am writing to you. It does not matter to you who cleans out your stables. Your Uncle Stanley and Gertie and Maud send their love. Maud has a fine big baby boy now. We call him Bertie and he is ever such a tartar. Please do that for me.

Your loving
AUNT KATE.

Curzon sat and fingered the letter. Aunt Kate was quite right when she said it did not matter to him who cleaned out his stables. Curzon really had not troubled his mind with regard to the dispensing of patronage at his headquarters. He had no knowledge of how the grooms and clerks and servants there had been appointed to their soft jobs — nor would he trouble as long as they were efficient. A single telephone message would suffice to give him Corporal Richard Cole's services — the 1/29 London was in Terry's Division and coming back to the line soon.

But Curzon had no intention of sending for him; he formed that resolution after only brief reflection. Cole had his duty to do like everyone else, and there was no reason why he should be selected rather than any other for a safe billet. Curzon had always frowned on favouritism — he reminded himself how he had sent back Horatio Winter-Willoughby to regimental duty. He was not going to deprive the fighting forces of the services of a valuable trained N.C.O. He tore the letter up slowly. He was glad that he had reached that decision, because otherwise a request by a lieutenant general for the services of a corporal would have been sure to excite comment, and Cole would be sure to talk about the relationship, and Greven would hear, and from Greven the news would reach the Duchess, and from the Duchess it would go on to Emily. He did not want Emily to know he had a Cockney cousin — to shake that thought from him he plunged back furiously into his work.

In fact he was able to forget all about his cousin again in the stress and strain of the last weeks of the battle of the Somme, and the excitement of the first entry into action of the tanks, and the need to combat the growing paralysis caused by the October rains and the exhaustion of his units. Only was he reminded of the affair when yet another letter, addressed in the same way, was put into his hands. There was a telegraph form inside addressed to Shoesmith Road, Brixton — "Regret to inform you Corporal R. Cole killed in action Nov. 1st." There was only one word on the sheet of notepaper enclosing the telegraph form, and that was printed large — MURDERER.

His hands shook a little as he tore the papers into fragments, and his face lost a little of its healthy colour. He had never been called that before. It was a hideous and unjust accusation, and it made him furiously angry; he was angrier still — although he did not know it — because he was subconsciously aware that there were plenty of people who would most unreasonably have agreed with Aunt Kate. He did not like to be thought a murderer even by fools with no knowledge of duty and honour.

The memory of the incident poisoned his thoughts for a long time afterwards. When he went on leave — his first leave for eleven months — he was almost moved to confide in Emily about it. He knew she would appreciate and approve of his motives, and he was in need of approval, but he put the insidious temptation aside. His common sense told him that a moment's sympathy would not be worth the humiliation of confessing the deceit he had practised for two years; and yet it was his need for sympathy which made him put his arms round Emily and kiss her with an urgency which brought colour to her cheeks and expectancy into her eyes.

After the stress and turmoil and overwork of active service it seemed like Paradise to be back in the quiet West country, to ride a horse through the deep Somerset lanes with Emily beside him and not a soldier in sight. The freakishness of Fate had placed him in a position wherein he was compelled to work with his brain and his nerves. He had been gifted with a temperament ideal for a soldier in the presence of the enemy, knowing no fear and careless of danger, and yet his duty now consisted in never encountering danger, in forcing responsibility on others, in desk work and paper work and telephone work which drained his vitality and sapped his health.

Emily was worried about him. Despite the healthy red-brown of his cheeks (nothing whatever would attenuate that) she fretted over the lines in his forehead and the increasing whiteness of his hair, even though she tried to look upon these changes in him as her sacrifice for King and Country. There was anxiety in her eyes when she looked at him while they were in the train returning to London — the Duke had expressed a wish to have a long talk with Curzon before he went back to France, and, as he could not leave his official duties, Curzon was spending a day and a night of his leave in London although Emily had met him at Folkestone and carried him straight off to her beloved Somerset.

The Duke was worried about the progress and conduct of the war. While talking with Curzon he seemed incapable of coming out with a downright statement or question or accusation. He listened to Curzon's bluff phrases, and said "H'm," and stroked his chin, but an instant later he harked back again, seeking reassurance. Curzon found it difficult to understand his drift. Curzon was quite ready to admit that the offensive on the Somme had been quenched in the mud without decisive results, but he was insistent that it had done much towards bringing victory within reach. The German Army was shattered, bled white; and if it had not rained so continuously in October, just when the offensive had reached Sailly-Saillisel and

Bouchavesnes on the crest of the ridge the decisive victory might have taken place then and there.

"H'm," said the Duke, and after a pause he harked back once more to the aspect of the question which was specially worrying to him. "The casualties are heavy."

The Duke felt that was a very mild way of putting it, considering the terrible length of the daily lists — Englishmen were dying far faster than in the Great Plague.

"Yes," said Curzon. "But they're nothing to what the German casualties are like. Intelligence says — "

The conclusions that the General Staff Intelligence drew from the material collected by their agents and routine workers were naturally as optimistic as they could be. The material was in general correct, but necessarily vague. Exact figures could not be expected, and the data accumulated only permitted of guesses. Pessimists would have guessed much lower. Equally naturally Curzon and his fellows approved of the conclusions reached by Intelligence. If this plan of attrition failed, there was no plan left to them, only the unthinkable alternative of stagnation in the trenches. With just that unmilitary confession of helplessness before them they would need a great deal of convincing that their only plan was unsuccessful.

"You're sure about this?" asked the Duke. He wanted to be convinced, too. The task of finding someone to win the war was a heavy one for the Cabinet.

"Quite sure," said Curzon, and he went on to say that as as soon as fine weather permitted a resumption of the offensive a breakdown of the German defence could be looked for quite early. Tanks? Yes, he imagined that tanks might be a useful tactical accessory; they had not yet fought on his front at all, so that he could not speak from experience. It would take a great number of tanks, all the same, to kill the number of Germans necessary for victory. Only infantry, of course, can really win battles — the Duke was so eager to learn that Curzon could restate this axiom of military science without impatience. Keep the infantry up to strength, build up new divisions if possible, keep the ammunition dumps full, and victory must come inevitably.

"I'm glad," said the Duke, "that I've had this chance of talking to you. We've been a bit despondent, lately, here in London."

"There's nothing to be despondent about," said Curzon. A despondent soldier means a bad soldier; Curzon would be as ashamed of being despondent as of being afraid — he would see little difference between the two conditions, in fact.

It may have been this conversation between the Duke and Curzon which turned the scale of history. Perhaps because of it the Cabinet allowed the Expeditionary Force to spend that winter preparing once more for an offensive on the present lines, and were only confirmed in their decision by the bloody failure of the great French attack launched by Nivelle with his new unlimited ideas. Curzon was at Arras when Nivelle failed, waiting to engage in his eternal task of sending divisions through the Moloch-fires of assaults on the German line. So serious was the news that a general assembly of British generals was called to discuss it — Curzon was there, and half a dozen other corps commanders, and Hudson and his chief, and Wayland-Leigh from the Sixth Army with Norton. When Curzon climbed out of his car with Miller behind him and saw the array of cars already arrived, and the different pennons drooping over the radiators, he guessed that something serious was in the wind. Wayland-Leigh's car stopped immediately after his, and Curzon waited to greet his old commander before going in. The Buffalo was lame with sciatica, and he took Curzon's arm as they went up the steps.

"Christ knows," said Wayland-Leigh, hobbling along, "what

this new how d'ye do's about. Ouch! I bet the French have got 'emselves into trouble again."

Wayland-Leigh's shrewd guess was correct. When everyone was seated on the gilt chairs in the big dining room of the château an officer on the General Staff at G.H.Q. rose to address the meeting. It was Hammond, very tall, very thin, with no chin and a lisp, but with a reputation which belied his appearance.

"Gentlemen," said Hammond. "The news I have to tell you is such that we have not dared to allow it to reach you by the ordinary channels. It must not be written about, or telephoned about, or even spoken about outside this room."

He paused and looked round him as he said this, and one general looked at another all round the room, before Hammond went on.

"The French Army has mutinied."

That made everyone stir in their seats. Half a dozen generals cleared their throats nervously. There were alarmists among them who had sometimes thought of mutiny.

"As you all know, gentlemen, the great French offensive on the Chemin-des-Dames has failed with very heavy losses, just as you all predicted. General Nivelle promised a great deal more than he could perform."

Wayland-Leigh and Norton grinned at the mention of Nivelle's name, and others followed their example. Nivelle, with his gift of the gab and his vaulting ambitions, was an object of amusement to the British staff. They smiled when he was spoken about, like a music hall audience when a comedian refers to Wigan or to kippers. But Hammond was deadly serious.

"The point is," he went on, "eight French divisions have refused to obey orders. It is not as serious as it might be, gentlemen. There has been no Socialist movement." The word

"Bolshevik" had not yet crept into the English language, or Hammond would have used it — "There are no political feelings at all in these divisions. They only objected to what they call unnecessary waste of life. It is a case of — "

"Cold feet," interjected Wayland-Leigh, and got a laugh.

"Objection to a continuance of the offensive," said Hammond. "Nivelle has resigned and Pétain has taken his place. He is rounding up the mutineers with loyal troops. I don't know what measures General Pétain will take — I suppose we all know what we should recommend to him. But the fact remains, gentlemen, that for this summer the duty of maintaining pressure upon the enemy will fall on us alone. We must attack, and attack again, and go on attacking. Otherwise the enemy will undoubtedly take the opportunity of falling on our gallant allies."

There was a sneer in Hammond's tone at these last two words — for some time there had been a tendency in the British Army to say those words with just that same intonation; for a year no English staff officer had spoken of "les braves Belges" and meant it.

"So, gentlemen, the battle at present in progress at Arras will continue. The Second Army will deliver the attack at Messines which they have had ready for some time, while plans will be perfected for a transference of pressure to the northern face of the Ypres salient and a drive to clear the Belgian coast. In this fashion, gentlemen — "

Hammond turned to the big map on the wall behind him, and introduced his hearers to the Third Battle of Ypres. It was not the Third Battle of Ypres as the long-suffering infantry were to know it. Polygon Wood and Passchendaele were mentioned, but only in passing. The concentrated efforts of the British Army for a whole summer would carry them far beyond these early objectives. Hammond indicated the vital railway junctions far to the rear which must eventually fall to them; and he lingered for a moment over the relief it would afford the Navy in the struggle against submarines if the whole Belgian coast should be cleared.

Hammond's optimism was infectious, and his lisping eloquence was subtle. Curzon's mood changed, like that of the others, from one of do-or-die to one of hope and expectancy. There were seventy divisions, and tanks for those who believed in them, guns in thousands, shells in tens of millions. Surely nothing could stop them this time, no ill fortune, no bad weather, certainly not machine guns or barbed wire. The enemy *must* give way this time. All a successful attack demanded was material and determination. They had the first in plenty, and they would not be found lacking in the second. Curzon felt resolution surging up within him. His hands clenched as they lay in his lap.

The mood endured as his car bore him back to his own headquarters, and when he called his staff about him his enthusiasm gave wings to his words as he sketched out the approaching duties of the Forty-Fourth Corps. Runcorn and Deane and Frobisher caught the infection. They began eagerly to outline the plans of attack which Army Headquarters demanded; they were deeply at work upon them while the divisions under their direction were expending themselves in the last long-drawn agony of Arras.

Chapter XXII

CURZON wrote to Emily that there was no chance at all of his taking leave this summer. He realised with a little regret that an officer at the head of an Army Corps would be far less easily spared for a few days than any regimental officer or divisional General. The troops of the line had their periods of rest, but he had none. His responsibility was always at full tension. He was signing plans for the future at the same time as he was executing those of the present. He was responsible for the discipline and movement and maintenance and activity of a force which sometimes exceeded a hundred thousand men.

And he was lonely in his responsibility, too, although loneliness meant little to him. Save for Emily he had gone friendless through the world among his innumerable acquaintances. He would sometimes, during that summer of 1918, have been desperately unhappy if he had stopped to think about happiness. But according to his simple code a man who had attained the rank of Lieutenant General, was the son-in-law of a Duke, and had a loving wife, could not possibly be unhappy. There could be no reason for it. Unreasonable unhappiness was the weakness of poets and others with long hair, not of soldiers, and so he believed himself to be happy as the British Army plunged forward into the slaughter of Passchendaele.

For fifteen days — half as long again as at the Somme — twice the number of guns as at the Somme had pounded the German lines. Curzon's staff, Hobday's staff on his right, the staffs of six other army corps and of three Armies had elaborated the most careful orders governing the targets to be searched for, the barrages to be laid, the tactics to be employed. The Tank Corps had early pointed out that this sort of bombardment would make the ground impassable for tanks, but after the success at Messines Curzon and all the other generals had decided that the tank was a weapon whose importance had been overrated, and it stood to reason that fortifications should not be attacked without preliminary bombardment.

Once more the reports came in describing the opening of the battle — large sections of the German line overrun, the advance once more held up, the usual heavy fighting in the German second line. Once more the weather broke, and the country, its drainage system battered to pieces, reverted under the unceasing rain to the condition of primeval swamp from which diligent Flemish peasants had reclaimed it in preceding centuries. Already intelligent privates in the ranks were discussing whether the Germans had a secret method of bringing rain whenever they wanted it for tactical purposes.

Curzon in his headquarters as the days went on and the rain roared on the roof, began almost to feel a sinking of heart. The toll of casualties was mounting, and, significantly, the number of the sick, while the progress was inordinately slow. Those optimistic early plans had envisaged advance a mile deep, and here they were creeping forward only a hundred yards at a time. Tanks had proved utterly useless in the swamp. The Germans with their usual ingenuity and foresight had studded the country with concrete fortresses to hold the line where trenches were impossible to dig, and attacks were horribly costly. There were moments when Curzon hesitated before forcing himself to read the casualty figures of the divisions he had sent into action.

His determination was maintained by the information which Army Headquarters supplied to him. The German losses were heavier than the British; the German morale was on the point of giving way; any moment might see a general collapse of the enemy's army. When Curzon rode out to inspect his long-suffering divisions in their rest billets he could see for himself that they were as reliable as ever, and that if they were not as high spirited and hopeful as the early divisions of Kitchener's Army they were still ready, as he knew British soldiers always would be, to pour out their blood at the command of their leaders — and three years of elimination had given the British Army leaders like Curzon, who could not be turned back by any difficulties, nor frightened by any responsibilities.

Cheered on by the encouragement of the highest command, Curzon threw himself into the work of maintaining the pressure upon the Germans, flinging his divisions each time they had been filled up with drafts once more in assaults upon the enemy's line, battering away with the fiercest determination to win through in the end. Under his direction and those of his colleagues the British Army used up its strength in wild struggles like those of a buffalo caught in a net, or a madman in a strait-jacket, rather than submit to what seemed the sole alternative, which was to do nothing.

A week or two more — no longer than that — of these nightmare losses and thwarted attacks would see the end of the war, a complete disintegration of the whole German front in the northeast; that was what the Army command deduced from their Intelligence reports. Victory was in sight. Then suddenly Hudson, the Army Chief of Staff, dropped in with a bombshell. The civilian government at home had grown frightened at the casualty lists, and were losing their nerve, as

[234]

might be expected of civilians. There was a suggestion that the government — the "frocks" as one famous staff officer significantly and humorously called them — were actually proposing to interfere with the military conduct of the war and to force some scheme of their own upon the command.

No self-respecting general could put up with that, of course. There would be wholesale resignations, and, if the government persisted and could withstand the effect of these resignations upon public opinion, there would be more than resignations. There would be dismissals, until the army was under the command of the pliant and subservient boot-licking type of general who always wins promotion under civilian command. It was not idle talk, but an imminent, urgent possibility; in fact, to such lengths were the civilians going that the politicians were actually coming out to France to see for themselves, not on the customary sight-seeing trip, but because they were pleased to doubt the word of the soldiers as to the present state of affairs. Something must be done to impress them immediately.

Curzon was in the heartiest agreement. He was genuinely horrified by what Hudson told him. Civilian interference in military affairs spelt ruin — all his teaching and experience told him that. If the present order of generals was swept away and their places taken by others (Bewly was an example of the type Curzon had in mind) there could be nothing but shame and disaster awaiting the British Army. Curzon did not tell himself that the present state of affairs must be the best possible because it was the present state of affairs, but that was a pointer to his line of thought. Innovations and charlatanry were indissolubly linked in his mind. He called upon his staff to make haste with their plans for the renewed attack upon Passchendaele. The surest reply to these busybodies would be a resounding success and thousands of prisoners.

Curzon was shaving early one morning, before the night's reports could arrive, on the third day of that last tragic offensive, when young Follett came into his room.

"G.H.Q. on the telephone, sir," he said — and the tone of his voice indicated the momentous nature of the occasion. "They want to speak to you personally."

Curzon hurried out with the lather drying on his cheeks. In the inmost room of his headquarters Miller was at the telephone, and handed the receiver over to him.

"Curzon speaking," he said.

"Right. You know who this is?" said the receiver.

"Yes," said Curzon.

"Is anyone else present in the room in which you are?"

"My B.G.G.S."

"Send him out."

Curzon dismissed Miller with a gesture, and, when the door had closed, he addressed himself again to the telephone.

"I'm alone now, sir," he said.

"Then listen, Curzon. You know about the visitors we're entertaining at present?"

"Yes, sir."

"They're coming to poke their noses about in your sector this morning."

"Yes, sir."

"They won't believe that the quality of the German Army is declining. They as good as told me to my face last night that I was lying."

"Good God!"

"You've got to show 'em they're wrong. You've got a good bag of Huns at the moment, haven't you?"

Curzon reflected for a moment. In the cages there would be the prisoners of the last four days.

"About two thousand, I should say."

"Well, the nosey-parker troupe will be round at Nine-tieth Division headquarters soon. See that the divisional cage has got a real good selection for 'em to see. Understand?"

"Yes, sir."

"Right. Good-bye."

In the outer room Miller was waiting.

"Send for my car," said Curzon abruptly. "And get through to the nearest ammunition column for ten lorries. Empty ones, of course."

With clear-headed rapidity Curzon shaved and completed dressing by the time the lorries were ready for him. He threw himself into the car with a rapid order to drive to Ninetieth Division headquarters. A little farther up the road was the divisional prisoners' cage — a rectangle of barbed wire with sentries at each corner. The inmates were a deplorable sight. They had been fighting for days in the inconceivable hardships of Passchendaele; they were worn out, nerve broken, covered with mud. Even those who had been taken prisoner some time before looked no better, thanks to confinement in the drizzling rain.

Curzon looked at them through the wire until the staff officer for whom Greven had been dispatched arrived, and then Curzon demanded and obtained admission. He walked round the miserable huddled groups.

"Bring that one out. And that one. And that one," he said, pointing with his stick. He left the boys, the undersized, the shell shocked, the sick, the dispirited. The giving of receipts, the formalities and redtape, were waived at the command of a Lieutenant General. The better specimens, wondering what new horror the war held in store for them, were packed into the lorries under the guard whom the staff officer summoned from the nearby billets.

Then they drove off to Eighty-Eighth Division, and at that

divisional cage Curzon went the opposite way to work. He picked out the weaker specimens, left a proportion of his stronger ones, and drove on to Seventy-Ninth Division, and then to Seventy-Seventh. By the time he got back to Ninetieth his ten lorries, which had rolled and pitched over the battered roads in the wake of his speeding car, were crammed with the least prepossessing of the prisoners from six divisional cages, and they were all turned in to join their companions in misery in the Ninetieth Division cage. The thing was hardly done, and Curzon had barely strolled into the headquarters, when an awed young staff officer looked up from his telephone and said, "They're coming."

In ten minutes a little fleet of motor cars came rolling up and stopped outside the house. From the radiators flew the pennons of G.H.Q. A motley crowd climbed out of the cars — the khaki and red of the General Staff, the new horizon blue of the French Army, officers in the "maternity jackets" of the Royal Flying Corps; and among the crowd of uniforms were half a dozen figures in ludicrous civilian clothes. Curzon noted their long hair and shapeless garments with contempt. They gawked about them like yokels at a fair. They were stoop-shouldered and slack. He came forward reluctantly to be introduced.

"This is Lieutenant General Curzon, sir, commanding the Forty-Fourth Corps," said the senior staff officer present. At the moment of making the introduction the staff officer, his face turned from the civilian, raised his eyebrows in inquiry, and Curzon nodded in return.

"Have you got any prisoners here, General?" asked the staff officer.

"Oh, yes," said Curzon. "There are five hundred, I should think, in that cage over there."

"Recent ones?"

"All taken in the last few days." The stilted artificiality of the conversation could hardly have escaped the notice of one of the keenest minds in Europe if the circumstances had not been so entirely natural.

"Oh, that's fine," said the staff officer. "You wanted to see some recent prisoners, didn't you, sir? Would you care to come this way and inspect a few?"

The party plodded off through the squelching mud, mackintoshes up to their ears, while Curzon turned away. He had done his best for the army. It would not be his fault if he and his brother soldiers were held back at the moment of victory.

But the rain which had poured down upon prisoners and politicians alike extinguished the last chance of victory. Passchendaele was taken — a statistician might have calculated that the miserable village cost, in the shells hurled against it and in pensions paid to the dependents of the dead, about three hundred times as much as a similar area in the most valuable part of New York covered with intact skyscrapers. The ridge was crowned, but the higher command had decided that there was nothing to be gained by trying to push on. The high hopes of capturing Bruges and Zeebrugge had vanished; even if further efforts could be asked of the troops (as Curzon maintained) there was no chance of keeping the troops in the front line supplied well enough to maintain an offensive across the three miles of shell-torn swamp which they had conquered.

Curzon was informed of this decision in the course of a visit to Sixth Army Headquarters; he was closeted alone with Hudson for a long time. Yet during that interview Hudson was disinclined to discuss the future of the war. His own efforts had ended in failure, and now the Third Army was planning a tank offensive in the Cambrai sector regarding which his opinion was not even being asked. Hudson skirted round controversial subjects with a good deal of tact. He was

[239]

full of appreciation for Curzon's recent work, and as well as Curzon's relentlessness in command he was pleased to approve of Curzon's handling of the matter of the prisoners.

"That was first rate," said Hudson, grinning. "It was absolutely convincing — took 'em in completely. Serve 'em right."

Curzon grinned back. There was joy in the thought that soldiers could outwit politicians in other things as well as military affairs.

"Oh yes, by the way," said Hudson. "You'd better take your leave now while things are quiet."

"Thank you very much," said Curzon. "I was intending to ask you."

"There'll be a special reason for it, though," said Hudson.

"Indeed?"

"Yes." Hudson's expression was one of ungainly whimsicality. He fumbled with the papers on his desk to prolong the dramatic moment. "You will have to be present at an investiture."

Curzon's heart leaped; he guessed now what Hudson was going to say — he had been modestly hoping for this ever since the Somme.

"The future Sir Herbert Curzon, K.C.M.G.," said Hudson. "Yes, I'm glad I'm the first to congratulate you. The very strongest recommendations have gone through both from here and from G.H.Q., and I'm glad that someone in London's got sense enough to act on them. You'd better take your leave from the day after to-morrow."

Curzon was genuinely delighted with the news. He was glad to be a knight. Socially it was a distinction, and professionally too — only a minority of corps commanders received knighthood. There would be a ribbon and star to wear with full dress uniform, and it would be pleasant to be addressed by servants as "Sir Herbert." Incidentally he had never really liked being announced with his wife as "General and Lady Emily Curzon." "Sir Herbert and Lady Emily Curzon," on the other hand, sounded much better.

When he reached England, Emily was inclined to agree; she was glad for Curzon's sake even though she herself was sorry because the investiture would take him from her side for a day and would compel them to stay in war-time November London, where the Duchess insisted on claiming (or, rather, assumed as a natural right) too much of his attention. The Duchess was full of gossip as usual — the Duke told Curzon that it beat him where she got it from — and although the Navy in its life and death struggle with German submarines was occupying more of her attention than the Army nowadays, she found time to try and pump Curzon about the new offensive, regarding which she had heard rumours.

Curzon was relieved to find that it was only rumours which she had heard — many of the leaks of information must have been stopped — and that the main reason for her curiosity was this very vagueness. Offensives of the ordinary sort had no more charm of novelty for London society by now than they had for the men in the trenches, but there was a quality about the new rumours which stimulated her interest. Curzon was tactfully reticent. He knew little enough about this Cambrai stunt as it was, and neither he nor his corps were to be employed. Moreover, it was to be a tank affair, and, frankly, he was not interested in tanks after they had disappointed him at Arras and Passchendaele. His unconcern actually deluded the Duchess into believing that the rumours had been exaggerated, and she went back to her new interest of trying to find out the latest about the new American Expeditionary Force.

However, she called upon Curzon and Emily at their hotel on the evening of the investiture — naturally she wanted to hear about that. So it came about that she was present when a servant came in with the information that the Duke of Bude would like to speak to Sir Herbert Curzon on the telephone.

"I wonder what your father wants, dear," said the Duchess to Emily during Curzon's absence.

"I can't imagine, mother," said Emily.

Meanwhile Curzon was standing in his little glass box (which was the home of the telephone at even luxurious hotels in 1917) listening in amazement to the Duke's voice and to the news it was conveying to him with excited volubility.

"There's good news, Curzon," said the Duke. "Best since the war began. There's no harm in my telling you — it's being made public as quickly as possible. We've won a big victory."

"Where?"

"On the Western front, of course. Cambrai."

"My God!"

"There's no doubt about it. Five miles advance up to now. Five thousand prisoners. Two hundred guns. The cavalry are being brought into action. The war's as good as won. It's the tanks that have done it."

"God bless my soul."

Three months of agony at Third Ypres had won no greater result.

"I'll come in later, if you're going to be in, and discuss it with you."

"Very good."

Emily and the Duchess thought that Curzon's expression on his return portended bad news; they were relieved when in reply to their startled "Whatever's the matter?" Curzon told them that England had won a victory. It was irritating in the extreme to Curzon to have to recount that in his absence from France a battle had been won in which his corps had played no part, and that the principal instrument of victory had been a weapon he despised — he remembered his cutting rudeness

[242]

to his tank staff officer when the latter had ventured to make suggestions. He could have swallowed the affront of the success of the tank if he and his men had shared in it. As it was, he was exceedingly angry; apprehensive, as well, because the Duke's preposterous optimism over the telephone had almost infected him with doubt lest the war should be won before his leave expired. He would be a fool in his own eyes then.

He was hardly as angry as the Duchess, all the same.

"I'll never forgive you, Bertie," she said, bitterly. "And as for young Gordon, he's finished as far as I'm concerned. Here have I been going round, and whenever anyone's said that there was going to be a big push soon I've said, 'Oh no, I'm quite sure you're wrong. There's not going to be anything of the kind. I know for certain.' I shan't be able to hold up my head again."

Fortunately the Duke on his arrival was able to suggest a very satisfactory way out of the difficulty, presumably by the aid of his political experience.

"Don't worry, my dear," he said. "You'll be able to say that you knew about it all the time, but denied the rumours so that the Germans would be lulled into insecurity. You can say that you were acting in obedience to a Royal command, because it was well known that whatever you said was given great attention in Berlin."

The Duchess thought that a brilliant suggestion.

Chapter XXIII

IN the morning the newspapers proclaimed England's victory in flaming headlines. There could be no doubt about it. Curzon's appetite for his war-time breakfast (not nearly as appetising as the ones served him at his headquarters in France) quite failed him as he read. Envy and apprehension between them stirred up strange passions within him, to such an extent that after breakfast he made an excuse to Emily and slipped away to telephone to General Mackenzie at the War Office. He did not dare tell Emily that he was going to suggest that he sacrifice the remainder of his leave in order to make sure of missing no more of the glory which was to be found in France.

But Mackenzie seemed to be in an odd mood.

"I shouldn't worry, if I were you, Curzon," he said.

"But I don't want to miss anything," persisted Curzon.

"Well — no, look here, Curzon, take my advice and don't worry."

"I don't understand, I'm afraid."

"Don't you? Perhaps that's my fault. But on the other hand perhaps it isn't. Now ring off, because I'm busy."

There was a small grain of comfort in the conversation, Curzon supposed, but it was woefully small. Out in the streets as he went for his walk with Emily the church bells were ring-ing a peal of victory, such as London had not heard for three dark years. Emily's happy chatter at his side received small attention from him. He brought tears into her eyes by declining flatly to go to Somerset for the rest of his leave — he felt that he did not dare quit the centre of affairs and put himself six hours farther away from France. He could picture in his mind's eye the rolling downland on which the victory had been won, and his mind dwelt on the armies pouring forward to victory at that very moment while he was left behind here in England and ignominy.

The evening papers told the same tale of a continued advance and of further captures. The whole press was jubilant, and Curzon remembered bitterly the cautious half praise which had been grudgingly dealt out to him in the press (not by name, of course, but by implication) for his greatest efforts at Third Ypres. He began to lose confidence in himself, and when a soldier of Curzon's type loses confidence in himself there is little else for him to lose. He told himself repeatedly, and with truth, that he was not jealous of the success of others. It was not that which was troubling him, but the thought that there were still six days of his leave left.

Then in the morning there was a change. Curzon was no literary critic, but he sensed, even although he would not have been able to label it, the note of caution in the newspaper comments on the progress of the battle of Cambrai. There was a decided tendency to warn the public not to expect too much. Curzon could imagine the sort of reports which would be coming in to corps commanders from divisional headquarters — he had received them often enough. Reports of a stiffening resistance, of the arrival of new German divisions in the front, of the establishment of a fresh defensive line which only a prolonged bombardment could reduce. He could read the symptoms with certainty, and he knew now that General Mackenzie had been right when he told him not to worry — enough details must already have trickled through to the Imperial General Staff at that early stage of the battle for Mackenzie to have formed his judgment.

So Curzon was fully reconciled to spending the rest of his leave in England, and he brought a new pleasure into Emily's heart by consenting to go down into Somersetshire with her for his last four days. Emily was more anxious and worried about him than she had previously been. Perhaps the revelation of Curzon's attitude during the battle of Cambrai had shown her an aspect of his character with which she had not been previously familiar, or perhaps with her woman's intuition she could guess at the changing state of affairs on the Western Front more accurately than Curzon could. In either case she had a premonition of danger. She clung to Bertie during those four idyllic days in Somerset.

There was just enough petrol in the Duke's reserves to supply the motor car which bore them across the loveliest and most typical stretches of the English countryside — lovely even in a war-time December — from Somerset to Folkestone at the end of Curzon's leave. Emily found it hard to keep her lips steady as she said good-bye to her husband at Folkestone Harbour, where the stream of khaki flowed steadily by on its way to the ships and to France; and Emily's cheeks were unashamedly wet with tears. Curzon actually had to swallow hard as he kissed her good-bye; he was moved inexpressibly by the renewal of the discovery that there was actually a woman on earth who could weep for him. His voice was gruff, and he patted her brusquely on the back before he turned away, spurs clinking, past the barriers where the red-hatted military police sprang to stiff attention, to where the steamer waited against the jetty, crammed nearly solid with pack-laden soldiers.

At the headquarters of the Forty-Fourth Corps Curzon

found a new atmosphere. The revelation of the efficacy of tanks to break the trench line had come too late. The alterations of plan forced on the Tank Corps Staff by G.H.Q. had reduced material results to a minimum, and occasioned such losses in tanks that it would be some time before a tank force sufficient to launch a new offensive could be accumulated. Meanwhile the collapse of Russia meant that Germany could transfer a million troops from East to West. Miller had ready for Curzon a long list of new German divisions already identified, and more were to be added to it every day. Where for three years three Allied soldiers confronted two Germans there was now an equality, and there seemed to be every prospect that before long the balance would alter farther yet until the Germans would possess a numerical superiority, which they had not been able to boast since First Ypres. The staff maps which showed the order of battle of the contending armies indicated an ominous clustering of the black squares of German divisions in front of the British line.

Curzon pored over them for long, scratching his cropped head, and turning repeatedly to the detailed trench maps as he forced himself to concentrate on this unusual problem of defence, with the help of the appreciations to which Miller and Frobisher devoted long hours in drawing up. He presided at long weary conferences with his divisional generals and their staffs, when defensive tactics were discussed. Universally the schemes laid before him took it for granted that ground would be lost in the first stages of the battle should the enemy attack, and he was puzzled at this. He tugged at his whitened moustache as he listened or read. This almost voluntary cession of soil was quite opposed to the traditions inherited from Wayland-Leigh, and the prospect irked him sorely. There had been a few occasions when the Forty-Fourth Corps had yielded up bloodsoaked fragments of trench in the height of a battle, but they had been very few. He would have preferred to have issued a few stringent orders to hold on to the front line to the last gasp, and threatening with a court martial any officer who retreated. That was the kind of order which he understood and would have been ready to execute.

But Miller was able to back up his suggestions with a huge mass of orders from Sixth Army, bearing Hudson's signature, in which the greatest urgency was laid upon the need for the economy of life. Two-thirds of a million casualties, incurred at Arras and Passchendaele, had forced the British army, for the first time in two years, to worry about losses. Curzon found the restriction irksome and unnatural. He had grown used to handling unlimited supplies of men and material, and in the Forty-Fourth Corps a convention had grown up under which the prowess of a division was measured by the number of its men who were killed.

"Confound it, Miller," he said, angrily. "You're surely not proposing that we should give up St. Victor like this?"

A hundred thousand men had died so that the ruins of St. Victor should be included in the British line.

"I think we'd better, sir," said Miller. "You see, it's like this. There's a weak flank *here*. We can't be sure of holding the sector along here to here. That'll mean a salient if we hang on to St. Victor. It would be all right if we could afford the men, but — "

"Oh, all right, have it your own way," said Curzon, testily. He could not withstand arguments about possible losses.

Into this atmosphere of nervous preparation there came a fresh bombshell from Sixth Army headquarters. The Forty-Fourth Corps was being taken out of the line they were preparing to hold and transferred to take over a sector held up to that time by the French.

"Yes, I'm sorry about it," said Hudson, when Curzon hotly

[248]

denounced the scheme over the telephone to him. "You don't think I wanted it, do you? My own idea is that G.H.Q. have been weak. We oughtn't to stretch our line any farther. But we've got to, old man, and there's an end of it. You'll find your new sector a bit weak. Buckle to, old man, and get it strengthened while you've got time."

Weak it certainly was. Divisional generals and brigadiers, when the transfer was effected, inundated corps headquarters with complaints regarding the inadequacy of the wiring, the absence of support trenches, and so on. Curzon passed on the complaints to Hudson.

"What do you expect from the French?" said Hudson. "They can't fight and they can't work, and they expect us to do both for them. I can't help it. We've picked the Forty-Fourth Corps for this sector for that special reason. If anyone can hold it, you can, Curzon, old son. We're relying on you."

Under this stimulus Curzon threw himself into the work of strengthening his line, while Miller and Frobisher and the others slaved at drawing up new orders to cover the changed conditions. Gone were the days when the front of the Forty-Fourth Corps was marked out from all others by nightly fireworks and exceptional activity. Curzon's major generals had no desire to attract hostile attention to themselves. The waste of a night of labour in consequence of a barrage put down by the enemy was a disaster. They sought to extract as much labour from their men as they could — as much as the sacrifices of Passchendaele had left spirit in the men to give.

Curzon studied the new orders which Miller drew up. There were three divisions in front line and one in support — the attenuated divisions which the recent reduction in establishments had left to him. It was a woefully weak force, and as far as he could gather from a study of Sixth Army orders, and those issued by Fifth and Second Armies, there was precious little reinforcement to expect. At first sight the prospect was gloomy. There could be no doubting the menace of the accumulation of German forces in front of him, and the reports which Intelligence kept sending in of the piling up of German artillery and transport. Curzon actually experienced a quailing in his stomach as he envisaged a future of ruin and defeat. The inconceivable was at hand.

Largely because it was inconceivable to him Curzon later took heart. He forced himself to remember the offensives he himself had commanded and directed. Once he had looked upon them as tremendous victories, but now, in a fresh light, he did not value them so highly. After all, what had they brought? A few square miles of ground, a few tens of thousands of casualities, and then stagnation. Why should he fear that the Germans would achieve more? They had no tanks worth mentioning with which to bring off a surprise like Cambrai. They had no new weapon, and would be compelled to fight with the old ones. When their bombardment commenced there would be ample time to move fresh divisions up to meet the assault — he remembered the number of times when he had imagined himself to be on the verge of victory, and had been held back by the arrival of German reserves; he remembered his exasperation on hearing of the identification of new divisions in his front. He forced himself to realise that he had launched attacks with a fourfold, fivefold superiority of numbers, and that not upon a settled piece of front, but on one hastily built up in the midst of a bombardment, and he had never broken through yet. He could rely upon his men to oppose a sturdier resistance than the Germans, and upon his own will to hold them together during the crisis — he set his mouth hard when he thought of that.

Moreover, the tactical arrangements of which he was approving would cost the Germans dear. There were a whole series of strong points against which the German waves would break in red ruin — how often had he not flung whole divisions unavailingly upon strong points in the enemy's line? He felt that he could await the attack with confidence, whatever might be the boastings of Ludendorff and his men.

"Intelligence," said Miller, shuffling through a sheaf of reports, "keep on insisting that the push is coming on March 21st. They say they've confirmed it a dozen different ways. Cavendish would bet his life on it. Sixth Army says so, too."

"They may be right," said Curzon. "It doesn't matter to a day or two, except that the later they leave it the stronger we can make our line. I should have liked another week or two, myself. But beggars can't be choosers — I mean when you're on the defensive you can't expect to choose the day to be attacked on."

"No, sir," said Miller.

Chapter XXIV

CURZON presided at the dinner of the staff of the Forty-Fourth Corps on the night of March 20th. He remembered how Wayland-Leigh had provided champagne on the eve of other battles, and he sent Greven all the way back to Amiens by car in order to obtain a full supply of the Clicquot 1900 which Curzon specially favoured. Conditions were a little different from those other evenings, for Terry and Whiteman, commanding two of the divisions in the line, had been compelled to refuse Curzon's invitation on the ground that they dared not leave their headquarters for so long. But Franklin was there, redfaced and beribboned, and Challis — for the glorious old Ninety-First Division had come back under Curzon's orders. Challis sat silently as usual, handling his knife and fork so as not to draw attention to his maimed hand, about which he was morbidly sensitive.

The dinner was dull enough at first, because everyone present was overtired, and the smooth flow of conversation was continually being checked by interruptions as messages came in which could only be dealt with by particular individuals. The wine only loosened tongues gradually, but by degrees a buzz of talk grew up round the table. Stanwell told his celebrated story of how once when he had a bad cold he had been deputed to show a sight-seeing party of important civilians round the front. They had arrived in the dark, and his sore throat had compelled him to whisper as he guided them to where they were spending the night — "Step wide here, please," "Stoop under this wire, please."

At last one of the civilians whispered back to him —

"How far off are the Germans?"

"Oh, about ten miles."

"Then what the hell are we whispering like this for?"

"I don't know why *you* are, but I've got a cold."

Everyone laughed at that, even those who had heard it before; it was always good to hear of civilians and politicians making fools of themselves. Milward, the Gas Officer, down at the foot of the table (the Irregulars were dining with the Regulars on this special occasion) was tempted to tell how he had pleaded for a year with Curzon to experiment with dichlorethyl sulphide — mustard gas — and had been put off because he could not guarantee many deaths, but only thousands of disablements.

"We want something that will kill," Curzon had said, and the British army postponed the mustard gas until the Germans had proved its efficiency.

Milward almost began to tell this story, but he caught Curzon's eye along the length of the table and forbore. Curzon noticed his change of expression, and with unusual sensitiveness felt Milward's slight hostility. As host it was his duty to keep the party running smoothly; as commanding officer it was his duty, too. He remembered Wayland-Leigh on the night before Loos quoting Shakespeare as he toasted the advance to the Rhine. He fingered his glass. There was no imminent advance before them, only a desperate defensive. Into his mind drifted a fragment which he remembered of one of Lewis Waller's speeches in the old days when he was playing Henry V.

"Come the four corners of the world in arms and we shall shock them," said Curzon, turning to Challis on his right.

"Er — yes. Yes. Quite," said Challis, taken by surprise.

The presence of so many senior officers and the small number of young subalterns present prevented the evening developing into the sort of wild entertainment which Curzon had so often experienced in cavalry messes. The junior ranks were unusually quiet, too. Several of them withdrew early on the truthful plea that they had work to do, and Franklin, who was a determined bridge player, quietly collected a four and settled down, rather rudely and unsociably, Curzon thought.

He went out and stared through the darkness towards the line. The night was absolutely still. There was an aeroplane or two droning in the distance, but the sound of their passage was louder than any noise of guns from the front. The bobbing points of light which marked the line of trenches on the horizon were far fewer than he had ever noticed before. There was no breath of wind; the stars were just visible in a misty sky. Curzon went to bed. If Intelligence's forecast was correct he would need all his energies for the morrow. He told Mason to call him at four o'clock.

Curzon was soundly asleep when Mason came in — he had the trick of sleeping soundly until the exact moment when he had planned to wake. Mason had to touch his shoulder to rouse him.

"Is it four o'clock?" said Curzon, moving his head on the pillow, with his moustache lopsided.

"It's three-thirty, sir," said Mason. "Here's Mr. Greven wants to speak to you, sir."

Curzon sat up.

"Bombardment's started, sir," said Greven. "Been going five minutes now."

The house was trembling to the sound. A thousand German

[254]

batteries — more guns than the whole world put together had possessed before the war — were firing at once.

"Mason, fill my bath," said Curzon, leaping from the bed in his blue and white pyjamas.

"I've done it, sir," said Mason.

"Any reports?" asked Curzon, flinging off his pyjamas.

"Not yet, sir," said Greven.

"No, of course there wouldn't be," said Curzon. Not for two days did he expect any vital report — the Germans would be fools if they attacked after a briefer bombardment than that.

Curzon had his bath, and shaved, and dressed, and walked into his headquarters office to hear the latest news before he had his breakfast.

"Bombardment's heavy, sir," said Miller, sitting at a telephone. "Gas, mostly. Queer that they're using gas at this stage of the preparation. And there's thick fog all along the line. I've warned everyone to expect local raids."

"Quite right," said Curzon, and went off to eat porridge and bacon and eggs.

When he had eaten his breakfast he came back again. Miller seemed unusually worried.

"Something very queer's going on, sir," he said. "Back areas are coming in for it as much as the front line. They're flooding places with gas."

He proffered half a dozen reports for inspection.

"And the cross-roads behind the line are catching it as well. We've never spread a bombardment out like this."

"I expect they think they know better than us," said Curzon lightly.

"Terry's reporting that all communication with his front line units has been broken already, but that's only to be expected, of course. But — " said Miller.

"Yes. Any raids?"

"Nothing yet, sir."

Curzon found his stolidity a little shaken by Miller's alarmist attitude. There must be a long bombardment before the attack; in theory there would be no need to do anything for days, and yet — Curzon could not bring himself to order his horse and take his customary morning's exercise. He paced restlessly about headquarters instead. The thick ground mist showed no sign of lifting; the roar of the bombardment seemed to have increased in intensity.

When next he came back Frobisher was speaking excitedly into a telephone.

"Yes," he was saying, "yes," and then he broke off. "Hallo! Hallo! Oh hell," and he put the receiver back with a gesture of annoyance.

"Wire's gone, I suppose. That was General Whiteman, sir. Attack's begun. That's all I could hear."

An orderly came running in with a message brought by a carrier pigeon and Frobisher snatched it from him. The attack had undoubtedly begun, and confusion descended upon headquarters.

Incredibly, it seemed, the line was crumbling along the whole corps front, and along the fronts of the corps on either flank as well. Curzon could hardly believe the reports which were coming in. One of the chief duties of a general is to sort out the true from the false, but here it was impossible to believe anything. One or two strong points in the front line whose communications had survived reported that they were holding out without difficulty; the entire absence of news from others might merely mean a rupture of communication. And yet from here and there in the second line came reports of the German advance — so far back in some places that Curzon felt inclined to dismiss them as the result of over-imagination on the part of the officers responsible. The mist and the gas were causing confusion; and the German bombardment had been cunningly directed so as to cause as much havoc as possible in the means of communication. Curzon found himself talking to an artillery Colonel who was reporting by telephone that the Germans were assaulting his battery positions.

"Are you sure?" asked Curzon.

"Sure? We're firing over open sights with fuses set at zero," blazed the Colonel at the other end. "God damn it, sir, d'you think I'm mad?"

Through all the weak places in the British line —and they were many — the German attack was pouring forward like a tide through a faulty dyke. The strong points were being steadily cut off and surrounded — there was no heroic expenditure of German life to storm them by main force. Little handfuls of machine gunners, assiduously trained, were creeping forward here and there, aided by the fog, taking up strategic positions which destroyed all possibility of unity in the defence.

Holnon and Dallon were lost. As the afternoon came Curzon sent orders to Challis and the Ninety-First Division to move up into the line and stop the advance. His old Ninety-First could be relied upon to do all their duty. Guns, ammunition dumps, bridges, all were falling intact into the hands of the enemy. At nightfall the British army seemed to be on the verge of the greatest disaster it had ever experienced, and Curzon's frantic appeals to Army headquarters were meeting with no response.

"We've got no reserves to give you at all," said Hudson. "You'll have to do the best you can with the Ninety-First. It'll be four days at least before we can give you any help. You've just got to hold on, Curzon. We know you'll do it."

All through the night the bombardment raved along the line. Challis was reporting difficulties in executing his orders. Roads were under fire, other roads were blocked with retreating transport. He could get no useful information from his fellow divisional Generals. But he was not despairing. He was deploying his division where it stood, to cover what he guessed to be the largest gap opening in the British line. Curzon clung to that hope. Surely the Ninety-First would stop the Huns.

At dawn Franklin reported that he was shifting his head-quarters — the German advance had reached that far. There was no news from Terry at all. He must have been surrounded, or his headquarters hit by a shell — four motor cyclists had been sent to find him, and none had returned. The coloured pins on Miller's map indicated incredible bulgings in the line.

"Message from Whiteman, sir," said Frobisher, white-cheeked. "He's lost all his guns. Doesn't know where Thomas's brigade is. And he says Stanton's is legging it back as fast as it can, what there is left of it."

That meant danger to the right flank of the Ninety-First. Before Curzon could reply Miller called to him.

"Challis on the telephone, sir. He says both flanks are turned. There are Huns in St. Felice, and nothing can get through Boncourt 'cause of mustard gas. Shall he hold on?"

Should he hold on? If he did the Ninety-First would be destroyed. If he did not there would be no solid point in the whole line, and in the absence of reserves there was no knowing how wide the gap would open. Could he trust the Ninety-First to hold together under the disintegrating stress of a retreat in the presence of the enemy? He went over to the telephone.

"Hallo, Challis."

"Yes, sir."

"What are your men like?"

"All right, sir. They'll do anything you ask of them — in reason."

"Well — "

Frobisher came running over to him at that moment with a scrap of paper which an orderly had brought in — a message dropped from an aeroplane. It bore only three important words, and they were "Enemy in Flécourt." At that rate the Germans were far behind Challis's right flank, and on the point of intercepting his retreat. There could be no extricating the Ninety-First now.

"I can't order you to retreat, Challis," said Curzon. "The Huns are in Flécourt."

"Christ!"

"There's nothing for it but for you to hold on while you can. You must maintain your present position to the last man, Challis."

"Very good, sir. Good-bye."

Those few words had condemned ten thousand men to death or mutilation.

"If the Huns are in Flécourt, sir," said Miller, "it's time we got out of here."

Half a dozen eager pairs of eyes looked up at Curzon when Miller said that. He was voicing the general opinion.

"Yes," said Curzon. What Miller said was only common sense. But Curzon suddenly felt very dispirited, almost apathetic. What was the use of withdrawing all this elaborate machinery of the corps command when there was no corps left? Three divisions were in ruins, and a fourth would be overwhelmed by converging attacks in the next two hours. And there was nothing to fill the gap. The Germans had achieved the break-through which the English had sought in vain for three years, and a break-through meant defeat and ruin. England had suffered a decisive military defeat at a vital point. Curzon went back in his mind through a list of victories which had settled the fate of Europe — Sedan, Sadowa, Waterloo. Now England was among the conquered. He tried to find a precedent in English military history, and he went farther and farther back in his mind through the centuries. Not until he reached Hastings could he find a parallel. Hastings had laid England at the feet of the Normans, and this defeat would lay England at the feet of the Germans.

"We'll move in the usual two echelons," Miller was saying. "Frobisher, you'll go with the first."

What was the use of it all? A vivid flash of imagination, like lightning at night, revealed the future to Curzon. He would return to England a defeated general, one of the men who had let England down. There would be public reproaches. Courts martial, perhaps. Emily would stand by him, but he did not want her to have to do so. In an excruciating moment he realised that even with Emily at his side he could not face a future of professional failure. Emily whom he loved would make it all the worse. He would rather die, the way the old Ninety-First was dying.

He swung round upon Greven, who was standing helpless, as was only to be expected, amid the bustle of preparation for the transfer.

"Send for my horse," he said.

Those who heard him gaped.

"The motor cars are just coming round, sir," said Miller, respectfully.

"I shan't want mine," replied Curzon. Even at that moment he sought to avoid the melodramatic by the use of curt military phrasing. "I'm going up the line. I shall leave you in charge, Miller."

"Up the line," someone whispered, echoing his words. They knew now what he intended.

"I'll send for my horse, too, sir," said Follett. As A.D.C. it was his duty to stay by his General's side, even when the General was riding to his death. One or two people looked instinctively at Greven.

"And me too, of course," said Greven, slowly.

"Right," said Curzon, harshly. "Miller, it'll be your duty to reorganize what's left of the corps. We can still go down, fighting."

"Yes, sir."

"Two minutes, Follett," said Curzon, and under the gaze of every eye he strode across the room and through the green baize door into his quarters.

Mason was running round like a squirrel in a cage packing his officer's things.

"Get me my sword," snapped Curzon.

"Your sword, sir?"

"Yes, you fool."

While Mason plunged in search of the sword into the rolled valise Curzon wrenched open the silver photograph frame upon the wall. He stuffed Emily's photograph into the breast of his tunic.

"Here it is, sir," said Mason.

Curzon slipped the sword into the frog of his Sam Browne. There was still a queer military pleasure to be found in the tap of the sheath against his left boot. Mason was talking some foolishness or other, but Curzon did not stop to listen. He walked out to the front of the house, where among the motor vehicles Greven and Follett were on horseback and a groom was holding his own horse. Curzon swung himself up into his saddle. The horse was full of oats and insufficiently exercised lately, besides being infected by the excitement and bustle. He plunged madly as Curzon's right foot found the stirrup. Curzon brought the brute back to the level with a cruel use of the curb, and swung his head round towards the gate. Then he dashed out to the road, with Greven and Follett clattering wildly behind him.

The road was crowded with evidences of a defeat. Transport of all sorts, ambulances, walking wounded, were all pouring down it with the one intention of escaping capture. Puzzled soldiers stared at the three red-tabbed officers, magnificently mounted, who were galloping so madly over the clattering *pavé* towards the enemy. Far ahead Curzon could hear the roar of the guns as the Ninety-First fought its last battle. His throat was dry although he swallowed repeatedly. There was no thought in his head as he abandoned himself to the smooth rhythm of his galloping horse. Suddenly a flash of colour penetrated into his consciousness. There was a group of unwounded soldiers on the road, and the little squares on their sleeves showed that they belonged to the Ninety-First. He pulled up his horse and turned upon them.

"What the hell are you doing here?" he demanded.

"We ain't got no officer, sir," said one.

They were stragglers escaped by a miracle from the shattered left wing of their division.

"D'you need an officer to show you how to do your duty? Turn back at once. Follett, bring them on with you. I expect you'll find others up the road."

Curzon wheeled his lathered horse round again and dashed on, only Greven following him now. They approached the cross-roads where a red-capped military policeman was still directing traffic. An officer there was trying to sort out the able-bodied from the others.

"Ah!" said Curzon.

At that very moment a German battery four miles away opened fire. They were shooting by the map, and they made extraordinarily good practice as they sought for the vital spots in the enemy's rear. Shells came shrieking down out of the blue and burst full upon the cross-roads, and Curzon was hit both by a flying fragment of red hot steel and by a jagged lump of *pavé*. His right leg was shattered, and his horse was killed.

Greven saved Curzon's life — or at least always thought he

did, although the credit ought really to be given to the two lightly wounded R.A.M.C. men who came to the rescue, and put on bandages and tourniquets, and stopped a passing lorry by the authority of Greven's red tabs, and hoisted Curzon in. Pain came almost at once. No torment the Inquisition devised could equal the agony Curzon knew as the lorry heaved and pitched over the uneven road, jolting his mangled leg so that the fragments of bone grated together. Soon he was groaning, with the sweat running over his chalk-white face, and when they reached the hospital he was crying out loud, a mere shattered fragment of a man despite his crossed sword and bâton and crown, and his red tabs and his silly sword.

They drugged him and they operated upon him, and they operated again and again, so that he lay for months in a muddle of pain and drugs while England fought with her back to the wall and closed by a miracle the gap which had been torn in her line at St. Quentin.

While he lay bathed in waves of agony, or inert under the drugs, he was sometimes conscious of Emily's presence beside him, and sometimes Emily was crying quietly, just as she had done at that revue he took her to the last night of his last leave after Passchendaele and someone sang "Roses of Picardy." It was a long time before he was sure enough of this solid world again to put out his hand to her.

And now Lieutenant General Sir Herbert Curzon and his wife Lady Emily are frequently to be seen on the promenade at Bournemouth, he in his Bath chair with a plaid rug, she in tweeds striding behind. He smiles his old maidish smile at his friends, and his friends are pleased with that distinction, although he plays such bad bridge and is a little inclined to irascibility when the east wind blows.

[263]